D0434805

AMERICAN LABOR UNIONS

Chart I. Union Membership in the United States, 1932-1962

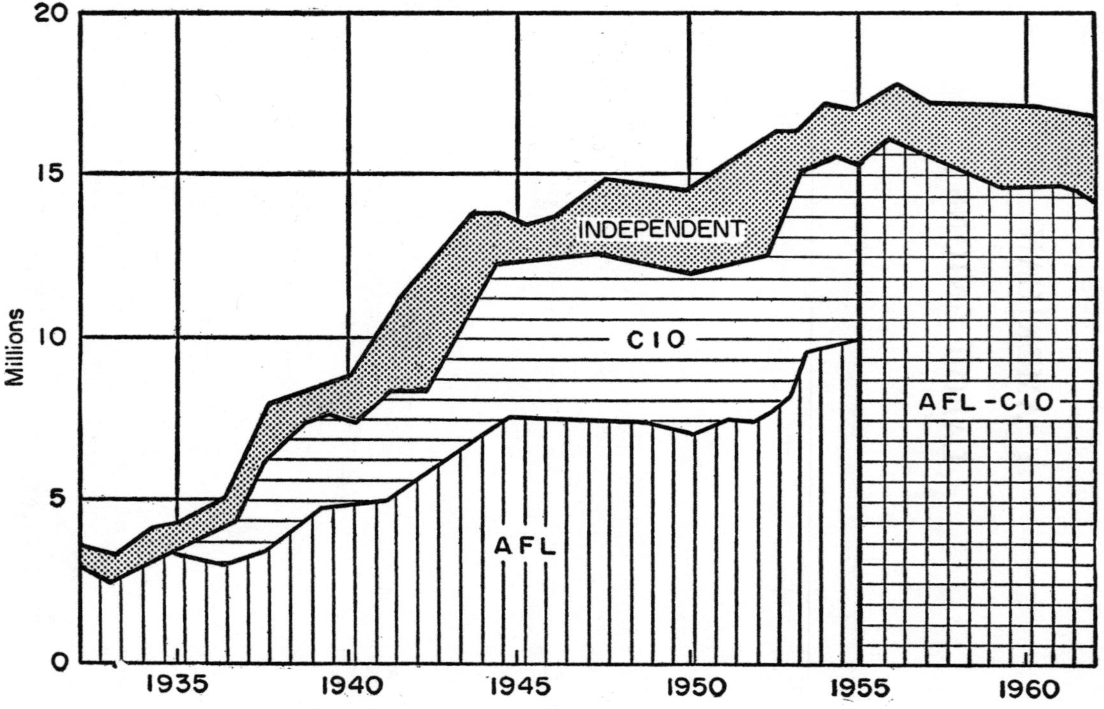

43676

AMERICAN LABOR UNIONS

WHAT THEY ARE AND HOW THEY WORK

Florence Peterson

FORMERLY, CHIEF, INDUSTRIAL RELATIONS DIVISION
U.S. BUREAU OF LABOR STATISTICS

SECOND
REVISED
EDITION

Harper & Row, Publishers
NEW YORK, EVANSTON,
AND LONDON

HD
6508
P42
1952

AMERICAN LABOR UNIONS. *Copyright © 1945, 1952, 1963 by Harper & Row, Publishers, Incorporated. Printed in the United States of America. All rights reserved. No part of this book may be used or reproduced in any manner whatsoever without written permission except in the case of brief quotations embodied in critical articles and reviews. For information address Harper & Row, Publishers, Incorporated, 49 East 33rd Street, New York 16, N. Y.*

L–N

LIBRARY OF CONGRESS CATALOG CARD NUMBER: 63–10629

CONTENTS

CHARTS AND TABLES

PREFACE

The life of every person in the United States, whether engaged in business or the professions, whether a politician, housewife, farmer or worker himself, is affected in some way by the existence and activities of labor organizations. This will continue so long as we maintain a democratic form of government and a system of free enterprise in business, because organizations of workers are a natural concomitant of a competitive economy and an evidence of a free society.

Although all of us are more or less conscious of the presence and influence of labor organizations, few of us have much understanding of why and how they came to be such an important factor in our industrial and national life; fewer still have much knowledge of their mechanism, their rules of procedure and internal government. Those not connected with labor unions are prone to think of them in connection with isolated actions which receive headline notices in the daily press; union members naturally think of them in terms of what their own unions are doing for them on the job; students of labor problems are inclined to think of organized labor as an amorphous movement whose direction, for good or bad, is controlled by a few dominant leaders. These are important, but are fragments of the whole.

The purpose of this volume is to describe how labor unions, as organisms, perform their functions and conduct their daily affairs. There are a number of books on labor problems and the labor movement, and much literature about individual labor leaders and particular actions of trade unions. This volume does not deal with those subjects commonly classified under "labor problems," nor is it an interpretative history of the labor movement. There has been little attempt to discuss the economic, political or sociological forces which have brought into being the modern labor union; neither does it discuss the labor leaders who have influenced the course of the trade union movement. The omission of these matters does not indicate that the author depreciates their importance, for personalities and circumstances are important factors in any movement. Nonetheless, the character and effectiveness of organized efforts are also strongly influenced by their internal mechanism and rules of operation.

This is the second revised edition of AMERICAN LABOR UNIONS. The original edition was published in 1945 and the first revision in 1952. Much has happened during the past decade which has necessitated major revisions throughout most of the chapters. Also, there is an important addition to the present volume, namely Part Three, which discusses the past and present legal status of labor unions and collective bargaining.

The widespread circulation of the first two editions of this book has given ample evidence of the need for this kind of factual presentation of the history, structure and operation of American labor organizations. Earlier editions have been translated into more than a dozen languages and are included in the libraries of the U.S. Information Agency throughout the world. Letters received by the author from the "four corners of the earth" are a sobering reminder of the concern people everywhere have with American institutions, and of their especial interest in labor organizations in these critical times.

FLORENCE PETERSON

March, 1963

AMERICAN LABOR UNIONS

PART ONE

GROWTH OF THE AMERICAN LABOR MOVEMENT

1

THE FIRST HUNDRED YEARS

The urge to combine with others for mutual protection and advancement is an inherent characteristic of human nature. In every form of society persons of similar economic pursuits and needs have tended to unite into associations for the purpose of promoting their common interests. The nature of these associations, and the methods pursued, differ according to the particular needs and desires of the members; they are also affected by legal and other forms of social control. Similar to any other kind of organized effort, the labor movement is an expression of group conciousness of common problems as well as convictions as to the remedies needed.

THE MEDIEVAL GILD—PRECURSOR OF MODERN UNIONISM

A labor union has been defined as "a continuous association of wage earners for the purpose of maintaining and improving the conditions of their employment." Spontaneous strikes and rebellions of oppressed and dissatisfied workers are as old as history itself, but labor unions are a product of comparatively modern times, since by definition they imply a wage system and more or less permanent and formal organizations of workers. Although there is no generic connection between the modern labor union and the medieval craft gild, there are significant similarities, as to both purposes and the methods by which these purposes were carried out.

The medieval gilds were based on a feeling of scarcity of opportunity. To protect their interests, the gilds brought influence upon the government to forbid anyone from practicing a trade who was not a member of the gild, and through their strict apprenticeship regulations and their restrictions of "foreigners" from other localities they saw that too many did not become gild members. Their work rules included quality standards to protect them from the competition of inferior workmanship, daily hours were limited, and night and holiday work was forbidden. The gilds, like many labor unions today, also performed certain fraternal functions such as providing financial aid in time of sickness or death of their members.

The medieval gild, however, was composed of both masters and journeymen and there was no conflict of interest between the two because the journeyman was serving a master only temporarily; in a few years he would also be a master and any advantages which he might gain from his master he would in turn have to give to *his* journeymen. The gild system was concurrent with an economy of local markets and no capital outlay except a few tools and a limited supply of raw materials. The gild was a group of craftsmen banded together for mutual protection and control of the local market. When the market was extended and more capital was needed to care for short credits and finished stock, the industrial grouping changed. The journeyman's opportunity for becoming a master grew more limited, and the great bulk of workers ceased to be independent producers who owned their tools and materials and disposed of the product of their labor. The journeymen came to constitute a distinct and permanent class, and many of them formed gilds of their own as their masters gradually converted the craft gild into merchant-employer gilds.

The use of power machines and the factory system widened the gap between employers and workers. The factory system, because of the increasing amount of capital required, necessitated combinations of capital resources which were legalized into corporations. The collective action of capital and management extended beyond the confines of a single corporation and found expression in trade and manufacturers' associations, chambers of commerce, and other permanent and *ad hoc* combinations to promote and protect the interests of the investors and managers of capital.

In response, ever seeking a semblance of equality in the bargaining relationship, workers' organizations have expanded both horizontally and vertically. Local unions of skilled craftsmen have grown into national and international unions; workers of all crafts in an industry have united into industrial unions; both craft and industrial unions have formed city, state, national and international federations.

INFLUENCES SHAPING THE AMERICAN LABOR MOVEMENT

A labor movement connotes a continuous association of wage earners for the purpose of improving their economic and social well-being. The motive force and central purpose of the labor movement in this country, as elsewhere, is the improvement of the status of workers *as* workers. Its appeal and challenge is based on the premise that wage earners can and should share in the good things of life while *remaining* wage earners; that economic well-being and its accompanying social prestige and privileges need not be solely contingent upon becoming an employer or self-employed businessman.

Ever adhering to this general purpose there nevertheless have been many changes in specific aims and procedures of organized labor as a whole, and many differences among its component parts. Upon occasion these differences have lead to schisms, and it could be questioned whether one can accurately speak of a "labor movement" in this country. But despite the changes and diversities in organizational structure and policies which have taken place throughout the years, there has been a common and permanent thread of unity. The cohesive forces have been sufficiently strong and enduring to outlive and outweigh the influences making for disruption, although upon numbers of occasions the presence of conflicting purposes and rivalries have retarded growth and weakened bargaining and political strength. Before going into the factual history let us review briefly some of the diversified and conflicting factors which have been responsible for the shaping of the labor movement in this country.

Labor organizations are an integral part of any industrial society. They emerge with the separation of workers from the ownership of the instruments of production and the marketing of their products, the impersonality and subdivision of labor under the factory system, and the competition resulting from widening of markets. These conditions make for class conciousness, but in this country class consciousness of workers did not develop as early as in some other countries with comparable industrial advancement. Nor did national organizations of workers parallel the rapid growth and power of large business corporations. There were several reasons for the relative lack of widespread class consciousness on the part of American wage earners, and the lag in the development of strong national labor organizations.

Geographical and Political Factors

A major factor was the abundance of free land, available almost for the asking, during most of the nineteenth century. This had a two-way effect. Thousands of discontented workers from the eastern industrial centers who otherwise would have sought redress of their grievances through collective action, migrated westward and became independent landowners. Their departure, in turn, tended to keep down the labor supply in the eastern states, especially of skilled workers, thus improving the individual bargaining strength of those who remained and reducing the pressure for concerted action.

Closely related to the factor of abundant lands for settlement was the rapid growth and geographical expansion of industry which provided opportunities for workers to rise to managerial positions or establish businesses of their own. The growth of business gave sufficient substance to the "American dream of unlimited opportunities" to enable each generation to maintain the hope and expectation of rising out of the wage-earner class. If fathers failed, there was the enduring faith that, given adequate education, their children would succeed. Moreover, the growth in size and sectional diversity of business interests tended to minimize horizontal class loyalties in favor of geographical groups associated with particular economic endeavors. Thus, during the period around the turn of the twentieth century, wage earners in the middle west were inclined to identify themselves with agriculture and small business in the fight against eastern bankers and railroad interests. It was a fight against monopoly, but for the purpose of "freeing" small business and farmers rather than wage earners from monopolistic control. Industrial workers tended to identify themselves with these other groups because of their family ties with farmers—most of them had come to the city from farms and their hope was that they soon would be able to buy farms or establish businesses for themselves. This was in contrast to the situation in Great Britain, for example, where there was little flow of peoples from agriculture to industry, and where successive generations of industrial workers without the agricultural individualistic background encouraged the growth of class solidarity.

Widespread voting privileges which were early enjoyed by workers in this country served in several ways to lessen their feeling of class consciousness. The very fact that they had the right to vote and participate in political activities tended to make them feel that they were a part of the body politic and not a class separate from the rest of the community. Secondly, unlike the situation in some of the older countries where the franchise was long reserved for the upper economic classes, it was not necessary for the industrial wage earners in this country to organize for the purpose of gaining the right to vote. Popular voting was the heritage of an evolving political democracy rather than a result of economic class struggle.[1] Finally, the opportunity which the ballot gave to workers to express their discontent tended to assuage their desire for more overt and pos-

[1] This does not imply that universal suffrage actually exists throughout the United States nor that the suffrage which exists was obtained without struggle. Property qualifications long existed in some of our Eastern states; women suffrage was granted in 1920 after years of agitation; the struggle to remove color restrictions still continues in some of our Southern states. For the most part, however, these efforts to broaden the right to vote do not represent economic class struggle so much as other kinds of group struggles.

sibly more violent economic action. There was always the hope that campaign promises of justice and equal opportunity for all would be carried out!

Effect of Immigration

A major influence in the development of the American labor movement, as many other of our cultural and social institutions, was the successive waves of immigrants from the different lands of Europe during the fifty years before the passage of restrictive legislation in 1924. This immigration had contrasting influences upon the attitude and actions of American workers, but its net effect was undoubtedly adverse to the development of the kind of class consciousness which would be conducive to the early growth of a labor movement. It tended to accentuate occupational and cultural cleavages rather than to promote unification of all workers. Language differences, racial, religious and national antagonisms among the various groups of immigrants, and between them and the native born, created formidable barriers to solidarity, and they became active forces against unity under the stimulus of employers who were prone to pit one group against another during strikes and organizational drives, thus utilizing group antagonisms to their own advantage.

It was not only the heterogeneity of the immigrant population but the background from which most of them came which influenced the development of the labor movement. The majority who came to our shores after the 1880's were peasants, used to hard work with meager pay, and with habits of docility and obedience. Most of them were unskilled and even those who had been skilled workers in "the old country" were forced to accept unskilled jobs because of language handicaps. This had a twofold effect: management tended to introduce devices to break down skilled jobs into semiskilled work suitable to their capacities, and the native born, while being pushed up the occupational ladder, were also ever aware of the competitive menace of the newcomers and were thus lead to organize into craft unions with membership confined to skilled workers.

Although the continual stream of immigrants tended to retard a crystallization of working class consciousness, their infusion into the American labor force wrought a positive and at times a decisive influence upon labor union action and policy. Many of the immigrants were persons of native ability and with qualities of leadership. Unable to rise to managerial positions or to political office because of language and prejudice against foreigners, they became leaders in the labor movement. With a background of racial and class oppression and convinced of the necessity for concerted action for the redress of grievances, they provided a vigor and kind of intellectual leadership which had a vital effect upon the basic philosophy and the numerical growth of organized labor.

Such factors as the existence of free lands, a fluid working population continually augmented by an influx of immigrants, widespread voting privileges, and an expanding economy with its consequent opportunities for individual advancement, were characteristics more or less unique to the American scene. They explain, in part at least, the relative lag in the growth as well as the differences in policies of the American labor movement in contrast to other industrial countries. Fundamentally, however, the world-wide forces set in motion as a result of mechanization of industry, large-scale production and widening of markets, had the same impact upon American workers as those in all other industrialized countries. Even though their standard of living has been generally better than elsewhere, the dream of America as the land of opportunity and abundance has provided the incentive for aggressive and continued efforts toward further advancement.

EARLY HISTORY

Machines and mass production have materially influenced the growth and character of labor organizations but labor unions in this country preceded the factory system. The earliest labor organizations, and some of the strongest today, were established in the skilled handicraft trades. The first organizations of labor in this country appeared among the carpenters, shoemakers, printers, and tailors in the east coast cities during the 1790's. These craft societies bargained over wages and hours, demanded closed shop conditions, engaged in strikes, boycotts, and picketing, paid strike benefits, regulated apprentices, and employed "walking delegates" to see that the terms agreed upon were enforced. These early workingmen's societies were local in scope, although there was some interchange of information among the societies of a given trade, and some concerted effort to deal with the problem of traveling journeymen who competed with resident workers.

Experiments Early in the Nineteenth Century

As the local craft societies became more numerous and active, more united efforts were made to alleviate some of the worst ills which beset the workingmen of that day. The various societies in the different cities united into "trades' unions" to provide common support during strikes, and frequently maintained a common strike fund accumulated through per capita taxes from each member society. Paralleling these city combinations, local societies of shoemakers, printers, carpenters, and weavers united into what they called "national" organizations, although in reality their membership was limited to the larger eastern cities. During the "wild-cat" prosperity and rising prices of the middle 1830's, members of these city and craft organizations formed a National Trades' Union. All these organizations, in addition to seeking improvements in wages and hours, were concerned with broad social reforms such as free public schools, abolition of imprisonment for debt, and elimination of property qualifications for voting.

The national organizations as well as most of the local unions collapsed during the panic of 1837 and the ensuing years of business dislocations. New workingmen's organizations appeared during the forties, but these were concerned more with cooperatives, land reform, and general social improvement programs than with bargaining with employers. Numerous local trade unions came into existence with the general expansion of industrial activity and the rising prices that followed the discovery and use of California gold. In contrast to the workingmen's associations established in the forties, the major concern of these local unions was bargaining for better wages and hours. It was during the 1850's that several of our present-day national unions had their beginnings—the typographers, hat finishers, machinists and blacksmiths, and molders. All the labor organizations suffered a serious setback in the depression which began in 1857 when unemployment and wage cuts affected union treasuries and morale.

POST-CIVIL WAR DEVELOPMENTS

Within a few years after the outbreak of the Civil War, many new local organizations and several national unions came into existence as a means of combating the soaring prices that resulted from the issuing of "greenbacks" and the lag in wage increases. There was a further interest in organization after the close of the war, when returning soldiers found that their skilled hand jobs had been supplanted by factory and machine production, when existing work standards were being menaced by the influx of immigrants willing to work for low wages, and when improved railroad transportation made it possible for goods manufactured in low-cost areas to be brought to higher wage markets.

Most of the organizations which emerged during the decade following the Civil War were craft unions. A progenitor of the modern industrial union was the Knights of St. Crispin, a shoe workers' union founded in 1869 for the purpose of protecting journeymen against the influx of "green-hands" into their industry. With its 50,000 members, it was probably the largest union in existence at that time, but within a decade the Crispins disintegrated because of drastic wage cuts and the introduction of new machinery which they were unable to prevent.

After several attempts to unite the numerous national and local organizations, the National Labor Union was formed in 1866; it was a loose federation of trade unions and of some reform organizations which were not strictly concerned with labor problems. At first it directed its chief attention toward obtaining an eight-hour day but later it turned more and more to political action and began to espouse varied kinds of reform measures, social and fiscal. Thereupon many of the trade unions became dissatisfied and withdrew. The National Labor Union finally disbanded in 1872, after an unsuccessful attempt to form a National Labor and Reform political party.

THE ORDER OF THE KNIGHTS OF LABOR

To circumvent employers' lockouts and black lists, workers were led to meet secretly and to organize a type of association so clothed in ritual, sign grips, and passwords that "no spy of the boss can find his way into the lodge room to betray his fellows." One of these organizations was the Noble Order of the Knights of Labor, which was established by some Philadelphia tailors in 1869. Soon the tailors were joined by shoemakers (mostly remnants of the St. Crispin lodges), carpenters, miners, railroadmen, and other organized and unorganized workers.

During the 1880's the Knights of Labor, having revoked its secrecy features, grew into a spectacular mass movement which included workers of all trades and degrees of skill. Discontented farmers, professional persons, and even some employers responded to its appeal for the amelioration of the hardships of the common man under the rallying cry, "An injury to one is the concern of all." The general and far-reaching aim of the Order was the substitution of a cooperative society for the existing wage system, a goal which it hoped could be attained through education and legislation. More immediately, it sought improvement in wages and hours and the abolition of convict and child labor.

Structurally, the Knights of Labor was composed of local assemblies (organized along either craft or mixed lines), combined into district assemblies[2] which had sole authority within their respective jurisdictions; at the head was the General Assembly, with "full and final jurisdiction." These mixed assemblies bargained with employers and conducted strikes, frequently calling out workers in various trades to aid strikers in a given trade or plant. Through these mixed assemblies, the superior bargaining power of the skilled workers could be utilized to help the unskilled workers.

The Knights of Labor reached its peak following the southwest railroad (Gould system) shopmen's strike in 1885, when for the first time officials of a large corporation met with and negotiated an

[2] Opposition by some of the trade groups to the mixed district assemblies forced the Knights of Labor to allow these groups to organize into district and national trade assemblies. Thus the telegraphers and the window glass and shoe workers finally obtained national craft autonomy, although the general officers of the Knights of Labor did everything they could to discourage trade autonomy.

agreement with the organization. This success brought enthusiastic response from workers throughout the country, and the Knights of Labor membership increased sevenfold within one year. By the autumn of 1886 the Order had over 700,000 members in more than 5,500 local assemblies—the equivalent of almost 10 per cent of the total industrial wage earners.[3]

Its day of power was brief. Railroad strikes in 1886 met with disastrous defeat, and the united opposition of employers caused the failure of numerous strikes for an eight-hour day which resulted in the disintegration of entire assemblies. Most important was the disaffection of most of the skilled workers, who were leaving the mixed assemblies in the Knights and forming trade unions. By 1900 the Order had practically ceased to exist as a national movement, although a number of local and district assemblies remained active for several decades.

The Knights of Labor was the first national labor organization in this country to be active for more than a year or two and its influence extended beyond its immediate membership and beyond the years of its active national existence. Its chief contribution was education. The workers learned the strength and weaknesses of the one-big-union type of organization, and the general public, as never before, was made conscious of the bitter discontent which existed among large sections of industrial wage earners.

THE AMERICAN FEDERATION OF LABOR

The conflict of interest between skilled craftsmen who worked with tools and the mass of semiskilled and unskilled wage earners led in 1881 to the formation of the Federation of Organized Trades and Labor Unions, which in 1886 became the American Federation of Labor. Samuel Gompers of the Cigarmakers' Union was elected the first president of the Federation and continued in that office,

[3] Grand Master Workman Powderly said regarding this: "In 1885 we had about 80,000 members in good standing: in one year the number jumped to 700,000, of which at least 400,000 came in from curiosity and caused more damage than good." (Terence V. Powderly, *The Path I Trod,* Columbia University Press, New York, 1940.) The newspapers at that time, greatly alarmed over the popularity of the mass movement, quoted a membership of 2½ million.

with the exception of one year, until his death in 1924. In contrast to the mixed assemblies of the Knights of Labor, complete autonomy was retained by each organized craft in the American Federation of Labor. Each national union (international if it included Canadian locals) had its own constitution, its own rules for internal government, and its own procedures for dealing with employers. In no case were outsiders—that is, persons not working at the trade but in sympathy with the union's aims—admitted to active membership.

General Policies of the AFL

For fifty years the American Federation of Labor was not only the dominant but practically the sole spokesman of the organized workers in this country. During this half century, while sweeping and fundamental changes were taking place in the nation's economic and industrial life, it maintained a consistent course of action and almost never deviated from the general policies adopted during its formative period.

The Federation was established at a time when many persons, both wage earners and intellectuals, believed that the ultimate solution of labor's problems was the elimination of employer-employee classes altogether through the substitution of a new industrial order of either producers' cooperatives or state socialism.[4] This could be achieved only through the solidarity of all workers, skilled and unskilled alike, who would not only engage in piecemeal efforts with individual employers, but also use their united economic and political strength to gain basic and general reforms throughout the industrial system.

The emergence of the AFL represented a decisive defeat for the one-big-union idea by which the superior strength and strategic advantages of the skilled workers could be used economically and

[4] Although Marxian socialism had a considerable following, there were many other proposed schemes whereby workers would share in the ownership, management, and profits of business. Similar philosophies were popular among workers in European countries. The French term for labor union, *syndicat,* implies direct action through general strikes and violence, if necessary, to establish control over the means and processes of production—a theory which the French labor movement later abandoned but resumed to some extent during a period after World War II.

politically to benefit the entire working class. Not only was the Federation founded upon the principle of craft autonomy, but it early adopted the policy of concentrating its efforts on the economic front and relegating political action to a minor role. Instead of engaging in political campaigns to obtain laws for the general improvement of working conditions, the AFL and its affiliated unions preferred to rely solely upon collective bargaining with employers. The only governmental assistance they sought was legal protection against actions of employers and public officials (such as court injunctions) which interfered with their freedom to exert the maximum economic pressure to gain better terms in their trade agreements.

The rise of a labor movement such as the American Federation of Labor resulted in the exclusion of an ever-increasing number of industrial workers from the benefits of unionization. Although the Federation from time to time made efforts to organize particular groups of factory workers, it received lukewarm support and sometimes opposition from its affiliated craft unions, which feared a dilution of their bargaining strength. The AFL type of organization had its advantages, however, for it was no doubt its limited coverage of skilled crafts which enabled it to carry on during periods when other forms of organization were unable to survive.

In contrast to the experience of unions during previous depression periods, the unions affiliated with the American Federation of Labor made substantial gains during the prolonged depression of the 1890's. On the return of business prosperity at the beginning of the present century, there was a further expansion in union organization and in collective bargaining. In the foundry and machinery industries, industry-wide bargaining was established between the unions and the employers' associations. In 1902, with the assistance of a federal government commission, collective bargaining arrangements were begun in the anthracite areas.

Membership in the American Federation of Labor increased from 350,000 in 1899 to over 1,675,000 in 1904, and some two dozen new national unions were established. By 1904 there were no less than 90 stable national unions, most of which, except the railroad and postal unions, were affiliated with the American Federation of

Labor. With the exception of the mine, brewery, garment, textile and shoe workers, practically all of them were craft unions. In the local organizations of the garment, textile, and shoe unions, moreover, craft distinctions were usually followed.

Employer Opposition

While the skilled workers in industries characterized by hand tools and small employers were able to establish new unions, factory and mill workers were facing the powerful opposition of large corporations which were assuming an ever-increasing importance in American industry. The American Railway Union, founded by the idealist Eugene V. Debs, was virtually extinguished after the strike in 1894 in which it faced the combined opposition of the Pullman Company and the Railway Managers' Association.[5]

Two years previously the Amalgamated Iron and Steel Workers, the most powerful trade union in existence at the time, had suffered a disastrous defeat in its strike at Homestead, Pennsylvania,[6] against the Carnegie Steel Company in protest against a wage reduction. Thereafter one large mill after another was put on a nonunion basis. After the formation of the United States Steel Corporation in 1901 and its adoption of a vigorous antiunion policy,[7] the once strong Iron and Steel Workers' Union was practically eliminated from all the major steel concerns in the country.

The influence and prestige of one large corporation were instrumental in driving unionization from the steel industry; in industries

[5] The Pullman strike is significant in labor history because of the numerous injunctions issued by the federal courts upon the initiative of the Department of Justice, and because President Cleveland sent United States troops to Chicago in spite of the protest of the governor of the state.

[6] One of the earliest instances of the use of a private detective agency in an industrial dispute was during the Homestead strike in 1892, when several hundred guards supplied by the Pinkerton Agency participated in riots in which scores of strikers were killed or injured.

[7] A congressional investigating committee, ten years after the adoption of this policy, said: "The great bulk of American union laboring men in the iron and steel industry understood they were not wanted at the works of the U. S. Steel Corporation. The process of filling the places of these union laborers is interesting and important. . . . Southern Europe was appealed to. Hordes . . . poured into the United States. They . . . knew absolutely nothing about iron and steel manufacture but they were sufficient to fight the labor unions." (House of Representatives, 62nd Congress, 2nd Session, Report No. 1127, p. 128.)

made up of many independent companies the employers combined into trade associations to combat the unions. Such organizations as the National Founders' Association, the National Metal Trades' Association, and the Structural Erectors' Association not only refused to enter into agreements with unions but engaged in activities directed toward their complete destruction. Local employers' associations and "citizens' alliances" also came into existence, their chief function being to break up strikes and otherwise aid employers who were having labor difficulties. In 1902 there was organized the American Anti-Boycott Association, a secret body of manufacturers who sought to attack unions through the courts.[8] About the same time the National Association of Manufacturers, originally organized for purely trade purposes, began to combat trade unions, chiefly through political and legislative means.

Paralleling these positive and belligerant campaigns against unions was the indirect effect of scientific management which was then being popularized by Frederick Taylor and his followers. Scientific management cut into union morale in two ways: The unions' opposition to its implied speed-up and the lessening of job opportunities through improved processes caused many employers to increase their determination to do away with the unions. Second, the wage incentive plans tended to discourage group loyalties and solidarity by encouraging individual workmen to seek better wages through their individual effort on the job, rather than through collective bargaining. The welfare programs which some employers were just beginning to adopt were a further means of winning employees away from "outside" unions.

LABOR DURING WORLD WAR I

The American Federation of Labor's prompt assurance of cooperation with the government upon its entry into World War I smoothed the way for the expansion in union organization which followed. In March, 1917, almost a month before the United States declared war, representatives of most of the unions met in Washington, where they voted unqualified support to the government and

[8] Among the many cases this Association took through the courts was the famous Danbury Hatters' case. (See Chapter 6.)

drew up a statement of labor's war policy. This statement expressed the demand that the organized labor movement be recognized by the government as the representative of all wage earners, including those "who have not yet organized," and that organized labor be given representation in all agencies determining and administering policies of national defense.

Government Labor Policy

The principle of labor representation on government committees was accepted. Never clearly defined was the policy with respect to organized labor's status in private industry—even in those industries upon which the government was directly dependent for carrying on the war. The Council of National Defense accepted the principle adopted by its labor advisory committee,[9] that "neither employers nor employees shall endeavor to take advantage of the country's necessities to change existing standards." The Secretary of Labor explained this as meaning that "where efforts to organize the workers are not interfered with and where a scale of wages is recognized that maintains the present standard of living . . . for the time being no stoppage of work should take place for the purpose of forcing recognition of the union." The National War Labor Board, which was established in the spring of 1918, adopted a more positive policy, namely, that "the right of workers to organize in trade unions and to bargain collectively, through chosen representatives, is recognized and affirmed. This right shall not be denied, abridged, or interfered with by the employers in any manner whatsoever."

Accompanying this positive declaration, however, was the statement that "the workers, in the exercise of their right to organize, shall not use coercive measures of any kind to induce persons to join their organizations, nor to induce employers to bargain or to deal therewith." Another statement specified that employers were not required to deal with union representatives who were not

[9] The Council of National Defense was established by the Army Appropriation Act of December, 1916. Early in 1917 an advisory committee on labor was established with Mr. Gompers as chairman; it consisted of over a hundred representatives of labor, capital, and members of organizations interested in social and industrial problems, as well as government officials and specialists.

employees of the company unless this had been the practice previously. This latter provision opened the way for the rapid growth of employees' works councils, which became a formidable rival of trade unions. These works councils (later more generally called employee representation plans or company unions) multiplied rapidly, some being installed by employers to avoid dealing with trade unions, others being established by award of government boards as an expedient compromise with firms which would have no other form of collective dealing.

In spite of this encouragement of the works councils, distinct advantages to trade unions resulted from the adoption of the principle of collective bargaining by this first National War Labor Board. With jobs plentiful enough to remove the fear of discharge and with sufficient grounds for discontent to encourage workers to seek to better their wages and hours, the established unions were able to carry on successful organization drives. Except in the steel industry, the unions connected with most of the industries important to the war effort made significant gains. The building- and metal-trades unions expanded and, on the intervention of the government, recognition was obtained from the large meat packers. The seamen were successful in getting agreements everywhere except on the Great Lakes, and the bituminous coal miners were able to extend their central competitive agreement into other areas. The shipbuilding unions obtained recognition, and the railroad brotherhoods were equally successful during the period the government took over the operation of the railroads.

INDUSTRIAL WORKERS OF THE WORLD

While the American Federation of Labor and the railroad unions were making notable gains, the war witnessed the virtual disappearance of the rival labor movement which had been active during the decade preceding the war, the Industrial Workers of the World. This organization, formally launched in 1905, was a "one big union" made up of the Western Federation of Miners[10] and the hitherto un-

[10] A metal miners' union organized in 1893. Its many bitter strikes against strongly organized employers who frequently had the active support of the sheriffs and other local government officials had made many of its members antigovernment. The more conservative faction gained control of the union in 1907

organized migratory workers of the wheat fields and lumber camps of the Northwest. It was a direct-action movement which was opposed to the signing of collective bargaining agreements with employers. Although its long-time program sought the substitution for the existing government of a workers' society in which the unions would own and operate all industry, its immediate efforts were directed toward improving conditions on the job.

At first largely confined to the unskilled workers of the West and Middle West, in 1912 the Industrial Workers of the World expanded into the East, especially among the foreign-born, low-wage textile workers. These campaigns, however, resulted in no lasting organizations although the lusty intervention of the IWW was instrumental in gaining some victories in a number of widely publicized strikes such as those of the textile workers in Lawrence, Massachusetts, in 1912 and Paterson, New Jersey, in 1913, and the Louisiana lumberjacks the same year. In Chicago[11] and farther west the IWW continued to expand until our entry into the First World War.

Many of the IWW members, including most of the leaders, refused to register for the draft. As a consequence of its antiwar position, the members were suspected and accused of acts inimicable to the pursuit of the war program, although the organizers main-

---

and the Western Federation of Miners withdrew from the Industrial Workers of the World.

[11] Chicago served not only as the editorial headquarters for the national organization but also as the local center for the midwest migratory workers. A former IWW leader gives this description of the Chicago headquarters and its environs: "In the busy season the streets were swarming with migratory workers resting up between jobs or ready to ship out—loggers, 'gandy-dancers,' lake seamen, harvest hands. . . . In prosperous times as many as a million men a year were cleared for seasonal jobs in all industries and in all parts of the country. In hard times it took on the characteristics of a labor ghetto. . . . Our general headquarters dominated the skid road.' . . . The old hall on Madison Street was full to overflowing day and night. There were big blackboards on the walls on which jobs throughout the harvest fields were listed. . . . The windows were ablaze with red lettering and a big IWW emblem. Every migratory worker on the 'skid road' wore a Wobbly button, and there were IWW stickerettes on every lamppost. Open air meetings were blocking traffic. Halls weren't large enough to accommodate crowds that turned out for Wobbly meetings and entertainments. The revolution was on! . . . Now at last, we were in a position to start 'building the structure of the new society within the shell of the old'!" (Ralph Chaplin, *Wobbly,* Chicago University Press, 1948, pp. 86–87, 198–199.)

tained that their numerous strikes were directed toward improving working conditions. Through action on the part of both the federal Department of Justice and local government, most of its leaders were imprisoned[12] and its headquarters were closed subsequent to our entry into the war. In the Northwest logging camps, where it had been most active, a representative of the War Department was successful in replacing the IWW with an organization composed of both workers and employers—the Loyal Legion of Loggers and Lumbermen—which remained in existence for more than twenty years. However, in the lumber towns and elsewhere on the Pacific coast, the IWW continued to be active throughout the war and took a prominent part in the numerous strikes following the armistice. During the tensions and hysteria of the postwar period, hundreds of its leaders were arrested under the criminal syndicalism laws. As a result of the legal suppression campaigns, as well as internal factional dissensions, the IWW lost all vitality as a general movement. Many of its most militant leaders joined the newly formed American Communist party.

STALEMATE OF THE TWENTIES

The close of the war in 1918 brought an end to active government participation in labor relations, as well as the unions' release from the wartime restraints. With the continued expansion in business and the rise in living costs following the signing of the Armistice, workers continued to join the unions in increasing numbers. In 1919 and 1920 more than one and a half million joined the various unions, bringing the total membership to over five million. This represented a peak not surpassed until 1937.

[12] In September, 1917, agents of the Department of Justice made simultaneous raids of offices of the IWW throughout the country and entered many members' homes without warrants to seize records and literature. Hundreds of members were indicted for violation of the Federal Espionage Act and sentenced to Leavenworth for terms of from one to twenty years. In 1919 a number were temporarily released on bail, including Secretary-Treasurer William ("Big Bill") Haywood. Haywood jumped his bail and went to Moscow where he lived until his death in 1928. His friends maintained that Moscow promised him that they would send some of the confiscated Russian crown jewels to this country to pay his bondsmen but that Moscow failed to keep its promise. By 1924 the sentences of practically all the IWW prisoners were commuted.

Postwar Adjustments

The unions' efforts to expand collective bargaining and raise wages led to many bitter disputes. The industrial unrest and the difficulties incident to getting industry back on a peacetime basis caused President Wilson in October, 1919, to call a conference of representatives of employers, labor, and the public to "discover such methods as had not already been tried out of bringing capital and labor into close cooperation." The conference immediately split on the question of collective bargaining and trade unions. Mr. Gompers submitted an eleven-point resolution, the first of which was the right of wage earners to organize into unions and to bargain collectively. The employer group adopted a resolution including "the right of employers to deal or not to deal with men or groups of men who are not their employees," stating that the arbitrary use of collective bargaining "was a menace to the institution of free peoples." The representatives of the public endorsed the principle of collective bargaining but insisted that employee representation "plans" be included as proper collective bargaining agencies. Unable to arrive at any common agreement on the fundamental basis of all employer-employee relations, the conference broke up within a few days.

The Open-shop Movement

Following this conference, employers throughout the country started a movement to destroy unionism. Manufacturers' associations, boards of trade, chambers of commerce, builders' associations, bankers' associations, so-called "citizens' associations," and even a farmers' organization—the National Grange—united in a program, which they called the "American Plan," to save workers from "the shackles of organization to their own detriment."[13] Open-shop organizations were established in practically every industrial center in the country. In addition to conducting "patronize the open shop" campaigns, these organizations extended direct aid to employers such as maintaining blacklists of union members and fur-

[13] From a statement of policy of the American Bankers' Association in the magazine *Industry*, January 1, 1921.

nishing money, spies, and strikebreakers to employers involved in strikes.

Union after union lost its war and postwar gains under the combined onslaught of the antiunion drives and the wage cuts introduced during the postwar depression of 1921–1922. Early in 1921 the "Big Five" packing companies declared that they no longer would be bound by the union agreement, and the packing industry once again became open-shop. The United States Shipping Board and private shipowners demanded the abolition of the three-watch system and the withdrawal of union preferential hiring. Seamen returned to the 12-hour day, 84-hour week, and the once powerful seamen's union was soon reduced to less than one-fifth its former size.

Even the strongly organized building trades did not escape the antiunion drives. When the building-trades unions in San Francisco rejected a wage reduction, employers conducted a general lockout until the workers returned under open-shop conditions. In Chicago, a citizens' committee organized by the Illinois Manufacturers' Association and the Chicago Chamber of Commerce was successful for several years in compelling unions and builders to maintain an open shop and to accept the wage rates determined by an arbitrator.

Efforts to break up the unions failed in a few industries, notably in the book and job printing industry and in the New York men's and women's clothing industry, although the unions were forced to engage in prolonged strikes in order to maintain their collective bargaining relations.

In spite of occasional victories for the unions, the employers' open-shop drives, aided by the postwar depression, resulted in large losses to organized labor. Union membership dropped from a peak of over 5 million in 1920 to 3½ million in 1924 and, contrary to all similar experience in the past, continued to decline after the return of business prosperity.

WELFARE CAPITALISM

The chief reason for the absence of trade union growth during the 1920's was the failure to organize the expanding mass-production industries. New machines and processes were substituting semi-skilled machine tenders for skilled craftsmen working with tools.

The bulk of the trade unions were composed of skilled craftsmen, and few of them made any serious attempts to broaden their field of interest to include the new type of factory worker. Whole industries, such as automobile and rubber, remained untouched; in others, such as steel, electrical products, furniture, and glass manufacture, only a fraction of certain groups of skilled workers belonged to any union.

Even if energetic organizing efforts had been undertaken, the response of many of these workers at that time might have been lukewarm, especially those in the newer expanding industries where relatively high wages were paid and where increasing production softened the incidence of technological displacements. The comparatively high wages received by these workers were not diluted by rising costs of living, for the prices which workers paid for what they bought remained stable through this period. If there had been a marked increase in the cost of living, no doubt many of the unorganized workers would have sought the assistance of already established unions or formed new ones, just as they had in the past when prices were rising.

It was in these industries, characterized by large corporations, that management was most active in the adoption of programs which many employers felt made unions unnecessary. The twenties marked the peak of welfare activities, when employees' pension plans, group life insurance, and medical services were offered by employers as security against the unavoidable hazards of life; when professional personnel managers were engaged to handle the grievances and problems arising on the job; and when plant baseball teams, glee clubs, and dances provided recreation off the job. To create an attitude of partnership with management, employee stock-ownership was encouraged and sometimes required.[14]

As a further substitute for trade unions, a number of employers established works councils or employee representation plans. Many

[14] The National Industrial Conference Board (*Employee-Stock Purchase Plans in 1928*) estimated that in 1928 over a million employees owned or had subscribed for over a billion dollars' worth of securities of the companies by which they were employed. In over 315 companies which reported having employee-stock-ownership plans, 30 per cent of the employees were stockholders. All the employees of the Firestone Tire and Rubber Company, and 70 per cent of those of the International Harvester Company, owned company stock.

of these company unions were established after an unsuccessful strike by trade unions. Shop councils were established on the Pennsylvania and a number of other railroad systems following the shopmen's strike in 1922; the General Electric Industrial Representation Plan was established subsequent to numerous strikes of the metal workers' unions; and some of the larger New England textile mills adopted employee representation plans as an aftermath of strikes by the textile unions.

UNION-MANAGEMENT COOPERATION

In response to the challenge offered by personnel managers and by company unions, a number of the trade unions adopted programs of union-management cooperation. The first such plan on a broad basis was entered into by the Baltimore and Ohio Railroad and the Machinists' Union soon after the railroad shopmen's strike in 1922, and was later accepted by other shop crafts and several other railroad systems not already entrenched in company unionism. The cooperative machinery provided for local, regional and system joint committees of union representatives and supervisors, which not only handled employee grievances but discussed all questions and problems relating to the greater efficiency and improvement of railroad service. Similar arrangements were entered into by the Association of Street and Railway Employees and the Philadelphia Rapid Transit Company whereby, under the Mitten Plan, the union shared with management the responsibility for promoting efficiency and reducing operating costs.

The Amalgamated Clothing Workers' Union was an outstanding example of a union's willingness to share in management responsibility. Employers were persuaded to allow union experts to go into the shop in order to reorganize the flow of work, subdivide processes, establish production standards, and even substitute machines for hand labor. When such innovations resulted in reductions of the staff, dismissal wages were sometimes provided for the employees laid off; in other instances, such workers were transferred to other plants by the union's centralized hiring hall. In addition to these aids for improving the competitive position of individual firms, the union sometimes loaned money to enable employers to stay in business.

Another instance of union-management cooperation took place in the coal industry. As an aftermath of a bitter strike in the Colorado coal fields in 1927, the United Mine Workers accepted the offer of one of the companies, the Rocky Mountain Fuel and Iron Company which was friendly to union organizations, to cooperate with management in order to obtain maximum efficiency so that the company might compete successfully with neighboring nonunion mines which paid lower wages. Later, cooperative relations progressed to such an extent that the union undertook sales promotion campaigns to bring more business to the company.

Union motives for entering into cooperative plans with management were twofold. They believed that efficiency provided the key to higher wages, and they also hoped that their endorsement of such programs would encourage nonunion employers to welcome unionization. During this period when the unions were unable to win new members through the customary organization drives, many of them adopted the "front-door" approach; that is, organizers went directly to employers and sought closed-shop contracts in return for promises of a more efficient and stable work force. Very few employers responded to this approach, and where unions were accepted on this basis, they usually lost vitality as employee organizations and became, in essence, little more than company unions.

Left-wing Movement

The close of the First World War and the return to "normalcy" ushered in a period of decline for the regular labor movement. A year before the signing of the armistice the Russian revolution had taken place which had immediate reverberations in this country. One was a solidifying of various left-wing groups—syndicalists, anarchists, radical socialists—with a focus toward Russia. The American Communist party was formally launched in 1920 and its members were ordered by the Communist International to join the unions of their craft and propagandize for the party and for revolution. This "boring from within" was done under the aegis of the Trade Union Educational League established by William Z. Foster, later president of the American Communist party, although he had disclaimed Communist affiliation when conducting the 1919 general steel strike.

The Trade Union Educational League was vigorously opposed by the American Federation of Labor and it never gained much headway. Unsuccessful with boring-from-within methods, the Party in 1928 established the Trade Union Unity League which was frankly a dual labor movement. Capitalizing upon the discontent of many workers who were dissatisfied with the passive role of the American Federation of Labor and the restrictive membership of the craft unions, the TUUL met with some success in some industries. It organized a number of industrial unions, the most important being in the mining, textile, and needle industries.

The National Miners' Union was active during the coal strikes in 1931, especially in and around Harlan County, Kentucky. Most of these coal strikes ended in defeat, the few settlements which were made being negotiated with the older United Mine Workers. The National Textile Workers' Union conducted a number of organization strikes among southern textile workers, the best known of which occurred in Gastonia, North Carolina. The establishment of a Needle Trades Workers Industrial Union was the outgrowth of years of bitter strife between the Communists and the regular trade unionists within the Ladies' Garment Workers. Although the League was active for a few years in these areas, its total membership was probably never over a hundred thousand.

In 1934 the Party decided it was better strategy to give up dualism and resume "boring from within." The League was dissolved as a separate organization and its members re-entered their respective unions. Before this took place, momentous changes were already underway within the main stream of the labor movement.

2

THE LAST THIRTY YEARS

The stalemate of the twenties was followed by a further decline in union membership and influence during the early 1930's depression, but conditions changed drastically during the ensuing New Deal period.

From a low ebb of fewer than three million members in 1933, union organizations developed into a dynamic and expanding movement with a membership of 10.5 million just before World War II. While a sympathetic government and favorable economic conditions provided the opportunity for this expansion, the workers themselves were responsible for the actual growth in numbers and influence. Given a break by the law and public opinion, large masses of workers showed a spontaneous desire for organized efforts to improve their living conditions, and vigorous labor leadership came to the fore.

During World War II and the postwar prosperity period union membership in the United States expanded to reach a peak of 17.5 million in 1956. During the 1957–1958 recession organized labor lost half a million members, which it has not been able to regain. The major reasons for the lack of growth have been the introduction of automatic processes throughout industry, with a resulting decline in employment in the occupations where unions had their greatest strength, and the inability of organized labor to attract members from the increasing numbers of white-collar workers who are entering the labor force. In 1956, for the first time in our history, the number of salesmen, clerical, technical and professional workers exceeded the total number of manual workers, and the trend in white-collar employment has been steadily upward.

THRESHOLD OF THE NEW DEAL

The unfolding events of the New Deal period, and their impact upon the labor movement, can be appreciated only in the light of the milieu from which they developed. The situation confronting workers in their efforts to organize and to bargain collectively *before* the dramatic political and social upheaval during the 1930's has been summarized thus:

> The workers were free to bargain collectively; their right to organize and bargain collectively was recognized and repeatedly affirmed by legislatures and by courts. Their right to strike was also recognized, though, as we have seen it, it was by no means unqualified. But the rights of employers and nonunion workers were also recognized and affirmed. Nonunion workers had the right to get and hold jobs; employers had the right to use yellow-dog contracts, to hire and fire for any or no reason, and to organize company unions. They also had the right of access to the commodity and labor markets, the right to operate their plants, and the general right to do business.
>
> Now these rights of workers and employers were bound to come into conflict. And the courts who were supposed to enforce the rights of both groups very frequently had to decide which rights to enforce. On the whole, their decisions in such cases tended to favor the employers, largely because their rights were better understood by lawyers and judges, and were more susceptible of protection through court proceedings.
>
> The right to bargain collectively certainly includes the right to join a union. Yet the protection of this right by forbidding discriminatory discharges and yellow-dog contracts was held to be an infringement of the employer's right to hire and fire. . . . While the courts enforced yellow-dog contracts which enabled employers to maintain *shops closed to union labor,* they often held illegal strikes to secure *shops closed to nonunion labor.* Again, collective action by workers cannot be effective unless it extends beyond the confines of a local craft union. Yet the courts, ignoring economic realities, condemned many kinds of sympathetic action on the ground that these workers had no legitimate interest in the dispute.
>
> Collective action by workers is more likely to interfere with the rights of the public than are the methods which employers use to combat it. Pickets must use the streets, agitation may lead to violence; but the firing of employees or the procuring of new ones is but an incident to the regular conduct of business. Hence the courts were more likely to interfere with the activities of workers.

Injunctions theoretically could be used to protect workers' rights as well as employers'. But the injunction can only be used to protect property rights from irreparable injury. For the most part, workers' rights were not recognized as property rights which could be protected in this way. . . . Thus in actual practice the law operated to protect those employers who strove to prevent organization among their workers, who refused to bargain collectively, or who were trying to break a strike. The workers had the right to bargain collectively, but in seeking to achieve this end they were allowed to use only those methods which did not interfere with the rights of employers and of nonunion workers.[1]

These concepts of "rights" and the court decisions which resulted from them did not go unchallenged. Large sections of the general public became more and more aware that the uneven hand of the law was suppressing many laudable purposes of organized workers and interfering with their basic right to improve their working conditions. Public recognition of the need for a counterpoise was evidenced by the passage of the Norris-LaGuardia Act in 1932, which placed strict limitations upon the injunctive powers of the federal courts and made yellow-dog contracts illegal.

LABOR GAINS UNDER THE NEW DEAL

Although the Norris-LaGuardia Act foreshadowed the legislation which was to come, the New Deal's influence on the progress of union organization amounted to much more than placing additional and strengthened laws on the statute books. Experience with similar legislation at the hands of the courts in the past made for a good deal of skepticism regarding the outcome of the Norris-LaGuardia Act at the time it was enacted. It was not until after the Supreme Court, in 1937, had taken cognizance of the change in public opinion which had occurred under the New Deal that any kind of labor legislation was reasonably secure from judicial invalidation.[2] Just

[1] J. R. Commons and J. B. Andrews, *Principles of Labor Legislation,* Harper & Brothers, New York, 1936, pp. 417–419.

[2] Regardless of the merits of President Roosevelt's efforts to "pack the Supreme Court," there is no doubt that his threat to increase the personnel of the court caused a drastic change in the attitude of its members toward all types of labor legislation—wage and hour controls as well as protection for collective bargaining. During the turmoil over the court-packing threat, in the spring of 1937, the

a year previously it had stated that "the relation of employer and employee is a local relation and consequently beyond the scope of Federal jurisdiction . . . the relation of employer and employee, at common law, is one of domestic relations . . . the powers which the general government may exercise are only those specifically enumerated in the Constitution, and such implied powers as are necessary and proper to carry into effect the enumerated powers. . . ."[3]

THE NATIONAL INDUSTRIAL RECOVERY ACT

The first legislation under the New Deal government which directly affected organized labor was the National Industrial Recovery Act, enacted in June, 1933. In addition to an extensive public works program, the Act provided that each industry establish codes of fair competition which were to include minimum working standards. Labor was given only an advisory status in the preparation of the codes, although in a few instance, such as clothing and mining, the union representatives were active in determining the labor terms and in seeing that they were enforced.

Of vital significance to organized labor was Section 7a of the Act, which required that each code contain the provision that "employees shall have the right to organize and to bargain collectively through representatives of their own choosing, and shall be free from the interference, restraint, or coercion of employers . . . in the designation of such representatives. . . ." Labor boards were created to handle disputes arising over the interpretation of this section and to conduct elections to determine bargaining representation.

Supreme Court declared three basic types of labor legislation to be constitutional, namely, the National Labor Relations Act, the Social Security Act and the Washington state minimum wage law for women. The preceding year it had declared unconstitutional the New York state minimum wage law which was similar to the Washington law. Actually, the change in opinion of the court during these few months represented a change in attitude on the part of only one or two justices, most of the cases in both years being five-four decisions.

[3] Carter *v.* Carter Coal Co. *et.al.*, 298 U.S. 238 (1936). This decision invalidated the 1935 National Bituminous Coal Conservation Act and, in effect, held that Congress had no power to regulate wages, hours of labor, and working conditions in an industry not directly engaged in interstate commerce; it declared that "mining is not interstate commerce, but, like manufacturing, is a local business."

A wave of union activity followed in the wake of the passage of the National Industrial Recovery Act. Much of this was the result of the planned efforts of unions which sought to organize the open-shop areas in their industries. In many nonunion industries and regions, however, the urge to organize emanated from the workers themselves, with union organizers in many instances unable to keep up with the demands made upon them. The biggest gains were made by the mine workers' and the men's and women's clothing unions which had suffered such severe losses during the twenties that the gains made under the National Industrial Recovery Act signified the virtual revival of these unions.

As a result of the twenty-two months' activity under the Act, membership in American Federation of Labor unions increased over 40 per cent. In 1935, for the first time since 1922, their total paid-up membership exceeded three million. The Railroad Brotherhoods, benefiting from the 1934 amendment to the Railway Labor Act, also expanded. Organized labor as a whole not only recouped its depression losses and regained some of the following it had lost during the 1920's, but began to enter a few of the hitherto nonunion industries. Scattered local unions appeared among the mass-production industries and even among white-collar and agricultural workers.

Company Unions Under the NIRA

During this time of union revival and expansion, many employers were active in setting up their substitute for trade unions, namely, company unions. Although Section 7a was interpreted by labor to mean the legal right of being represented by unions which were co-extensive with employers' trade associations, many employers insisted that dealing exclusively with their own employee representatives fulfilled the requirements of the law and that the workers' freedom "from interference, restraint, and coercion" did not preclude assistance from employers in establishing and maintaining company unions. Accordingly, employee representation plans which had been formed before the depression and had become moribund were revived, and new ones were established.

By the spring of 1934, probably one-fourth of all industrial workers were employed in plants which maintained company unions. Almost two-thirds of these unions were established while the National Industrial Recovery Act was in force—a majority of them after a strike had taken place or a trade union had made headway in the plant. Most of the larger steel, rubber, petroleum, and chemical companies had company unions, as well as many of the utility companies and manufacturing concerns of all kinds. A good deal of the time of the National Recovery Administration labor boards was devoted to the disputes arising from the conflicting claims of unions and employers over the interpretation of Section 7a with respect to company unions.

GROWTH UNDER THE NLRA

The protections afforded labor under the National Industrial Recovery Act had become sufficiently acceptable to induce Congress, a few months after the Supreme Court's invalidation[4] of that Act in May, 1935, to enact a law exclusively dealing with labor's rights and privileges. The National Labor Relations Act guaranteed employees "the right to self-organization, to form, join, or assist labor organizations, to bargain collectively through representatives of their own choosing, and to engage in concerted activities for the purpose of collective bargaining or other mutual aid or protection." But passage of a law does not always insure immediate observance, and for almost two years the operation of this Act was seriously impeded by the resistance of many employers who were firmly convinced that the Act would be invalidated in the courts. Much to their surprise, its constitutionality was affirmed by the Supreme Court in April, 1937, and a number of Supreme Court decisions thereafter clarified the coverage of the Act and strengthened the power of the board created to enforce it.

The National Labor Relations Act (Wagner Act) signified governmental assistance of the first magnitude to organized labor. Na-

[4] When the labor provisions of the NIRA are under consideration it must be remembered that the other clauses of the Act providing for codes of fair competition accorded certain rights of collective action to employers which were forbidden under the antitrust laws. It was the price-fixing and similar features of the Act which were the points at issue in the Schechter case when the Supreme Court nullified the law.

tional unions successfully entered the mass-production industries such as the steel, automobile, rubber, and electrical products industries. Workers in industrial centers in the Southern states, as well as in many of the smaller communities in the Northern states, were aroused to trade union consciousness for the first time. Union organization made some headway among agricultural hired laborers, sharecroppers, and cannery workers. Coal miners were organized in sections where formerly employer hostility, aided by local government officials, had been an effective barrier against unionization. Interest in organization extended into certain groups of white-collar workers, such as newspaper reporters, as well as office workers and retail clerks in some cities. Unions expanded among federal government workers and were established for the first time for many state and local government employees.

These organization drives were accompanied by many strikes, some of which were called as a means of rallying workers to the unions, while others were resorted to when employers refused recognition after the union had obtained majority representation. Most of these strikes took the conventional form of a walkout with picketing, but a considerable number were sit-down strikes and these received a great deal of adverse public criticism. Within a very few years, however, organization strikes declined as unions were able to take advantage of the legal rights afforded by the Wagner Act to gain recognition through employee elections and certification by the National Labor Relations Board.

FORMATION OF THE CIO

Concurrently with the passage and validation of the National Labor Relations Act, momentous changes had taken place within the labor movement itself. Since the beginning of the labor movement there have been differences of opinion as to whether unions should be organized along occupation or craft lines, or whether they should be coterminous with the industries concerned. The American Federation of Labor unions were predominantly craft organizations, although some were established on an industrial basis, and others gradually expanded their coverage to include most or all of the employees within a plant or industry regardless of occupation.

When the organization of the mass-production industries was undertaken during the National Recovery Administration, the issue of craft versus industrial unionism became acute. At the 1934 AFL convention a resolution was adopted which recognized that there had been "a change in the nature of the work performed by millions of workers in industries which it has been most difficult or impossible to organize into craft unions." The same resolution stated, however: "We consider it our duty to formulate policies which will fully protect the jurisdictional rights of all trade unions organized upon craft lines." The controversy came to a head at the 1935 convention, when jurisdiction coextensive with the industry was denied the rubber, automobile, radio and other unions.

A month after this convention the presidents of eight AFL unions, under the leadership and driving force of John L. Lewis,[5] created a Committee for Industrial Organization "for the purpose of encouraging and promoting the organization of the unorganized workers in mass-production and other industries upon an industrial basis." The AFL interpreted the formation of this Committee as dual in character and as decidedly menacing to its success and welfare; and in May, 1938, the AFL expelled the unions participating in the Committee. A few months later, the thirty-two national unions, together with the city and state bodies then forming the Committee, met in constitutional convention and established the Congress of Industrial Organizations.

The formation of the CIO caused a spectacular growth in unionization of the mass-production industries. But the dynamics and influence of the new labor movement extended beyond its immediate membership. Many of the older craft unions, responding to the challenge of the newer unions, extended their jurisdictions to include semiskilled and unskilled workers and in many plants functioned as industrial unions. Likewise the boldness and vigor dis-

[5] John L. Lewis president of the United Mine Workers, became the first president of the CIO. He resigned following the 1940 national elections after he failed to divert labor's support of President Roosevelt. A few years previously, Lewis had been a vigorous supporter of Roosevelt, and the United Mine Workers had contributed a half million dollars to the 1936 Roosevelt campaign. The subsequent estrangement has been attributed to the fact that Roosevelt refused "to come across" on all the demands Lewis made upon him, and which Lewis felt he was entitled to because of his campaign support.

played by some of the young leaders in the CIO influenced other union leaders to strive for greater gains for their members.

At the time of the attack upon Pearl Harbor, unions affiliated with the CIO had become well established in all the major steel, automobile, rubber and other mass-production plants, and, as war production expanded, both AFL and CIO unions were able to obtain contractual relations in the new aircraft, shipbuilding, maritime and other war plants.

WORLD WAR II AND ITS AFTERMATH

All branches of organized labor took an active part in many phases of the war production program. At the outset, President Roosevelt indicated that the safeguards afforded labor by the National Labor Relations Act, the Fair Labor Standards Act, and the Public Contracts Act were not to be sacrificed but rather to be utilized to strengthen morale and improve productive efficiency. On the whole, cordial relations with organized labor were maintained by the War and Navy Departments, both of which employed labor relations experts at their Washington headquarters, as well as in the important production centers, to plan and direct labor policies and assist in settling differences between unions and military authorities. As a morale builder, union leaders were taken to training centers and foreign combat areas to see how guns and ammunition were being used and to gain first-hand knowledge of war production needs.

Direct participation in government administration was provided in the tripartite National War Labor Board which was established as a "supreme court for labor disputes." So long as this Board confined its activities to the original purpose, organized labor enthusiastically endorsed it as an example of voluntary cooperation by management, labor, and government. There was considerable dissatisfaction, however, after the Board was given responsibility for administering the wage stabilization program.

Postwar Strains

When the last bomb was dropped over Japan, the semblance of union-management cooperation which had been fostered during the war disappeared in large sections of our industry. Workers had become more and more restive under the wage stablization program, and when overtime and other war bonus payments ended they were determined to have their wage rates increased. Moreover, they insisted that employers, with their accumulated war profits and bright outlook for an era of high production, could afford pay increases without jeopardizing the price stabilization program. The employers, on the other hand, contended that this was impossible and gave as one reason the decline in worker efficiency which they stated had taken place during the war years when jobs were plentiful.

Underlying the wage disputes was the old, unresolved issue of what constitutes the necessary functions and prerogatives of management, and to what degree and along what lines workers shall participate in the making and administration of plant policies. Concretely, this is a question of the interpretation of collective bargaining, and many employers who asserted they were in favor of the principle of collective bargaining were nevertheless in wide disagreement with their unions over important matters pertaining to shop management.

With the hope that some workable solution of these major issues could be found, President Truman called a Labor-Management Conference on Industrial Relations in November, 1945. After several weeks' discussion, the conference adjourned with no agreement between management and labor on the issue, as stated in the agenda, of "management's right to manage." This conference was a disappointment in so far as it was unable to achieve any meeting of minds on the major specific problems facing industry and labor. In contrast to the similar conference after the First World War, however, there was no disagreement over the principle or right of collective bargaining *per se*.

THE 1947 LABOR-MANAGEMENT RELATIONS ACT

The discontent of workers was expressed in the numerous and prolonged strikes which took place during the winter and spring of 1945–1946. The strikes resulted in a general lifting of wage levels, but this was a Pyrrhic victory because price controls were simultaneously relaxed and the cost of living advanced. Organized labor suffered a serious setback after the 1946 elections when conservative Republicans gained control of Congress. The Eightieth Congress enacted practically none of the legislation which the unions sponsored as a means of smoothing the transition from a war to a peacetime economy. Proposed bills to control prices, guarantee full employment, raise the minimum legal wage level, liberalize and extend the coverage of social security and unemployment benefits, provide health insurance and housing programs, were either rejected entirely or amended to such a degree that they had little resemblance to the original measures which organized labor had sponsored.

Much more disconcerting to organized labor than congressional inaction on proposed legislation to bring new benefits, was its enactment of a new labor relations law which completely altered the philosophy of the 1935 Wagner Act and nullified portions of the 1932 Anti-injunction Law. The Wagner Act dealt solely with the establishment of the collective bargaining *process,* and its regulations were concerned only with removing those employer practices which impeded the ability of workers to engage in collective bargaining, that is, their combining in the collective mechanism of labor unions. The 1947 Taft-Hartley Act extended government regulation beyond the establishment of conditions *for* collective bargaining into the substantive terms in the collective bargaining contract in addition to setting up restrictions against certain kinds of union activity.

The majority in Congress maintained that the 1947 Taft-Hartley Act, enacted over President Truman's veto, was for the purpose of restoring the equality of bargaining rights between employers and employees, thus rectifying the one-sided protections given unions by the previous legislation. Organized labor declared it was a vindictive attack on unions, dubbed it a "slave labor act," and immediately started a campaign for its repeal.

CIO and the Communists

When the American Communist party, presumably under instructions from Moscow, abandoned its unsuccessful dual unionism (Trade Union Unity League), it found a haven for its "boring-from-within" tactics in the newly established, militant CIO. The new movement, in need of vigorous leaders, was happy to benefit from the organizing skill and indefatigable zeal of its Communist members, and assumed that political differences could be ignored. The Communists were in the vanguard of many of the early organizing drives and, benefiting from the atmosphere of goodwill toward our Russian ally during the war, they obtained positions of leadership in a number of the CIO unions and in the high councils of the CIO itself. Vociferously proclaiming the need for labor unity, they were able to form a tightly knit and closely disciplined core within the CIO which never became assimilated into its trade union program.

Although the majority non-Communist elements in the CIO recognized the Communists' presence as a constant threat to democratic unionism, they were tolerated as long as the "party line" did not conflict with fundamental CIO policy. The inevitable and final showdown came over some concrete and specific issues—issues which were reflections of the same differences which have divided the entire world into two hostile camps.

The first concrete issue which brought the long-smoldering friction within the CIO into the open was the question of endorsement of the Marshall Plan to aid the recovery of war-stricken Europe. The bitter debate which took place when the CIO 1947 convention endorsed the government program clearly revealed which CIO officers were following the "party line" in support of the Soviet opposition to the Marshall Plan and the Atlantic Pact.

The crucial issue which caused the final showdown between the Communist and anti-Communist factions in the CIO was the question of affiliation with the World Federation of Trade Unions. During the few months of optimistic hope for a united world which prevailed in 1945, the labor movements from the various countries formed a new World Federation of Trade Unions. The American Federation of Labor never joined the WFTU, but the CIO became an enthusiastic member.[6] It soon became evident that the new world organization was being dominated by its Soviet members, and in 1949 the CIO, as well as the British and other national federa-

[6] See Chapter 14 for an account of the formation of the World Federation of Trade Unions.

tions, formally severed connections with the World Federation of Trade Unions. The Communist-dominated unions within the CIO refused to abide by this action and insisted upon their right to continue association with the WFTU and its subsidiary organizations. Decisive action was taken at the 1949 CIO convention, when the constitution was amended to give the executive board power to expel any union for pro-Communist actions. During the ensuing months the charters of eleven unions were revoked.

Corruption in Unions

Racketeering has been a perennial problem in the labor movement, especially in the trucking, longshore, construction and garment trades. This is only one of the many areas in which racketeers operate in modern American society, but unions are especially vulnerable and union members suffer more directly than most other individuals from racketeers' manipulations. The labor racketeers, most of whom have criminal records, worm themselves into the labor movement and either take over existing organizations or establish "paper" organizations for the purpose of extortion. In addition to outright theft of union funds, dishonest union officials often sign substandard contracts with employers in exchange for bribes, thereby forcing employees to work for less pay and under poorer conditions than a legitimate union contract would bring them. Opportunities and temptations for dishonest practices have been vastly increased since the taking over by many unions of the administration of pension and welfare funds negotiated through bargaining.

Corruption and racketeering in all their devious forms were brought to the attention of the general public through the hearings of a Senate committee during 1955 and subsequent years.[7] Most of the testimony was concerned with top officials of the Teamsters' Union, but a half dozen other unions were also involved. The officers of the AFL–CIO unequivocally endorsed the "full exposure of corruption wherever it exists," and co-operated with the Senate committee whenever called upon. In an effort to clean its own

[7] The Select Committee on Improper Activities in the Labor and Management Field. Its chairman was Senator J. I. McClellan, and it was thus popularly identified with his name.

house, the Executive Council adopted a Code of Ethics and established an Ethical Practices Committee to act upon members' complaints and to investigate on its own initiative wherever circumstances warranted. By the time of the 1957 AFL–CIO convention the disclosures of the Senate committee hearings, as well as by its own committees, were so devastating that the convention voted to expel the Teamsters' Union and two smaller unions, and to place several more on probation.

THE LANDRUM-GRIFFIN ACT

This same convention, even as it took drastic action against corruption among its affiliates, also voiced concern that the McClellan Committee might permit itself to be used for "political retaliation" and as a "forum for the display of antiunion proposals." During the next two sessions of Congress labor fought strenuously to prevent the passage of legislation designed to extend far beyond the prevention of corruption. Several years previously the AFL–CIO had recommended legislation for the filing of financial reports and punishment of malfeasance. This in itself was a departure from labor's traditional policy of "no government intervention in internal union affairs." But the many bills considered by the Eighty-sixth Congress included restrictions on some activities in which unions had engaged for a hundred years, as well as proposals for "tightening" some of the Taft-Hartley restrictions which the unions considered onerous as they were.

The congressional battle was prolonged and bitter, and labor believed it had met with a major defeat when the Landrum-Griffin Act was finally passed[8] although some harsh measures which had been proposed were not included. The fundamental significance of the Act was that it opened the door for government's entrance into the "house of labor." Previous legislation, such as the Norris-LaGuardia and Taft-Hartley acts, had been confined to external activities of unions, especially in their dealings with employers. Since 1960 the government has laid down rules as to how union officers are to be elected and removed, how funds are to be handled, the circumstances under which a union may revoke a local's charter,

[8] Formally titled the Labor-Management Reporting and Disclosure Act. It was signed by President Eisenhower on September 14, 1959. (See Chapter 7.)

and procedures for the protection of members who criticize their union officers. The new law is a tacit recognition that labor unions, like corporations and financial institutions, are quasi-public in character and therefore subject to the watchful attention of government.

DISUNITY AND UNITY

For twenty years after the formation of the Congress of Industrial Organizations the labor movement in the United States was divided into several camps. The American Federation of Labor continued as the dominant movement although the CIO was firmly established in the great mass-production industries and wielded an influence extending far beyond its membership. Aggressively active in rallying the masses of unskilled and semiskilled workers, the CIO had not neglected the skilled workers. Although it had been based on the concept of industrial unionism, it soon found that there was no one formula for labor organization; consequently it began to include all types of unions—craft, industrial and mixtures of both. In self-protection, the AFL began to pay more than lip service to the needs of the great mass of workers, and many of its affiliates, which hitherto had closed their doors to all but craftsmen, actively sought recruits from all classes of labor. Within a few years after the split, there was little difference in structure or program between the AFL and the CIO.

Gradually, at the local as well as the national level, the two groups began to undertake an increasing number of joint efforts, especially in legislative and political matters, and there was soon much discussion about means of attaining organic unity. Since both organizations had expanded into many of the same industries and occupations, unscrambling the scrambled jurisdictional lines involved delicate decisions by the top leaders, as well as support from the rank-and-file members whose very jobs were at stake.

The first practical step toward structural unity was to get the various rival unions to agree upon terms of an armistice—that is, to cease raiding activities and establish a working basis for cooperative action. Rivalry was costly in terms of prestige as well as of money. During a three-year period it was reported that the various unions had spent well over $11 million in raiding campaigns or in defending themselves against raiding. In 1953 both the AFL and the CIO conventions approved a no-raiding agreement, with final determination of jurisdiction to be given to an umpire chosen by the AFL and CIO presidents. Although the agreement was voluntary, a number of unions availed themselves of this machinery for the settlement of their jurisdictional quarrels.

FORMATION OF THE AFL–CIO

Unity at the top was finally achieved when the 1955 conventions of both organizations decided "to create a single trade union center through the process of merger which will preserve the integrity of each affiliated union." The name which was adopted implied unity on an equal basis, rather than the absorption of the smaller CIO by the larger AFL which the latter had insisted upon for many years. Thus the twenty-year split was ended with the uniting of the American Federation of Labor, founded in 1881, and the Congress of Industrial Organizations, founded in 1935. Their combined membership of fifteen million did not, however, include the United Mine Workers, the Railroad Brotherhoods or a number of other independent unions. Moreover, just two years after the merger the new organization lost more than a million members when it expelled the Teamsters' Union and several others because of corruption.

The constitution of the AFL-CIO specifically provides for equal status of craft and industrial unions and the preservation of existing unions except by voluntary action on their part. State federations and local central bodies were required to unite within two years—although it was actually to be six years before all the state federations finally achieved structural unity. The unity at the top facilitated the merger of a number of dual unions which as separate AFL and CIO organizations had operated in the same industries and trades. But the formation of one central labor body by no means solved the problem of jurisdictional and raiding disputes between craft and industrial unions, and much time has been spent by union officers and their conventions in airing these quarrels and devising plans for their solution.[9] The present formula calls for

[9] An area which involves especially serious jurisdictional conflict is that of

referral to an outside umpire with final appeal to the AFL–CIO Executive Board.

Independent unions are of course not subject to the controls established by the affiliated organizations. Since its expulsion, the Teamsters' Union has frankly extended its jurisdictional claims to include any and all workers whom it can induce to become members. The United Mine Workers have also enlisted members outside the mining industry, and in Hawaii the west-coast Longshoremen's Union has extended far beyond longshoring. This presents one aspect of a complex problem comparable to that faced by the United Nations. Is it preferable to take in all unions or nations with the hope of bringing them into line, or to exclude or banish them as punishment for their misdeeds?

THE LABOR MOVEMENT TODAY

The growth of labor unions in membership and influence during the twenty-year period between 1935 and 1955 can accurately be called phenomenal. It brought about a revolutionary change in the way our private enterprise system is conducted. It has materially affected the political balance of power and has been a strong influence in numerous economic and social reforms. It has changed the attitude of all workers, nonunion as well as union members.

Employers continue to oppose unions over specific issues, but most of them no longer claim the "natural right" of determining wages and work conditions on a unilateral basis. The law of the land unequivocally proclaims the right of workers to form unions and to bargain collectively, even though specific provisions of the laws seem to organize labor to be unduly restrictive to the full implementation of these rights. Politically, unions are a power to be reckoned with, at least during election campaigns. And the great mass of workers have come to rely upon unions as their "rod and staff" for protection against unfair treatment on the job. Even

---

plant maintenance and the installing and repairing of machinery and equipment. The industrial union—the Automobile Workers, for example—seeks to have such jobs performed by its members, while the Carpenters or Machinists want this work "contracted out" to construction firms with whom they have contracts. To the union it is a matter of prestige and size; to the workers it is a bread-and-butter matter of job rights.

in unorganized plants employees are conscious that unions are available if their conditions become too unsatisfactory.

Visible evidences of the growth and prosperity of unions are their impressive headquarters in Washington and elsewhere, the size of their staffs, and the salaries paid to many of their officers. The administration of many of the larger unions is not unlike that of a business corporation. In addition to the traditional staff of organizers employed to supervise and assist their local affiliates, the national unions now require fiscal experts to administer their welfare funds, publicity personnel for their numerous publications, and lawyers to protect and advise them on the intricacies of all the laws now in effect having to do with unions, as well as numerous clerks to attend to the increased paper work incidental to the reporting now required by law.

As unions have acquired status and relative stability, there is some concern that they may have lost the dynamism and militancy of the 1930's and 1940's. The young, enthusiastic leaders who organized the CIO unions are now as old as their counterparts in the former AFL unions, and some observers say they have acquired the same "business unionism" attitude[10] as was prevalent among the

TABLE 1. Union Membership in the United States, 1900–1962[a]

Year	Membership	Year	Membership
1900	868,500	1936	4,700,000
1905	2,022,300	1939	8,200,000
1910	2,140,500	1942	12,000,000
1915	2,582,600	1945	13,600,000
1917	3,061,400	1948	14,600,000
1920	5,047,800	1951	15,300,000
1925	3,519,400	1954	17,000,000
1930	3,392,800	1956	17,500,000
1933	2,973,000	1958	17,000,000
1934	3,608,600	1962	17,000,000

[a] Includes members in unaffiliated as well as AFL-CIO unions but excludes the million or more Canadian members of unions having headquarters in the United States.

[10] Students of labor have attached the term "business unionism" to an organization with the limited objective of improving the condition of its own members

pre-New Deal unions. For whatever cause, there has been a slowing down in the momentum of union growth.

The approximate total membership of affiliated and independent unions has remained at about seventeen million since the middle of the 1950's—a time when the AFL–CIO president, George Meany, had admitted that there were still some twenty-five million "organizable" workers in industries then completely nonunion or in pockets of industries that were otherwise unionized. Moreover, union membership is weakest where employment is expanding most rapidly, namely the trade, finance, clerical and service occupations.

The task of increasing membership is difficult and expensive since most of these unorganized workers are employees in small businesses or in areas, for example the South, where state laws and customs are unfriendly to unions. The problem in the Southern states has worsened during the racial strife of recent years. The AFL–CIO has openly espoused integration of schools and unions, with the result that organizing efforts are interpreted by white Southerners to be "Northern interference." Efforts to bring into unions the two million hired farm workers in the South, on the West Coast and elsewhere have been conspicuously unsuccessful. Several expensive organizing drives have been conducted, especially among the migratory workers, but have resulted in no permanent agricultural workers' unions.

Instead of expanding, unions may find it more and more difficult to maintain their present strength as automation displaces more and more of the semiskilled workers who make up the bulk of their membership. If, on the other hand, business growth and new job opportunities do not keep pace with the labor displacement resulting from technological improvements, automation may lead to a renewed expansion of unionization. If the displaced workers and young people seeking jobs for the first time are unable to find work, they will naturally seek redress through organized efforts. Despite periods of relative quiescence, the potential strength of the labor movement remains, and its achievements and approach to problems will fluctuate as leadership and the needs of workers change from time to time.

---

in contrast to an organization which also considers itself an agent or catalyst for broad social and economic reforms.

PART TWO

STRUCTURE AND INTERNAL GOVERNMENT

3

FEDERATED ORGANIZATIONS

"Organized labor" refers to those workers who have combined into organizational units of one kind or another for the purpose of improving their economic status. The "labor movement" connotes the unified purpose, activities, and aspirations of such workers. Neither term relates specifically to the structural arrangement by which workers group themselves, although structural arrangements are basic elements of any general movement. Personalities and external circumstances may be controlling forces in the development of any movement, but its character and effectiveness are influenced strongly by its internal mechanism and rules of operation.

Organized labor is a composite of different types and hierarchies of organizations with varying kinds of relationships and lines of control. At the base are the local unions to which every member belongs and to which he pays his dues. These local unions have lateral and vertical affiliations, the most important of which are the national unions.[1] The national unions, in turn, may be federated with other national and international organizations.

[1] Labor organizations in this country are commonly called "international" unions because most of them have members in Canada as well as in the United

AFL–CIO STRUCTURE AND GOVERNMENT

Most labor unions at the present time are affiliated with the AFL–CIO although there are important exceptions. Several railroad unions, for instance, have never belonged to any federated group except the Railway Labor Executives' Association. Other unions have at various times belonged to either the American Federation of Labor or the Congress of Industrial Organizations, or to both, but for some specific reasons have withdrawn or been expelled. In 1962 the AFL–CIO was composed of 132 national unions, 50 state federations, more than 800 city and county central bodies and approximately 60,000 locals in the United States. More than 80 per cent of all union members in the U.S. belong to unions affiliated with the AFL–CIO.

The preamble to the AFL–CIO constitution, as adopted at the time of the merger in 1955, reads:

> The establishment of this Federation through the merger of the American Federation of Labor and the Congress of Industrial Organizations is an expression of the hopes and aspirations of the working people of America.
>
> We seek the fulfillment of these hopes and aspirations through democratic processes within the framework of our constitutional government and consistent with our institutions and traditions.
>
> At the collective bargaining table, in the community, in the exercise of the rights and responsibilities of citizenship, we shall responsibly serve the interests of all the American people.
>
> We pledge ourselves to the more effective organization of working men and women; to the securing to them of full recognition and enjoyment of the rights to which they are justly entitled; to the achievement of ever higher standards of living and working conditions; to the attainment of security for all the people; to the enjoyment of the leisure which their skills make possible; and to the strengthening and extension of our way of life and the fundamental freedoms which are the basis of our democratic society.

States. Because the use of the term "international" when referring to American unions causes confusion with labor organizations of broader international character (see Part 5), the term "national" is used throughout this volume when referring to any of the unions in this country, even though many of them have locals in Canada.

Chart 2.
STRUCTURE OF THE AFL-CIO

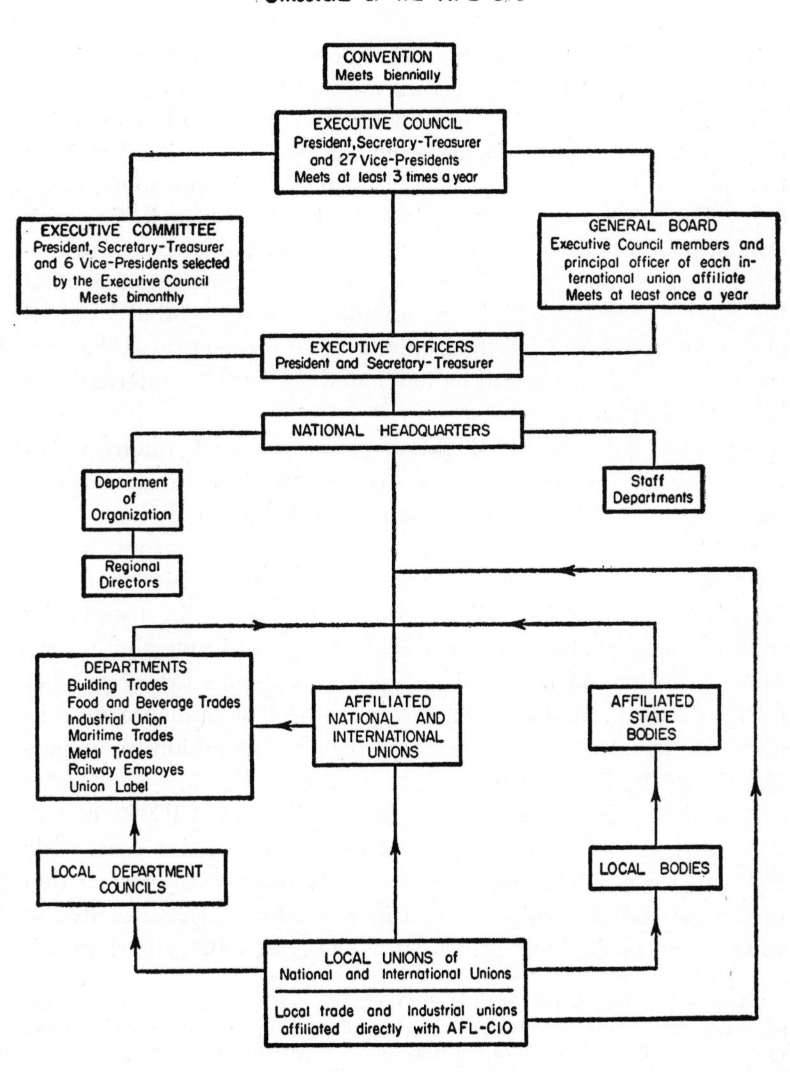

We shall combat resolutely the forces which seek to undermine the democratic institutions of our nation and to enslave the human soul. We shall strive always to win full respect for the dignity of the human individual whom our unions serve.

The major functions of the AFL–CIO are to promote the interests of workers and unions before the legislative, judicial and administrative branches of government; to expand union organizations, both directly and by assisting the member national unions; to provide research, legal and other technical assistance to the member unions; to publish periodicals and other literature dealing with economic problems and general matters of interest to labor; to represent and promote the cause of labor before the general public; to determine the jurisdictional boundaries of the affiliated unions and to protect them from dual unionism; and to serve as spokesman for member unions on international affairs, especially international labor movements.

The AFL–CIO is a federation of autonomous unions which serves as their spokesman and acts on matters which concern more than one trade or group of workers. Historically and structurally, the Federation is an agent of its constituent organizations, having only such powers and engaging in only those activities that have been assigned it by its affiliated unions. It has no direct authority over the internal affairs or the activities of any of its member unions so long as they do not impinge upon the jurisdiction of another affiliated union. While it exerts a great deal of influence over its members, its only actual power is the power of expulsion from membership in the Federation.

A national union becomes a part of the AFL–CIO in one of two ways: (1) An already organized independent union may apply for a charter of affiliation. If it does not trespass on the jurisdiction of already affiliated unions, and if its general characteristics are not in violation of the basic principles of the AFL–CIO[2], the charter is

[2] Article III, Sec. 9 of the AFL-CIO constitution states: "No organization officered, controlled or dominated by communists, fascists, or other totalitarians, or whose policies and activities are consistently directed toward the achievement of the program or purposes of the Communist Party, and any fascist organization, or other totalitarian movement, shall be permitted as an affiliate of this Federation or any of its state or local central bodies."

usually granted. (2) The AFL–CIO may itself create a national union by combining an appropriate group of its directly affiliated local unions.

GOVERNMENT OF THE AFL–CIO

The biennial convention is the supreme governing body of the Federation. Decisions and instructions of the conventions are carried out by the Executive Council, which meets at least three times a year. In addition there are an Executive Committee which meets every two months, a General Board which meets at least once a year, and various standing committees appointed by the President. The responsible administrative agents are the President and the Secretary-Treasurer, who devote full time to the Federation's work.

Biennial conventions are held during the last quarter of odd-numbered years, at a time and place designated by the Executive Council. A convention generally lasts about two weeks and is attended by delegates representing all the affiliated bodies. Each department, state federation, city central and directly affiliated local union is entitled to one delegate. Each national union has at least one delegate regardless of size. The formula for unions with more than 4,000 members is a graduated scale allowing up to nine delegates for unions with over 175,000 members, plus one additional delegate for each 75,000 members over 175,000. Membership is based on the average number of persons for whom the union has paid per capita taxes during the preceding two-year period. In a roll-call vote, held upon demand of 30 per cent of the delegates, each national union delegate casts one vote for every member whom he represents.

DUTIES OF THE EXECUTIVE COUNCIL

The Council is the governing body between conventions, and the President, as chief executive officer, has authority to interpret the constitution and convention decisions between meetings of the Executive Council. The Council is composed of the President, the Secretary-Treasurer, and twenty-seven Vice-Presidents elected by a majority vote at the convention. By custom, the Vice-Presidents are selected from among the presidents of the Nationals, who continue to hold the latter office in their respective unions. Although the President and the Secretary-Treasurer must be members of some affiliated union, after election they devote their full time to the AFL–CIO.

The duties of the Council are both promotional and administrative. It carries out the decisions of the convention and submits a report to each convention on the activities of the Federation, with recommendations for further action. During the interim between conventions the Council "may take any action which may become necessary to safeguard and promote the best interests of the Federation and of its affiliated unions." It is the duty of the Council to watch legislative measures affecting the interests of workers and to initiate, whenever necessary, such legislative action as the convention may direct. In its office at Washington the Federation maintains a staff of economic and legal advisers and assistants, who prepare data to be used at congressional hearings and work in close cooperation with the various governmental agencies concerned with labor.

The Executive Council is also responsible for conducting organizing campaigns in unorganized trades and industries not included within the jurisdiction of any of its affiliated Nationals. When a sufficient number of new members have been enlisted, they are organized into locals that are directly subordinate to the AFL–CIO, that is, they have the same relation to the AFL–CIO as other locals have to their Nationals. This arrangement is intended to be temporary, however, lasting only until such a local is transferred to an already established national union having appropriate jurisdiction or, if none exists, until a new National is established. In order to protect the jurisdictional rights of its affiliated national unions, no new charters may be granted if the jurisdiction is claimed by existing Nationals without their consent, and no affiliated National may change its name or its jurisdiction without the approval of the Council.

Among the duties of the Council is that of keeping the Federation free from corrupt or Communist influences. The Council has the right to investigate any affiliate or its officers and, by a two-thirds vote, may suspend a union found guilty of corruption or subversion.

The Council may recommend final expulsion, but no affiliate's charter may be revoked except by a two-thirds majority roll-call vote at the convention. Since every national union is autonomous, disciplinary action is limited to expulsion, for the AFL–CIO has no power to dissolve or take over the property of any National union or any of its locals.

The situation is different with respect to the state federations, city centrals, and directly affiliated locals. The President, subject to appeal to the Executive Council and thereafter to the next convention, is empowered to discipline, suspend or expel any of these organizations, their officers and members, for disobeying the constitution and rules of the Federation. Upon suspension or revocation of the charter, all funds and property revert to the Federation.

EXECUTIVE COMMITTEE

This smaller group, chosen from among and by the Executive Council, meets every two months in order to advise and consult with the President and Secretary-Treasurer on policy matters.

GENERAL BOARD

The largest decision-making body, aside from the biennial convention, is the General Board, consisting of all the members of the Council and one officer from each of the affiliated national unions and from each department. The Board meets at the call of the President, with a constitutional minimum of one meeting a year. It decides all policy questions referred to it by the Council. Unlike members of the Executive Council or the Executive Committee, General Board members vote as representatives of their unions, whose voting strength is based upon their respective memberships.

COMMITTEES

The scope of the AFL–CIO's interests is indicated by its constitutionally established committees, namely Legislation, Civil Rights, Political Education, Ethical Practices, International Affairs, Education, Social Security, Economic Policy, Community Services, Housing, Research, Public Relations, Safety and Occupational Health, and Veterans' Affairs. Members of these committees are appointed by the President and are under his direction, subject to the authority of the Executive Council and the convention.

AFL–CIO Finances

Most of the revenue for the support of the activities of the AFL–CIO is derived from per capita taxes upon members and, when necessary, from special assessments. The tax upon the paid-up membership of each affiliated National is 7 cents per member per month. From its directly affiliated locals the Federation receives at least 80 cents per member per month—more if the Executive Council so determines. Each state federation and city central pays an annual fee of $20. The Executive Council is empowered to declare a special levy, not to exceed 4 cents per member per month for a period not to exceed six months in any one year, when "the interests of the Federation require."

DEPARTMENTS OF THE AFL–CIO

The 1907 convention of the American Federation of Labor declared that "for the greater development of the labor movement, departments subordinate to the American Federation of Labor are to be established from time to time . . . each department is to manage and finance its own affairs . . . but no department shall enact laws, rules or regulations in conflict with the laws and procedure of the American Federation of Labor." Soon after this action by the convention, four departments were established: the Building and Construction Trades, the Metal Trades, the Railway Employees', and the Union Label Trades. In 1946 a Maritime Trades Department was established. When the AFL–CIO constitution was adopted, recognition of industrial unions was provided by the addition of an Industrial Union Department. In 1961 a Food and Beverage Trades Department was established, composed of nine affiliates with members engaged in the manufacturing, processing, sale and distribution of food and beverages.

The departments usually hold their conventions in the same city during the week preceding the AFL–CIO convention. Their officers are required to submit quarterly reports to the AFL–CIO Executive Council, and at each of the latter's meeting the officers of the various departments appear to discuss matters of mutual interest.

According to the AFL–CIO constitution, "Each department is to be considered an official method of the Federation for transacting the portion of its business indicated by the name of the department, in consequence of which affiliated and eligible organizations should be part of their respective departments and should comply with the actions and decisions of such departments, subject to appeal therefrom to the Executive Council and the convention of the Federation. An organization affiliated with one or more departments shall pay per capita tax to each such department upon the number of members whose occupation comes under such department."

A major function of the departments is to extend union organization within its appropriate industries and trades, as well as to settle jurisdictional disputes between member unions and appeal jurisdictional disputes with unions outside their departments to the Executive Council. The departments also represent their unions before Congress and other agencies of the government. Thus the officers of the Building and Construction Trades Department took an active part in the passage of the 1936 Public Contracts Act and were signatories to the Building Trades Stabilization Agreement during World War II. The Metal Trades Department has direct representation on the Navy Wage Board, which fixes wages for the various occupations in the government navy yards.

RAILWAY EMPLOYEES' DEPARTMENT

The Railway Employees' Department, which represents the members of the craft unions who work in railroad shops, takes a more direct part in collective bargaining than the other departments, although the Metal Trades Department frequently enters into the negotiations where large shipbuilding concerns are involved. The Railway Employees' Department organizes what is known as "system federations" which are composed of all its members in the various craft unions working for the same carrier or railroad company. Each craft union on a system elects a general chairman, and these several chairmen constitute the Executive Board of the system federation which carries on the collective bargaining with the railroad company.

The Department maintains general supervision over the activities of the system federations. Sanction must be obtained from the Department on all proposed agreements with employers as well as contemplated strike action, and all matters of general or common concern to all the railroad shopmen must be cleared through the Department. Jurisdictional disputes between the crafts as well as concerted demands for wage increases are referred to the Department for action. Any grievance which cannot be settled by the system federation or the national union involved is referred to the Department, which decides whether or not it should go to the Railway Adjustment Board (see Chapter 10). Only the Department may invoke the services of the National Mediation Board or enter into any arbitration of disputes between system federations and railroad companies. In addition to the activities concerning matters pertaining to its members, the Department cooperates with the operating railroad unions on matters of common interest to all railroad workers, such as general wage increases, federal and state legislation, and issues before the Interstate Commerce Commission which affect railroad employment.

Union Label Trades Department

The Union Label Trades Department is composed of all the affiliated AFL–CIO unions which use labels, cards, buttons or other insignia to designate the products or services performed by their members. The purpose of the union label is to promote union organization and union standards of workmanship by appealing to the consumer. The label is especially designed to channel the purchasing power of union members, who make up a large portion of the consuming public, toward buying union-made goods and services. The Department conducts advertising campaigns, issues union label directories, and in union conventions and literature urges members and their families to purchase union goods.

The Department has no authority to require union members to purchase label products; neither does it control the issuance of the labels. Each union concerned establishes its own standards and requirements governing the use of its labels by employers, and controls their issuance and withdrawal. The Department is an educational and publicity medium for promoting a demand for union label goods and services. In addition to publishing its directory which lists all affiliated unions together with facsimiles of their insignia, it conducts Union Industries Shows where manufacturers display products made by AFL-CIO members.

STATE AND CITY CENTRAL BODIES

The National unions and their locals are primarily concerned with protecting and improving the working conditions of members within their *particular* trades or industries. To take care of the many matters of common interest to workers in all trades, and to provide a means for unified effort for the general improvement of conditions of labor, unions representing *different* trades and industries affiliate for concerted action. The AFL–CIO represents such affiliation at the top level. Locally there are city and county central organizations of local unions, and on the state level are the state federations of labor.

These city and state organizations are delegate bodies. The city organizations are composed of representatives from all the member local unions, while the state organizations include delegates from the city organizations as well as all the affiliated local unions within the state. Membership in the city and state organizations is optional with a few unions, but most Nationals require their locals to belong. However, no local that does not belong to a National affiliated with the AFL–CIO may belong to any city central or state federation. If a local resigns or is expelled from its National, it automatically loses its membership. Likewise, if a National resigns or is expelled from the AFL–CIO none of its locals are entitled to belong to the city and state central bodies.

State federations are concerned chiefly with legislative and educational matters; they are not permitted to issue certificates of affiliation. They hold annual conventions where programs of general interest to all the workers in the state are formulated; they initiate legislation, appear before state legislatures, and in various ways promote organized labor's interests before the public. Most state federations take an active part in workers' educational programs, independently or in cooperation with other union organizations.

The city centrals go by various names—for example, Trades and Labor Assembly, Trades and Labor Council, Central Labor Council, Central Labor Union. As compared with the state organizations, these city bodies deal more on the economic front, serving as clearinghouses for their locals and assisting them in dealing with employers. However, they are not permitted to order strikes or boycotts, or to negotiate agreements, unless authorized by the Nationals of their respective locals. During recent years the city central organizations have become increasingly concerned with general community activities. In most cities they take an active part in the Community Funds and other educational and recreational programs which directly and indirectly bring services to their members.

JOINT BOARDS AND COUNCILS

Joint boards and trades councils are combinations of locals having jurisdiction within related trades or the same industry. In some unions they are referred to as joint boards, while in others they are called city or district trades councils. Whatever their title or exact geographical coverage, their primary purpose is to secure united action in collective bargaining and uniform working conditions among the employers within the same industry in a given city or area. With most unions it is mandatory to have a joint board or council whenever the union has a given number (usually three or more) of locals within the city or area, and most Nationals require all their locals within the community to belong to the council after it is once established.

Joint boards or trades councils are delegate bodies composed of representatives from all the locals affiliated with them. Their authority and responsibilities vary. In a few instances they are not much more than advisory bodies; most generally, however, they have supreme authority over the member locals and become their governing body. They may have broad powers to determine jurisdictional disputes between locals, to try cases against local unions and officers, and to hear appeals from disciplined and expelled members. Frequently the joint board or council negotiates the agreements with employers and has the sole authority to call strikes.

There are two types of joint boards or councils: (1) those composed of locals of the same National, usually referred to as joint boards and (2) those composed of locals of different Nationals having jurisdiction over allied trades in the same industry, usually referred to as trades councils.

In the clothing and textile industries, as an example, the joint boards are made up of locals of the same Nationals. Although these Nationals are industrial in character, their locals may be organized on a craft basis, on a plant basis, by section of the industry, or may be "mixed," i.e., include workers of various occupations within the industry. The joint boards may represent all or most of the various craft and mixed locals within the entire industry in a city or region. In a large clothing center, there may be joint boards for different branches of the industry, such as knit goods, dresses, coats and suits, custom tailoring, neckwear, etc. Similarly, the Teamsters' joint councils may be composed of locals covering distinct types of trucking or delivery service, for example, milk delivery, department store or parcel delivery, heavy trucking and moving vans.

Because of the scattered nature of the coal industry, the district council is the autonomous unit over the locals of the United Mine Workers which has thirty district organizations in coal mining. Some of these districts cover parts of states, some entire states, while a few extend across state lines. For administrative purposes the United Steelworkers has the steel-producing centers divided into districts, in each of which is a representative from the national Office. Likewise, the United Automobile Workers, the Teamsters, and other unions have district organizations whose jurisdictions have a broader geographical coverage than a local area.

The printing, building, and metal trades councils are made up of locals belonging to the several national unions whose jurisdictions cover allied crafts. City allied printing trades councils, for example, include the locals of the five allied printing trades unions, namely, the Typographical, Pressmen, Bookbinders', Stereotypers' and Electrotypers', and Photo-Engravers' unions. The local councils are chartered by the Allied Printing Trades Association which has jurisdiction over the label which is issued to all employers who deal with the printing trades locals and observe union conditions of work.

Joint action among the building and metal trades unions starts at the top level with the Building and Construction Trades and the Metal Trades Departments, which charter the local councils and maintain supervision over them. In large cities all the locals in the same craft may belong to a joint council which in turn is affiliated with the trades council composed of the locals in the various crafts of the same industry.

Once a joint board or district council has been established, the Nationals involved require all their locals in the area to belong in order to promote harmony among the different crafts within a community as well as to obtain unified action with the employers. For example, some of the trades councils negotiate city-wide agreements covering all their respective crafts. In lieu of a combined agreement, a council may see that the agreements of its various locals terminate at the same date and that no agreement of any member local contains any clause which will prohibit it from assisting another member union. These trades councils have supreme authority over their member locals except that they may not force locals to take any action contrary to the policies of their Nationals.

RAILWAY LABOR EXECUTIVES ASSOCIATION

Labor organization in the railroad industry is predominantly along craft or occupational lines. While many of the unions are confined solely to railroad employees, a substantial number of railroad workers belong to unions which cover workers of similar crafts in other industries. Many dining car employees, for example, belong to the Hotel and Restaurant Employees' International Alliance; railroad shopmen are members of the several unions to which workers of those particular crafts in other industries also belong. Recognizing the special problems and needs of their railroad members, the AFL-CIO Railway Department, described above, serves as a unified agency for all crafts of railroad shopmen.

Unlike the craft unions of railroad shopmen, the brotherhoods of operating railroad workers (those engaged in running the trains) remained independent from either the AFL or the CIO until recent years. In their relations both with their employers and with the government, they considered it to their advantage to remain free to pursue those measures which are of peculiar benefit to themselves.[3] Within recent years, however, all the railroad brotherhoods but two, the Locomotive Engineers and the Railway Conductors and Brakemen, have affiliated with the AFL-CIO.

Despite their AFL-CIO ties, railroad unions have considered it advisable to maintain their own organization, the Railway Labor Executives Association, which was formed soon after the passage of the Railway Labor Act in 1926 for the purpose of "cooperative action and to obtain and develop constant interpretations and utilization of all the privileges of the Act." As its name indicates, it is an association composed of the chief executives or presidents of the member unions. At present, twenty-four unions are represented in the Association. These include all the AFL-CIO unions having members employed in the railroad industry, plus the two independent Brotherhoods and two AFL-CIO maritime unions.

The Railway Labor Executives Association functions as a coordinating and policy body in legislative and other fields of concern to railroad employees. Its entire program is based upon voluntary action and no member union is bound by any action of the Association. Unlike the AFL-CIO, it does not intervene in the jurisdictional disputes between its member organizations. Its chief concern at the present time is the problem of railroad mergers, which threaten the jobs of some 200,000 railroad employees.

[3] In the field of legislation, railroad unions were successful in getting a law to protect them in collective bargaining nine years before the National Labor Relations Act was passed in 1935. The Railroad Retirement and Unemployment Insurance laws provide more generous benefits than does the Social Security Act.

4

NATIONAL AND LOCAL UNIONS

The national unions are the autonomous, self-governing units of the labor movement. Even when a National is affiliated with a larger body such as the AFL-CIO, it retains its independence as a self-governing organization so far as its internal affairs are concerned. Likewise, an affiliated union exercises wide latitude with respect to outside activities. It may, for instance, sponsor political programs and legislative measures on its own initiative—so long as such endorsements do not violate the fundamental principles and policies of the general labor movement.

The one major restriction placed upon affiliated unions is that they shall confine themselves to the trade jurisdiction assigned them by the AFL-CIO; a counterpart of this cardinal rule is that they shall not participate in dual unionism. However, although refusal to abide by the jurisdictional rulings of the federated body means expulsion, it does not mean the disintegration of the union itself since it may carry on as an independent organization and expand its jurisdiction at will. Nevertheless, there is overlapping within the AFL-CIO at the present time because the former AFL and CIO affiliates united in the new Federation as fully autonomous unions and now retain the same jurisdictional rights that they held prior to the merger in 1955. The new constitution states: "The integrity of each . . . affiliate of this Federation shall be maintained and preserved. Each . . . affiliate shall respect the established collective bargaining relationships of every other affiliate and no affiliate shall raid the established collective bargaining relationship of any other affiliate. . . ."

NATIONAL UNIONS

There are at present 179 labor organizations whose jurisdictions are broad enough to justify their being called national unions. Of these, 132 are affiliated with the AFL-CIO; they have a membership in the United States of approximately 14 million. Of the three million members belonging to unaffiliated unions, almost half are members of the Teamsters' Union.

SIZE OF NATIONALS

National unions vary in size from fewer than 100 members to over a million. Twelve national unions have fewer than 1,000 members each. By contrast, seven have over half a million members each: the Teamsters with almost a million and a half; the Automobile and Steel Workers, each with slightly over one million; the Machinists, the Carpenters, the Brotherhood of Electrical Workers and the Mine Workers, each with between 600,000 and 900,000 members. Fourteen of the largest unions include one-half of all union members.

TABLE 2. Unions by Number of Members, 1962

Membership	Number of Unions	
	AFL-CIO	Independent
Over 1,000,000	2	1
500,000 to 1,000,000	3	1
400,000 to 500,000	3	–
300,000 to 400,000	4	–
200,000 to 300,000	7	–
100,000 to 200,000	20	2
50,000 to 100,000	26	5
25,000 to 50,000	17	6
Under 25,000	50	32
Total	132	47

Differences in size may be due to one or more of the following reasons: the jurisdictional character of the union; the extent to which the union has been able to organize the trade or industry in which it has jurisdiction; the number of workers employed in the trade or industry. In general, unions covering entire industries, or several categories or trades, tend to be larger than those confined to single crafts. Practically all the very small unions are confined to particular skilled trades, and some are in trades now becoming obsolete.

The seven unions with over a half million members each include employees in all or most of the occupations within an entire industry, or even several industries. That of the Automobile, Aircraft and Agricultural Implement Workers, as its name implies, covers three industries. The United Steelworkers' jurisdiction covers workers in both steel and aluminum production and fabrication plants. The United Mine Workers include not only bituminous and anthracite miners but workers engaged in coal processing, chemical and other industries. While the Brotherhood of Carpenters, the Association of Machinists and the Brotherhood of Electrical Workers originally were confined largely to particular skilled groups, they now accept persons employed in all or most of the occupations in a number of related industries and plants. The Teamsters' large membership is the result both of the vast network of our motor transportation and of the fact that the Teamsters include many "inside" employees in brewery, packing and other plants.

Nationals whose jurisdictions cover related but somewhat distinct sections of an industry may be organized into departments or branches which retain a large measure of autonomy. In some instances this branch form of organization represents an amalgamation of formerly separate unions, as for example the Actors' Equity and several other organizations which comprise the Associated Actors and Artistes of America; the men's hat and millinery sections of the United Hatters, Cap and Millinery Workers; the Sailors' Union of the Pacific and several other maritime organizations which are units of the Seafarers' International Union. Some branches are the result of a union's extension into related industries, as for example District 50 of the United Mine Workers, which includes members in a variety of industries and trades outside of coal mining.[1]

[1] District 50 originally covered workers in coal-processing plants and coke ovens, but in 1942 the United Mine Workers' constitution was changed to include "such other industries as may be designated and approved by the Executive

In contrast to such consolidations as are represented by departments or branches within a National, there may be several unions in the same industry, each union covering a distinct branch of the industry. Unions of glass workers, for example, are divided among the glassware, glass container and flat glass sections of the industry. In the maritime industry the dock workers belong to different unions from the sea-going personnel, and the licensed personnel are in different unions from the ordinary seamen.

CRAFT *VS.* INDUSTRIAL UNIONS

The kinds of occupations included within a union's jurisdiction and the extent of their variety, have far-reaching effects on employer-union bargaining relations and on interunion relations, as well as upon the size and character of the union itself. What the jurisdiction of a union is at any given time is determined by the union, subject to the approval of the AFL-CIO if it is so affiliated. For an independent union the only limitation is its ability to enlist the support of the workers it wishes to have as members.

The great expansion era of the labor movement during the 1930's and 1940's was marked by a trend toward industrial unionism. The CIO was definitely committed to organize on a broad basis, and to meet the CIO competition many of the AFL craft unions began to admit semiskilled and unskilled workers in the plants where formerly they accepted only craftsmen. The AFL-CIO constitution recognizes that "both craft and industrial unions are appropriate, equal, and necessary as methods of trade union organization. . . ." It acknowledges the existence of overlapping jurisdiction brought about with the merger and urges the various affiliates to eliminate jurisdictional conflicts "through the process of voluntary agreement or voluntary merger in consultation with the appropriate officials of the Federation."

Although the constitutions and sometimes the names of the unions are designed to indicate their claim to coverage, jurisdictional lines are never fixed or settled over a long period of time.

Board." Coal mining has always been organized on a geographical district basis. When the union began organizing the coal-processing workers they termed the unit a "district" although it has no territorial significance.

Unions tend to respond to the changes taking place in industry itself, and in a dynamic industrial situation there necessarily are frequent amalgamations as well as divisions, transfers and expansions of jurisdictions. Realignments in the corporate or managerial units of business, increasing mechanization, changes in materials and processes, bring about conditions which call for adjustments in union jurisdiction.

Craft Unions

A strictly craft union consists of workers who have undergone an apprentice training and whose acquired skills enable them to carry through to completion a particular process, usually requiring manual dexterity with tools. A craft union crosses industry lines, that is, it has members in *various* industries, since industries producing entirely different commodities or services include some occupations which are similar. In contrast, an industrial union is identified with a *particular* industry and covers all the workers, skilled and unskilled, who are employed in that industry.

As a matter of fact, few unions at the present time fall within either of these extreme categories of craft *versus* industrial organizations, and no two persons would classify existing unions alike. As an example of some which most nearly approximate pure craft unionism might be cited the Journeymen Horse Shoers, the Association of Siderographers, the Marine Engineers' Beneficial Association and the Brotherhood of Locomotive Engineers.

A number of unions are multicraft, that is, they include several parallel and somewhat related occupations. Usually these represent an amalgamation of two or more unions which in some instances is indicated by their names—for example, Bricklayers, Masons and Plasterers Union and the Plate Printers, Die Stampers and Engravers' Union.

The majority of unions are variants of craft and industrial unionism. They may include one or more skilled groups along with several semiskilled trades, or they may have a broad jurisdiction and take in all the production workers within an industry except certain specified technical and skilled workers. The former category may represent a movement in the direction of industrial unionism; the latter is usually an indication that the skilled workers were already organized and were unwilling to lose their identity when the movement was started to unionize the entire industry.

As the result of recent changes in the industrial process, there are signs of some modification in industrial union structure and bargaining methods. For example, the Automobile Workers have been much concerned with the shift in the occupational composition of the labor force owing to technological changes. Recognizing the industry's increasing proportion of skilled craftsmen and technical workers, the union in 1957 changed its constitution to permit these groups to negotiate supplementary agreements, and to strike on a unit basis after review by the union's Executive Board. This drastic departure from solidarity was stated to be a "necessary refinement of industrial unionism."

FLEXIBLE JURISDICTIONS

Not only do unions readjust their jurisdictions from time to time in response to industrial changes, but the same union may function on a craft basis in some branches of an industry and as an industrial union in others. The Brotherhood of Carpenters and Joiners, for example, operates as a craft union in building construction and as an industrial union in logging camps and in furniture plants. This union is sometimes referred to as a "vertical" union since its jurisdiction is built around the commodity of wood—from the tree to lumber to building and furniture.

The Meat Cutters and Butcher Workmen functions as a craft union in local retail stores but as an industrial union in the packing industry. The Brotherhood of Electrical Workers operates as a craft union in construction work but is frequently organized on an industrial basis in plants manufacturing electrical products. Although the Association of Machinists functions as a craft union in railroad shops and confines its members to the skilled crafts in some other plants, in an increasing number of instances it is including all production workers. The Boilermakers, Iron Ship Builders and Helpers operates as a craft union in most industries but in some shipyards it has jurisdiction over practically all production and maintenance workers. The Teamsters' Union functions both as a craft and as a semi-industrial union: many of its locals are composed of specific types of drivers; others include drivers of all kinds; some locals include garage mechanics; and in the dairy and brewery industries the union's membership may cover inside employees as well as deliverymen.

In some national unions which claim jurisdiction over an entire industry, many or all of their locals may be formed on craft lines. This is especially true with the clothing and shoe unions where members of different occupations in the same plants frequently belong to different locals. The present jurisdictions of some national unions represent expedient compromises. For example, the Brotherhood of Paper Makers and the Brotherhood of Pulp, Sulphite and Paper Mill Workers reached an agreement in 1909 which gives jurisdiction over the skilled workers in the machine and beater rooms to the Paper Makers and all other workers in the industry to the Pulp Workers. In 1911 the Bricklayers', Masons' and Plasterers' Union and the Operative Plasterers' and Cement Masons' Association entered into a working agreement which grants the latter the sole right to organize unions composed exclusively of plasterers, although the former may accept plasterers in their mixed locals in communities where there are limited numbers of plasterers employed.

Although all the railroad unions are craft organizations, there is a great deal of overlapping jurisdiction. Through the numerous elections held by the National Mediation Board among the workers on the various railroad systems in different localities, persons employed in similar occupations have chosen different unions as their bargaining agents. On some systems the Brotherhood of Railroad Trainmen represents conductors although usually they are represented by the Order of Railway Conductors. Also, switchmen may belong to the Switchmen's Union or to the Trainmen Brotherhood. The yardmasters are scattered among half a dozen different unions, including two which are for yardmasters exclusively. Most of the dining car cooks and waiters belong to the Hotel and Restaurant Employees' but some belong to the Railway Conductors and some to the United Transport Service Employees.

INTERNAL GOVERNMENT OF NATIONAL UNIONS

The supreme authority and sole legislative body of the national union is the general convention, composed of delegates from all its local organizations. Because of the importance of the conventions as the final authority on all union matters, the frequency and regularity with which they are held, the distribution of voting power, and the manner in which business is conducted, are important criteria of a union's democratic administration. Ever-tighter control by a few officers inevitably results, for instance, when conventions are postponed from year to year, and if the attending delegates are predominantly the paid organizers or representatives chosen by the officers.

About 60 per cent of the national unions hold their conventions either annually or biennially. Almost 30 per cent, including the railroad brotherhoods, hold conventions every three or four years. About a dozen unions hold their conventions every five years; an equal number, mostly unions with small memberships, decide at each convention when the next shall be held. The cost of holding conventions represents a considerable item in total union administrative expenses and is the chief reason some unions do not hold conventions more frequently. For some of the larger unions, the cost of holding one convention amounts to half a million dollars or more.

To take care of unforeseen or emergency problems, practically all unions provide for the calling of special conventions. Sometimes these may be called only upon the initiative, or at least with the approval, of the General Executive Board; many, on the other hand, provide for the calling of special conventions upon majority vote in a membership referendum initiated by a specified number of locals located in at least several different states. Usually only such matters as are announced in the referendum vote may be discussed at such special conventions.

Conventions are attended by delegates from all the locals, the number and voting strength depending upon their paid-up membership. The basis of representation, that is the number of members required per delegate, varies considerably among the unions although the general practice is to allow a decreasing ratio of delegates as the size of the local increases in order to avoid too great domination by the large locals. The Presidents and other officers of the locals are customarily chosen to be delegates; in large locals they are accompanied by other members elected by the membership.

General Executive Boards

Every National has a General Executive Board, or Executive Council as it is sometimes called, which is responsible for the administration of the union's affairs and which serves as an appellate body on matters referred to it by the locals as well as individual members. Typically, national unions' constitutions say: "The General Executive Board shall execute the instructions of the convention and shall be the highest authority of the union between conventions, and shall decide all questions of interpretation of the constitution between conventions."

Although not the same in all unions, most General Executive Boards have the responsibility and authority to issue and withdraw local charters and to repeal any local's by-laws which do not conform to the National's constitution; to remove any officer for incompetency or nonperformance of duties, and to fill the vacancy until the next convention; to take charge of the affairs of any local when it is decided this is necessary "to protect or advance the interests of the union"; to pass upon all claims, grievances and appeals from locals and other subordinate bodies; to reverse or repeal any action of any National officers; to select auditors for the auditing of books, and to prepare the report for the forthcoming convention; to have supervision over the policy and publication of the official journal; to determine the amount and methods of bonding all officers who handle union funds, and to levy assessments in accordance with the terms of the constitution.

In unions having strike and death benefits, the General Executive Board is usually responsible for these funds and their disbursement. Some unions, especially those which maintain pension and disability programs, or a home for aged members, have a Board of Trustees whose members may also be members of the General

Executive Board or may be other members elected at the convention.

Most General Executive Boards are composed of the National President and Secretary-Treasurer together with a specified number of Vice-Presidents. The President and Secretary-Treasurer are usually full-time officers, their salaries generally being specified in the constitutions. Most generally the Vice-Presidents, who are chosen on a regional or branch of industry basis, also hold office in their local or district organizations which they continue to hold while serving as members of the Executive Board.

DUTIES OF THE PRESIDENT

The General President is necessarily vested with the chief responsibility for the day-to-day conduct of the union's affairs. As in any other organization, the actual powers and influence exercised by an elected leader depend about as much upon the will and ability of the person holding the office as upon the authorities formally granted by the constitution. Through the prestige of his office, as a presiding chairman and ex officio member of committees, the President has great influence in determining what and how matters are discussed and voted upon at Executive Board meetings and general conventions. As administrator of the union's day-to-day activities, his decisions and course of action vitally affect not only the internal affairs of the union and its members but also the general public.

Most union constitutions describe the general duties of the President somewhat as follows: "The General President as chief executive officer shall have full authority to direct the working of the organization within the provisions of the constitution; he shall convene and preside at all General Executive Board and convention meetings and between sessions execute their instructions; he shall be an ex officio member of all committees and appoint all committees not otherwise provided for; he shall supervise and be responsible for the work of all organizers and levy assessments according to the provisions of the constitution and make a full report of all union activities to the General Executive Board and the convention."

While there is a great deal of uniformity in the various constitutions as to the specific duties assigned to their Presidents, the degree of final authority vested in the President differs. A majority of the constitutions specify that the President shall have authority, subject to the approval of the General Executive Board and appeal to the convention, to decide all questions of interpretation of the constitution, to issue and revoke charters to locals, and joint councils, to appoint and dismiss organizers and other union employees, to remove or suspend local officers, to sanction strikes and allocate strike benefits.

Before 1959 several unions gave their Presidents broad powers which enabled them to initiate basic rules and policies, as well as to exercise final authority to expel members and officers and to revoke charters of locals. The Landrum-Griffin Act limits such autocratic powers through its provisions concerning methods of holding elections, the defining of rights of members and the holding of trusteeships. (See Chapter 7.)

Organizers

An important part of the national union's staff are the organizers, commonly referred to as "representatives." They may be permanently assigned to particular districts or regions or they may work out from central headquarters and travel from place to place wherever the union has members or potential members. While the initial function of an organizer is to solicit new members and establish new local organizations, his continuing function is to act as adviser to all the locals within his region with regard to both their internal union affairs and their relations with employers. An organizer is the point of contact between the national office and the local organizations. It is his responsibility to interpret the aims and policies of the National to the local officers and members and to keep the national officers informed of the conditions and problems of the locals.

In some unions the organizers are elected by the convention and may serve as delegates with voting power. In most unions they are appointed by the General President or Executive Board and are considered staff employees even though they usually, but not always, have been active union members. When appointed, they generally are not allowed a voice or vote at the convention—a measure obviously designed to discourage one group of officers from perpetuating its administrative control.

ELECTION OF OFFICERS

In more than three-fourths of the national unions the general officers are elected by the delegates assembled at their regular conventions, while less than one-fourth of the unions choose their officers by referendum vote of the general membership. In a few of the latter, candidates are nominated by convention but elected by majority vote through referendum.

Differences in method of electing officers, i.e., by convention or referendum, have no significant relationship to the size or age of the unions or their affiliations: While many of the small unions use the referendum method, some of the largest organizations also elect their officers by referendum, for example, the Machinists, the Steelworkers, the Amalgamated Clothing Workers and the National Maritime Union. On the other hand, the Automobile Workers, the Brotherhood of Electrical Workers and the Teamsters elect their officers by convention vote, as do all the standard railroad unions. The long-established printing trades unions use the referendum method.

As with the election procedure of any private organization or political body, both methods have their advantages and disadvantages, theoretical and practical. While the referendum system would seem to offer a more democratic means of expression, many unions feel that this is an unwieldy method to use where members are widely scattered throughout the country; that in actual practice it is not so conducive to popular choice of officers as the convention method where assembled delegates have an opportunity to discuss the relative merits of candidates before casting their ballots. From union experience there is nothing to indicate that one method is inherently better than the other, or that the results of most union elections would have been materially different if the reverse method had been used. Personality and other factors seem to have a greater bearing on the choice of union officials than the mere mechanics of the election procedure.

Whatever the reasons, union practice follows more closely that of business corporations than political governments in that the same persons tend to be re-elected year after year. It has been the experience with most unions, at least with respect to the presidency, that once having been elected to office, the same incumbent usually retains office until retirement or death.

Continuation of the same persons in office year after year may be an indication that such persons are providing the kind of effective leadership which the members want or think is obtainable; it may be due simply to long-standing custom, or a reflection of workers' feelings about security of tenure with its implication that one who has given satisfactory service should be retained on the job until retirement. On the other hand, repeated re-election of the same persons may not be conclusive evidence of the wishes of a majority of the members but a result of the difficulties in the way of their making a change.

This points to the very heart of the problem of union administration, namely, the need to maintain a united front with strong, unchallenged leadership for effective employer dealing and, at the same time, to preserve maximum freedom of expression among members. Opposition to those in office may be a manifestation of a healthy and legitimate desire for change in personnel and policy, but to those favoring retention of existing officers it may be interpreted as an effort to disrupt and weaken the union. Some unions have gone far to discourage any opposition movements; it was for this reason that the Landrum-Griffin Act prescribed certain minimum procedures for the nomination and election of officers. Beyond these minimum legal requirements, elections are conducted in accordance with each union's constitution; and only a very small number of unions were required to make any substantial changes in their procedures upon the passage of the law in 1959.

LOCAL ORGANIZATIONS

Most local unions are subordinate units of Nationals which define their locals' powers and duties and through which the Nationals reach and control the activities of their members.[2] To the union

[2] In addition to the locals that belong to the Nationals, there are locals that are directly affiliated with the AFL-CIO. These are usually confined to trades or industries for which there are no suitable Nationals, and as soon as a sufficient number have been organized within any industry they generally form into a National.

member his local is the point of contact with other organized workers in his trade; it is the agency to which he expresses his demands for better working conditions and through which he both seeks settlement of his grievances and participates in the broader political and educational programs of his union.

SIZE AND JURISDICTION OF LOCALS

There are at present approximately 71,000 local unions in the United States.[3] They range in size from as few as seven or a dozen members—the approximate minimum specified in most national constitutions—to memberships of over 100,000. The large majority have memberships of less than two or three hundred; probably about 10 per cent have more than a thousand; while only a half dozen have more than 30,000. Three postal unions account for 20 per cent of the total number of locals, and the building trades unions about the same proportion. More than 40 per cent of all Nationals have fewer than 100 locals, while seventeen Nationals have more than 1,000 locals each.

Locals may be organized on an occupational or craft basis and/or on a plant or multiplant basis. The unit of organization of a local does not necessarily parallel the jurisdictional boundaries of its parent body; e.g., many locals of the clothing and other industrial unions are organized on a craft basis. Locals for each craft covering numerous employers in the same city or area are common in the building, printing, metal and trucking industries. Railroad locals are organized on a craft basis by railroad systems.

In manufacturing, locals confined to single plants are most common in unions whose jurisdictions cover all occupations within an industry. However, large locals covering all or most workers in a number of establishments in the same city and industry are not uncommon. These latter are sometimes referred to as amalgamated locals, the membership in each plant constituting a branch of the amalgamated local. Each branch elects its own stewards or bargaining officials and holds its own membership meetings, although some amalgamated locals also hold general membership meetings.

[3] National unions whose headquarters are in the U.S. also have 6,200 locals in Canada and about 200 locals in Puerto Rico, the Panama Canal Zone and elsewhere.

Relation of Locals to Their Nationals

Although the degree of centralized control varies considerably among the various national unions, every local is subordinate to its National. It must abide by its National's constitution, which specifies the general rules by which the locals are to operate, and it must accept all the regulations adopted by its National's conventions. A National's constitution, for example, not only defines the conditions under which a local may be chartered, but it may (although it does not always) specify the amounts in dues and initiation fees its locals may charge, the requirements for acceptance of members, the procedures for dealing with employers and calling of strikes, and even work rules which the local members must observe.

The national organization has the authority to examine the books of its locals at any time, and in most instances the locals are required to submit audited reports at regular intervals. Violation of established rules and regulations may result in the National's taking over the local and all its assets by establishing a trusteeship over it.

While subject to the rules of their Nationals, each local has a voice in the formulation of these rules and policies through representation at the general conventions. The number of delegates which a local may send to the convention, the highest governing body of the national union, is dependent upon its paid-up membership as prescribed in the National's constitution. Even though not specified in the constitution, the President of the local is ordinarily selected as a delegate and will be accompanied by others elected by the membership if the local is of sufficient size to permit more than one delegate.

Local Officers

The constitutions of most Nationals specify the various officers which their locals are required to maintain although the choice of individuals to hold these offices and their pay are determined by the locals. The election procedure which locals must follow is usually outlined in their National's constitution and these rules usually require notice to all members of the pending election, open nominations and majority vote in a secret ballot. Officers are usually elected for one-year terms, although in some unions longer terms up to four years are specified.

The qualifications for local union officials are sometimes more rigid than qualifications for mere membership. In all cases nominees must be in good standing with the local and in some instances must have been a member a certain length of time, such as one year, before becoming candidates for office. Procedures to be followed and causes for the removal of local officials are usually outlined in the Nationals' constitutions. If a local officer violates his National's constitution, the National may expel him. For other causes a specified proportion of the local membership may file charges and demand an investigation and trial. An expelled local officer has the right of appeal to his National Executive Board and finally to the convention.

In small locals the elected officers usually continue to work at their trade and receive no regular salary from the union; the Presidents and Vice-Presidents are generally paid a few dollars for each meeting over which they preside, while the Secretary-Treasurers are paid a few hundred dollars a year for keeping the books.

Although it is more common to have the Secretary-Treasurer on a full-time basis than the other officers, a number of larger locals have found from experience that it is better to employ trained bookkeepers than to have members elected from among their ranks to perform the detailed duties connected with maintaining membership roles and recording the dues of hundreds and thousands of members scattered among numerous plants, and collecting and disbursing thousands of dollars a year.

Business Agents and Shop Stewards

In addition to the regularly elected officers, most unions have so-called "business agents" who are full-time paid employees of the locals with no definite term of office, thus providing continuity to the local's activities. Most business agents have served as officers and have been experienced workers in the industry, and thus know the language of the trade. As employees of the locals, they have no vote but may give advice and suggestions to the membership and elected officials. As a practical matter, the business agent usually exercises a great deal of leadership over the local and its affairs. To the rank-and-file members, the business agent is "Mr. Union."

The functions of a business agent cover the entire field of the local's activities. He usually accompanies the grievance chairman or goes by himself to the higher officers of the firm to settle those grievances which the shop steward is unable to settle with the foreman. In smaller locals with no other full-time officers, he maintains the union's office and files and sometimes collects dues, especially from delinquent members. His duties may include such activities as preparing the local's newspaper and other publicity, arranging social functions, and setting up the agenda for local meetings as well as participate in the negotiating of agreements. In the building trades and some other unions, the business agent often performs an additional function in maintaining the union's hiring hall.

Strictly speaking, a shop steward is not an officer of the local, although he is the union representative who comes in closest contact with the members. It is his job to see that union conditions are maintained in the shop. Unless there is a checkoff arrangement, he may also collect the dues from members in his department or plant. His chief function is to handle the grievances which members have against their employers or foremen.

Stewards are not elected in general union membership meetings, but are usually elected by the members in each department of a plant. In large plants the various department stewards, or in some cases the workers in the plant as a whole, elect a chief steward who represents the union in negotiations with higher plant officials. If the local covers only one plant, the President of the local may function as the chief steward and, in many cases, the plant grievance committee is in reality the executive board of the local.

Membership Meetings

The local union meeting is the medium through which the membership controls the policies and activities of the union. Many national constitutions specify the minimum number of membership meetings that must be held each year. Although the monthly meeting is the rule, two or even more meetings are held every month by some locals. Special meetings are called whenever necessary by the local's executive board and, in some unions, special meetings may be initiated by a petition signed by a specified number of members. In some cases the National outlines the program to be followed by its locals, especially concerning such matters as the proper reporting of finances and activities to the membership.

As with other kinds of voluntary organizations, many unions experience great difficulty in getting full attendance at meetings. Although poor attendance is no indication of lukewarm loyalty to the union, as is evidenced by the wholehearted response during a crisis such as a strike, nevertheless the character and effectiveness of a union are strongly influenced by the attendance at local meetings, since control of any organization's affairs inevitably goes to the few faithful attendants who may or may not be representative of the entire membership.

In order to ensure maximum attendance and avoid complaints from members that measures were adopted about which they had no knowledge, many unions require their members to attend all or a specified minimum number of meetings a year. For unexcused absences fines are sometimes imposed, especially for absences from the annual meeting where financial reports are read and new officers are elected; other unions charge double their usual fines for non-attendance at such special meetings.

5

MEMBERSHIP RULES AND FINANCES

In any trade or industry in which labor organizations are active, every worker and employer is directly or indirectly affected by the rules and regulations having to do with the acceptance and retention of members in the union. Membership rules are of paramount importance in the trades and plants whose contracts require union membership as a condition of employment. In all plants where collective bargaining exists, the nonunion employee as well as the union member is bound by the terms of the contract negotiated by the union. If a nonunion employee is dissatisfied with those terms and decides to join the union in order to bring about changes in the employment contract, he immediately becomes interested in the union's qualifications for acceptance.

The aim of a union generally is to take in as many as possible of those employed within its jurisdiction. Although some unions may place certain restrictions on the acceptance of candidates for membership, the tendency is in the opposite direction, since it is the chief aim of the unions to expand their membership by accepting any and all persons who can liberally be interpreted as being employed within their jurisdictions.

The broad provisions specified in the national unions' constitutions necessarily allow wide latitude in practice within any local organization. Also, a local union may be able to circumvent the spirit if not the letter of its National's constitution. For example, the constitution may specify that there shall be no discrimination as to race, but the members of a local organization may have a tacit understanding among themselves not to recommend any one of the colored race for membership. Likewise, a broad requirement that all applicants must be "of good moral character" may be interpreted variously upon different occasions.

CITIZENSHIP, SEX, AND RACE QUALIFICATIONS

The attitude of unions on citizenship, sex, and racial requirements has been dominated by the fear that recent immigrants, women, and Negroes are a competitive menace to the wage and working standards which the unions have already obtained or hope to gain. Negroes and immigrants, for example, have frequently been employed for strikebreaking and antiunion purposes, and women have been hired for wages which are below union standards. Throughout the years there have been conflicting opinions within the labor movement as to the best course to follow: whether to debar these groups from membership and seek to keep them out of the trade altogether, or whether to allow them into the union and thus reduce the hazard of having entrants into the trade accept jobs under competitive nonunion conditions.

Most generally, unions have deemed it wisest in the long run to alleviate the competitive menace of persons willing to accept jobs at low standards by taking them into the unions. Almost all of the national unions are nonrestrictive although some of the unions which were established during the time of the heavy influx of immigrants into this country, specify that applicants for membership shall be citizens or at least have applied for their first citizenship papers.

WOMEN

While a dozen of the craft unions restrict membership to males, most of these are in building and other trades where few, if any, women are employed. Several of these unions have accepted women as temporary members during war emergency periods, and others would probably modify their sex restrictions if there were pressing need to do so. In some trades as, for example, in the maritime industry, employment and hence membership in the unions is dependent upon licenses and certificates issued by the government.

Although the law does not specifically prohibit the issuance of seamen's certificates and officers' licenses to women, none in fact have been issued in this country for ocean marine service although there are a few licensed women operators for river and lake vessels.

At the present time one out of every six union members is a woman. About 25 per cent of the Nationals have no women members and in another 30 per cent women comprise fewer than 10 per cent of the membership. In contrast, women comprise at least 75 per cent of the total membership in eight unions, including the clothing unions, the communications and telephone unions, the hotel and retail clerks unions. Other unions with more than 50,000 women members are the Automobile, Building Service, Machinists, and Meat Cutters, and both the Electrical Workers' unions. Women comprise about 60 per cent of the membership in the Federation of Teachers—a lesser proportion than that of women teaching in the elementary and secondary schools.

Political Beliefs

Provisions with respect to political beliefs and affiliations have always presented a delicate problem to unions. In line with organized labor's traditional policy of political nonpartisanship, unions have adhered to the general principle that there should be no political qualifications or requirements for individual members.

An important qualification to this general expression of political freedom is specified in some union constitutions and implied in others, namely, that members shall not be identified with any political organization which is considered to be inimical to the present form of American democracy. Thus, a number of constitutions state: "No person shall be excluded by reason of his religious belief or political affiliation *provided* he is not a member of any organization hostile to the American form of government." In view of the current world situation, a number of unions have adopted more specific requirements such as: "Membership shall be denied anyone proven to be a member or in any way affiliated with the Communist or other totalitarian party, or any organization that has for its purpose the overthrow of our democratic government."

The absence of such qualifications in a union's constitution, or a provision which seemingly places no restrictions upon political action, does not in itself indicate that the union would accept or retain persons who engage in activities commonly considered to be contrary to American union philosophy. It may merely indicate that no situation or problem has arisen within the union which would cause it to adopt a specific restriction in its constitution.

NEGRO MEMBERSHIP

By and large, labor unions have been much more liberal in their attitude toward acceptance of Negroes into membership on an equal basis then have most other groups in this country, including churches, educational and professional organizations. Racial equalitarianism has been the policy adopted by most of the labor movement since earliest times. For many years after its formation the American Federation of Labor insisted that all its affiliated unions eliminate color restrictions in line with its declared policy that "working people must unite and organize irrespective of creed, color, sex, nationality. . . ." Much like the initially declared policy of the AFL was the stated objective in the CIO constitution, namely "to bring about the effective organization of working men and women of America regardless of race, creed, color or nationality."

The precepts adopted at conventions, however, have sometimes been ignored or abandoned altogether because of the insistence of rank-and-file members. Not many years after its formation, the AFL began to admit unions with color restrictions; and the CIO frequently had to bring pressure upon local groups not to deny Negroes the full benefits of union membership and rights established by collective agreements, particularly with respect to upgrading and seniority.

The AFL-CIO constitution contains no outright prohibition of racial discrimination, but it does provide for a Committee on Civil Rights ". . . to assist the Executive Council to bring about at the earliest possible date the effective implementation of the principle . . . of non-discrimination. . . ." Although there is no exclusion of Negroes in the constitutions of any of the affiliates of the AFL-CIO, a number of unions, especially in the railroad industry, maintain segregated locals.

Negroes comprise about 10 per cent of the total union membership. Although this is considerably less than their ratio in the total labor force, a large proportion of Negroes are employed in occupations such as farming, domestic service and the service trades, which are not unionized. In the train and mail service there are three unions whose membership is composed largely of Negroes—the Transport Service Employees, who are mostly redcaps; the Brotherhood of Sleeping Car Porters; and the Alliance of Postal Employees.

Membership Restrictions and the Law

During recent years union control over their admissions into membership has been qualified by two kinds of laws—the 1947 National Labor-Management Relations Act, and the Fair Employment Practices laws which have been enacted by a number of states.

The Labor-Management Relations Act (Taft-Hartley law) specifically says unions have the right to prescribe their own rules with respect to the acquisition or retention of members *but* the Act makes it an unfair labor practice for an employer to deny employment under a union-shop contract, or in any way to penalize an employee for nonmembership, if the employer has reasonable grounds for believing that union membership was not available to the employee on the same terms applicable to other members, or if the employee was expelled from the union for any reason other than nonpayment of regular dues and assessments. According to this law, therefore, a union can establish any membership rules it wishes, but it cannot enter into a union-shop agreement with an employer if its regular membership rolls are not open to all individuals and groups whose occupations and skills come within the union's jurisdiction.

Since 1945 a number of states have enacted Fair Employment Practices laws. As the term implies, these laws are aimed at the hiring policies of employers as well as the membership policies of unions. Typically, the laws forbid an employer to refuse to employ, or to discharge from employment, or otherwise to discriminate against an individual in conditions or privileges of employment; or for a labor organization to exclude or to expel from membership or to discriminate in any way against any of its members because of race, creed, color or national origin.

FOREMEN AND SUPERVISORS

The question of whether or not to allow or require foremen and supervisors to belong to unions has always been a troublesome problem to all parties concerned—management, unions, and the foremen themselves. Most foremen have been promoted from the machine or workbench and in organized shops were union members before promotion. If they belonged to unions which maintain pension and other benefit programs, they naturally do not want to lose these benefits toward which they have contributed for many years. Even more important, perhaps, is the risk of losing their seniority rights with the privilege of bumping[1] when no longer needed or wanted as foremen. This hazard is increased in seasonal industries where workmen are promoted to foremen during peak seasons and return to the machine or bench during dull seasons.

The urge to belong to unions is the same for foremen as that of workers, namely, to exert group pressure in order to improve their economic status. In large mass-production industries, the authority and prestige of the foreman's position have sometimes depreciated to the point where he participates very little, if any, in formulating company policies, and is given limited leeway in the application of such policies within his particular bailiwick. One among hundreds of others of his same status in the company, he is almost as anonymous to top management as the rank-and-file workers and thus feels that he has little chance for individual recognition and redress of grievances.

Some of the oldest unions have always favored the practice of having their foremen belong to their unions because, as members, they serve to ensure adherence to union work rules, and in dealing with higher management they can sympathetically interpret union aims and policies. Many unions, on the other hand, have been reluctant to allow members who have been promoted to foremen

[1] "Bumping" implies displacement of someone with less seniority. In most instances bumping according to seniority is confined to those employees covered by the employer-union agreement. However, in some plants where foremen are not union members, special clauses have been negotiated which give displaced foremen the right to return to their former or similar jobs according to their seniority standing before promotion to foremanship or, in some cases, according to their accrued seniority including the time spent as foreman.

to continue their membership; much less willing have they been to allow foremen to join who have not previously belonged. This policy is based on the belief that the inherent nature of a foreman's job makes him an instrumentality of management in dealing with employees and that there can be no satisfactory commingling of management and union functions. Furthermore, many union members fear the dominant role foremen might take in union affairs if they were permitted to be active members. Foremen necessarily have leadership qualities which other members may feel might be exercised in union meetings to the disadvantage of rank-and-file members. It is for this reason that some unions which allow foremen to be members place some restrictions upon their participation in union affairs.

The alternative, however, is not necessarily between foremen not belonging to any union and being members of the same union to which their employees belong. Foremen may be organized into unions confined to persons of their own rank. There are several long-established craft unions which are composed solely of foremen and supervisors. Unionization of foremen in the mass-production industries was an active issue during the 1940's when the Foremen's Association of America obtained recognition from the Ford Motor Company but met with determined opposition from other corporations. After hearing the Association's numerous requests for elections and certifications, the National Labor Relations Board finally held that independent unions composed of foremen only were entitled to protection under the law. Employers actively opposed this interpretation and were instrumental in getting foremen and supervisors excluded from the definition of "employees" in the 1947 Labor-Management Relations Act. While this Act specifically states that nothing in the Act shall prohibit foremen and supervisors from belonging to unions, it exempts employers from being required to bargain collectively with them. The Ford Motor Company withdrew its recognition, and the Foremen's Association soon disbanded.

Foremen in Craft Unions

Many of the craft unions which are composed primarily of journeymen also permit, and in some cases require, foremen to be members. Usually, these foremen have restricted voting privileges and union rules protect them from union discipline for actions necessary to their duties as foremen; in other words, while card members of their unions, they are considered to be directly responsible to their employers for the conduct of the men under them.

In the printing trades, union membership of foremen is a long-established practice. Foremen in the building trades who work with tools along with the men they supervise are required to be union members. Although the metal trades unions generally exclude foremen in the mass-production industries, elsewhere it is the tradition for them to belong to the same unions as the men under them. This is true in shipyards under agreements with the metal trades councils, although foremen in the government navy yards may belong to a separate organization, the Master Mechanics and Foremen of Naval Shore Establishments.

Separate organization by supervisory groups has long been the practice in the maritime industry, in parts of the railroad industry, and in the postal service. The Masters, Mates and Pilots and the Marine Engineers' Beneficial Association are organizations for licensed personnel and officers in the maritime industry. In the postal service there are organizations of Postal Supervisors and of District Postmasters. There is extensive organization of supervisory personnel on the railroads and airlines although the type or organization varies. In yard service, some of the supervisors belong to the yardmasters' unions while others are members of the train service and the switchmen's unions. The railway clerks', telegraphers', signalmen's and maintenance-of-way unions accept supervisors as members. Foremen in railroad shops and in the airline industry belong to the Railway and Airline Supervisors Association.

APPRENTICES

In trades which require prolonged apprenticeship, the unions are concerned with the intake of apprentices into the trade as well as the acceptance of journeymen members. Regulations restricting the number of entrants into a trade and rules for training apprentices are for the purpose of maintaining standards of skill and workmanship as well as to protect the job opportunities and wage rates of journeymen members.

Rules regarding apprentices are included in the constitutions of most of the national unions whose jurisdictions include skilled crafts, although some leave the matter to be settled locally. Most apprenticeship rules set age requirements for entrance and qualifications for journeyman status, and regulate the number or proportion of apprentices admitted and the length of the apprenticeship period. Some constitutions specify that apprentices must join the union as soon as accepted; sometimes they are not taken in until they qualify as journeymen, although almost always they are required to be registered with the union.

ACCEPTANCE AND RETENTION OF MEMBERSHIP

The recruiting of new members and the passing upon their qualifications are primarily the responsibility of the local unions, although most of the national constitutions specify certain broad precepts to be applied by their locals. Many of these consist of minimum qualifications; others are specific restrictions which their locals are required not to impose. A common phrase is "all persons working within the union's jurisdiction" or "all persons in the trade." Some unions specify that members are to be "of good moral character" and "of sober and industrious habits."

Applicants' names presented at the local union meetings are usually accepted as a matter of course; indeed, according to the present law, under union-shop contracts the union is virtually bound to accept all persons hired by the employer. Where unions supply workmen for the employer through the union hiring hall, as in some of the skilled trades, the union assumes responsibility for the competency of its members and an applicant must be endorsed by journeymen members who have knowledge of his ability. In order to avoid discrimination, some national unions restrict nonacceptance of candidates except for specified reasons and provide appeal to the General Executive Board. In a few of the small craft unions in trades where job opportunities are limited, permission from the National President is required before a local may finally accept a new member.

SUSPENSION AND REINSTATEMENT

After once joining the union a member is expected to continue his membership so long as he remains employed in the industry or trade within the union's jurisdiction. For that reason the term "resignation" is seldom, if ever, used by unions. If a member changes jobs but remains in the trade or industry over which his union has jurisdiction, he obtains a transfer; if he retires or changes his occupation to one outside the jurisdiction of his union, he applies for an honorable withdrawal or retiring card. If a member fails to pay his dues for a certain length of time—most commonly two or three months—he is automatically suspended and, if working under a union-shop agreement, he must be dismissed from his job.

In unions with low initiation fees, where there is no union-shop agreement, members may be inclined to allow their dues to lapse, if rejoining at any time is too easy. Such lapses in membership tend to take place after a wage increase or other improvement in working conditions has been obtained or, conversely, during times when the union is not able to gain immediate benefits for its members. In unions with relatively high initiation fees, the membership is more likely to be stable, since the cost of re-establishing good standing more than offsets continued payment of dues.

As a deterrent to frequent lapses in membership, most unions require the full payment of all back dues and assessments in addition to a specified reinstatement fee if the person has been continually employed in the interim. In some cases the reinstatement fee, or rejoining fee as it is sometimes called, is less than the original initiation fee; where the latter is nominal, the reinstatement fee is likely to be somewhat higher. Some unions make no distinction but require their suspended members to pay the regular initiation fee in addition to all back dues and assessments. A few require no payment of back dues or assessments but have a relatively high reinstatement fee. On the other hand, if a union, because of depressed business conditions or for other reasons, has suffered heavy losses in membership, it may offer the cancellation of all back dues as an inducement for mass rejoining during the period of an organization drive.

EXPULSION

While expulsion for causes other than nonpayment of dues is infrequent, it nevertheless is a serious matter and may prove a hardship in individual cases. Unions naturally consider those actions which jeopardize the existence or prestige of the union to be the most serious offenses, such as instigating internal factional disruption, promoting or aiding a rival union, or going to court about internal union matters. Here unions face the same problem as any political or other organization; namely, the inherent contradictions of group solidarity versus individual freedom.

In their day-to-day functioning, unions and union officers are continually faced with the problem of how to impose the discipline that is necessary for effective group action and at the same time preserve maximum freedom of speech of the individual; how to maintain organizational cohesion and unity of purpose and at the same time retain sufficient flexibility to permit group protests which might result in changes in customary procedures. Permissible grounds for expulsion and the methods by which they are consummated are important criteria of the way a union seeks to reconcile the necessities of efficient administration with maximum freedom of expression and action by its members.

Causes for Expulsion

Although some union constitutions do not specify particular causes for expulsion, all of them carefully outline the procedure to be used when charges are brought against a member. In many, the grounds for expulsion are described in such general terms as "violation of union rules" or "continued offense against the union." A number add to these general expressions such specific offenses as intemperance, accepting a job declared unfair by the union, working in a nonunion shop, strikebreaking or, conversely, going out on strike without the sanction of the union. Essentially such constitutional provisions are designed to permit expulsion only when basic union rules are violated.

In contrast are the provisions in a number of constitutions which itemize numerous causes for expulsion which, if enforced, might result in the expulsion of a member who openly voiced dissatisfaction or who sought to solicit votes for a change in union program or officers. Such potential infringements on members' freedom of speech generally turn on such clauses as "making untruthful statements," "impugning the motives of officers," "misrepresenting the union and its officers." The distinction between allowable and forbidden activities in connection with members' efforts to bring about changes in union government and program hinges on what constitutes "attempts to create dissension among members," "advocating or attempting to bring about a withdrawal of any member or group of members," "working in the interests of any cause which is detrimental to the union," "hampering any local or national officer."

PROCEDURE FOR EXPULSION

Obviously such clauses are subject to various interpretations under given circumstances. Their potential dangers are greatly mitigated, if not eliminated, if accused members are ensured a fair trial before a heavy fine or expulsion is imposed. The common procedure in a discipline case is for a member or officer to file specific charges at a local membership meeting. A trial committee is thereupon chosen by the President or elected by the members to investigate and conduct hearings. In some unions the committee's report to the local membership consists of a statement of findings only; in most unions the trial committee submits a verdict and recommendation for action, along with the evidence. In either case the accused member has the right to appear before the entire membership in his own defense. Most unions require a two-thirds affirmative vote of all members present at the meeting for the levying of fines or for expulsion. If the accused is acquitted, according to the rules of some unions, the committee may "investigate the intent of the accuser."

The constitution of practically every union gives a member expelled by his local the right to appeal to his National Executive Board and, finally, to the convention. Right of such appeal is provided also where heavy fines, which might be tantamount to expulsion, are voted by the local for disciplinary purposes. In most cases a member who is expelled from one local may not be admitted by another without the approval of the first local, and some unions also require the approval of the National Executive Board. A few unions put a time limit of six months or a year before any expelled member may rejoin; in all cases, of course, the expelled member must pay all outstanding fines as well as the usual, or sometimes a higher, rejoining fee.

In a few unions, the National President may take the initiative in the disciplining of members although theoretically, at least, appeal is possible to the general convention. Most generally, the power of the President to suspend a member is limited to actions which jeopardize the union's existence or reputation, such as "promoting dual unionism," going to civil courts over "internal union matters," or publicly attacking the union. Several unions require as part of their oath of office or admission to membership, a promise not to resort to any court "to secure redress of wrongs" before exhausting all the remedies provided by the union, and if a member goes to court the President may automatically suspend him.

Legal Protections

The Taft-Hartley Act protects employees working under union-shop contracts from losing their jobs because of expulsion from the union for any reason other than the nonpayment of dues. To protect members from the autocratic powers which a few union officers have exercised, the Landrum-Griffin Act specifies that no member shall be disciplined, fined or expelled without first receiving a written list of charges, a reasonable time to prepare a defense, and a "full and fair hearing." The Act also gives members the right to testify before governmental bodies and to sue their unions or union officers without retaliation, provided the members have first made use of any "reasonable" procedures the union itself has for adjusting complaints.

TRANSFERS AND WITHDRAWALS

A change-of-job situation may cause or require a change in union membership. A member may accept employment in another locality even though he continues in his same trade, or he may accept employment in an entirely different line of work; he may be promoted or demoted to an occupation lying outside the jurisdiction of his union, or he may be unemployed for a prolonged period of time. Transfers between locals of the same National are usually accepted as a matter of course. However, if a local already has unemployed members it may refuse to accept requests for transfers, although some Nationals require their locals to accept all requests for transfers, especially to members of at least two to five years' standing. A few Nationals permit transfers from any other National on the same basis as they provide for transfers between their own locals.

For special or temporary assignments, "courtesy privileges" may be extended a member from an outside local. Some of the craft unions issue "traveling cards" which permit the holders to take jobs for a limited length of time in any community without formal application for a transfer, provided, of course, the local in that community is not on strike. To make a permanent transfer he must obtain a "clearance card" from the local to which he belongs, which indicates he is a member in good standing with paid-up dues and assessments. Most generally the transfer or clearance card relieves the member from paying any initiation dues to the local to which he transfers. Since the amount of initiation fees may vary between the locals of the same national union, it is general practice to require those who have not been members for as long as one or two years to make up the difference when transferring to a local having higher initiation fees.

When a member changes his line of work or accepts a job in an occupation or industry outside the jurisdiction of his union, he usually obtains an honorable withdrawal card which gives him the privilege of returning to his original union whenever he wishes. He may, however, choose to retain his membership, especially if he has accrued old-age or other benefit rights. Membership in more than one union is allowable, provided there is no active rivalry between the unions within the plant or trade.

Some unions permit a member who is promoted to a foremanship (in unions which exclude foremen from membership) or retires because of old age or disability to obtain a retirement or, as it is sometimes called, an honorary membership card. An honorary member, although he may take no active part in the union's affairs during the period of retirement, is entitled to reinstatement, usually without payment of any fees, if his situation changes and he wishes to rejoin as an active member.

Unemployment and Military Service

A problem of considerable practical importance to the union as well as to its individual members is the question of membership status during periods of unemployment. All unions naturally want their members to retain their connection with the union, and various means are provided to carry unemployed members during periods when they are unable to pay their regular dues. In some unions the dues are reduced to a nominal sum, for example 10 cents a month, while in others members are permitted to remain in arrears for as long as six months without being dropped. Some rules specify that those working less than forty hours in any month shall be granted a dues-exemption stamp; others grant out-of-work stamps to members who have had less than ten days' employment, while some merely provide that those unemployed "the major portion of the month" shall be exempt from dues payment for that month.

Most unions provide that members drafted into the armed forces are to be retained as members in good standing but relieved of all dues payments until a specified time, usually sixty days, after discharge. Unions with relatively high initiation fees sometimes accept into membership without payment of initiation fees any honorably discharged veteran who has acquired "reasonable" skill in the trade while serving in the armed forces.

FINANCES AND DUES

Aside from disbursements under benefit plans, the bulk of the unions' funds is used to advance the general economic interests of the millions of workers who support the unions, and to promote legislation and other measures which will improve the well-being of workers, nonunion[2] as well as union. In union bookkeeping the

[2] For example, wage and hour legislation, and safety, health, and social security programs, both federal and state. Not only does organized labor employ

furtherance of these activities is chargeable to general administration, organizing, and strike expenses.

COSTS OF ADMINISTRATION

On an average, over the years, the greatest items of expense to unions are the salaries and traveling expenses connected with administration and organization work, although at certain times other expenditures may be much greater. (A prolonged strike, for example, may involve many times the outlay of ordinary administrative expenses, in addition to loss of dues.) The number of full- and part-time persons on a union's staff will vary not only in relation to the size of the organization but also in accordance with the activities conducted by the union. During an active membership campaign a union will employ additional organizers; if engaged in litigation or negotiating an agreement involving the preparation of a good deal of statistical and legal data, extra lawyers and economists will be employed. Unions which engage in benefit programs must employ actuaries and accountants to administer these activities.

Since practice varies as to the relative amount of the services performed by the national office and its locals, the comparative costs as between National and local administration are not uniform. In some unions most of the organizing work emanates from the national office; elsewhere the locals and district councils assume much of the organizing responsibility. In general, the paid organizers and enforcement officers comprise the bulk of the unions' staffs. On the average there is probably one full-time paid representative for each 1,000 members.

In most of the Nationals the only elected officers who are paid on a full-time basis are the President and Secretary-Treasurer. Their salaries differ not only according to the union's ability to pay but also according to its general theory of remuneration for such offi-

---

economists, lawyers, and others to take an active part in promoting such legislation, but representatives of the unions are frequently called upon to serve on tripartite advisory committees and in other ways to assist in the effective administration of the laws. To the extent of the cost of these salaries and other expenses, the dues-paying members of unions are bearing the costs of benefits which are shared by all workers affected by the legislation, nonunion as well as union.

cials, as well as the attitude of the membership toward the particular person holding the office. Some unions, especially the smaller craft unions, base the salaries of their officers at about or slightly above the highest level of wages earned by their members at their trades. Other unions, especially those which deal with large corporations, feel that the prestige and effectiveness of their officers are enhanced if their salaries approximate those received by the employer representatives with whom they deal. In many instances the salary paid a particular President or other official is a token of recognition and appreciation of his long service rather than an established remuneration for the office as such.

Almost 80 per cent of the national unions pay their Presidents less than $20,000 a year, the most common salary being in the $10,000-to-$15,000 bracket. With a very few exceptions the unions that pay less than $15,000 are relatively small, with fewer than 200,000 members. By contrast, the salary of the President of the United Steelworkers is $50,000; that of the Railway Clerks $60,000; that of the Teamsters' Union $75,000. In general, the salaries of the Vice-Presidents and Secretary-Treasurers are about 20 per cent less than those of the Presidents.

Dues and Assessments

Members contribute to the support of their unions by payment of (1) membership dues, usually on a monthly basis; (2) special assessments, usually for some particular purpose; (3) initiation fees when they first join the union, and reinstatement fees if they have withdrawn or allowed their membership to lapse and seek to rejoin. On rare occasions fines may be levied upon members, but these are disciplinary measures and not for revenue purposes.

With a few exceptions, all money is collected by the local unions, either directly from the members or through the employers when the unions have checkoff arrangements. The locals in turn forward certain specified sums to their national union and the other organizations with which they are affiliated, such as joint boards, city centrals and state federations. The payments to the latter amount to only a few cents per capita a month, but the locals' payments to their Nationals are greater—usually one dollar or more a month per

Chart 3. DUES AND INITIATION FEES, 1960 *

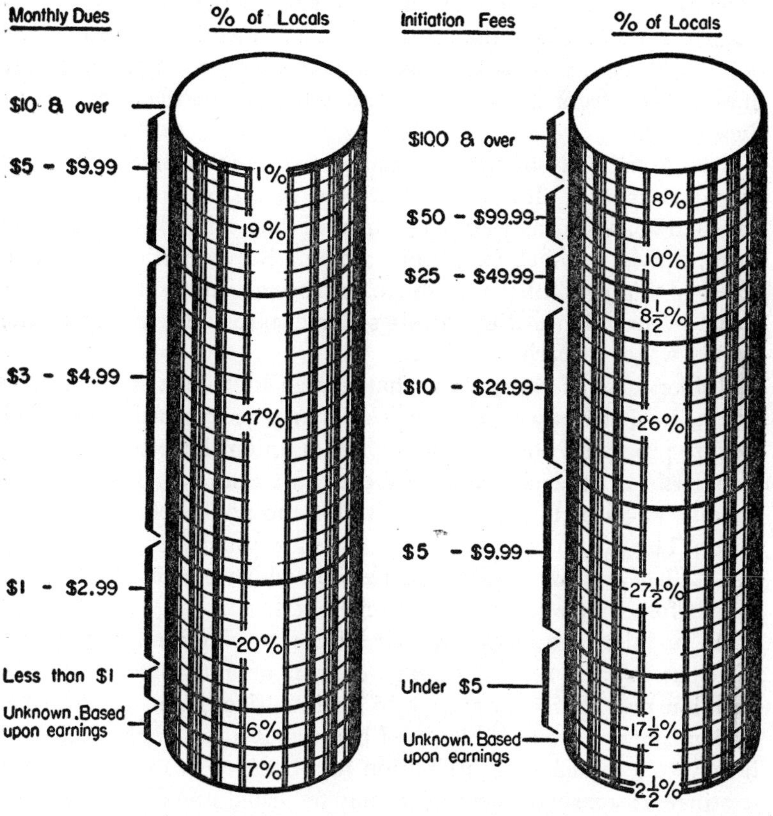

Monthly Dues
% of Locals
$10 & over
1%
$5 - $9.99
19%
$3 - $4.99
47%
$1 - $2.99
20%
Less than $1
6%
Unknown. Based upon earnings
7%

Initiation Fees
% of Locals
$100 & over
8%
$50 - $99.99
10%
$25 - $49.99
$8\frac{1}{2}$%
$10 - $24.99
26%
$5 - $9.99
$27\frac{1}{2}$%
Under $5
$17\frac{1}{2}$%
Unknown. Based upon earnings
$2\frac{1}{2}$%

SOURCE: Bureau of Labor-Management Reports, Fiscal Year, 1960

* The proportion of the total membership paying relatively low dues and fees is much greater than the percentages shown above would indicate. High fees are limited to skilled workers belonging to craft unions, which have smaller memberships, on the average, than the low-fee industrial unions. Also it must be noted that the above percentages are based on both prevailing and maximum fees. In many locals which have relatively high maximum fees for their skilled members, a large majority of their members actually pay less than the maximum amounts allowed by the locals' constitutions.

member, according to the relative degree of responsibility the National assumes in financing organization and strike activities. From these taxes the Nationals in turn pay per capita taxes to any organizations with which they are affiliated—the AFL–CIO and its departments, and any international labor organizations to which they may belong. In a few instances the national unions collect dues directly from the members and return a specified amount to their locals.

A large majority of union members are now paying dues of $3 or $4 per month, although 26 per cent of all locals have dues of less than $3, and nearly 20 per cent have dues of $5 or more. These latter, almost without exception, are relatively small unions composed of highly skilled craftsmen. In several unions the dues are levied in accordance with earnings—for example, 2 per cent of the weekly wages of each member.

Unlike most of the unions that charge high dues, none of the unions having comparatively low dues engage in pension or other welfare programs. Some of the high-dues unions have two classes of membership, beneficial and nonbeneficial; dues for the first class amount to $5 or more, while those for the nonbeneficial class are lower. The members of the latter class are usually engaged in the less skilled occupations, or are persons who were middle-aged or over before they were taken in as members.

On occasion the money received from regular dues may be insufficient to meet all the union's current or anticipated expenses. A union may decide to engage in an intensive organization drive; its funds may have been depleted because of a prolonged strike; or it may vote to make a contribution to a benevolent cause. For such contingencies a single assessment may be levied upon each member, or a specified assessment may be levied for a given number of months.

Assessments may be levied by the national office, in which event all members pay alike; or they may be levied by individual locals. Most commonly, assessments may be levied only after a two-thirds favorable referendum vote of the membership affected. Some constitutions impose a limitation even with referendum voting, for example "not to exceed $5 a year" or "not more than 10 cents in any one month." On the other hand, in a number of unions the executive board is given wide latitude and has authority to levy special assessments "whenever necessary" or "whenever necessary to meet an emergency."

INITIATION FEES

Unlike monthly dues, initiation fees are levied only once and they are not levied primarily for revenue purposes. During periods of stabilized membership little is collected, no matter how high the individual fees may be. During organizing drives many unions suspend their initiation-fee requirements as a means for attracting new members. A large majority of the present union members paid a fee of less than $5 when they were initiated into their unions. Although more than one-half of all locals have prevailing and maximum initiation fees of more than $10 (one-fifth ask $50 or more), a considerably smaller proportion of all union members have paid these higher fees. High initiation fees are limited to skilled workers belonging to craft unions, which have much smaller memberships than the low-fee industrial unions. High fees are almost always paid in installments; thus, for those who pay them, they amount to an extra levy in addition to regular dues from their weekly wages.

Unions which charge relatively high initiation fees regard them as in the nature of a fine as well as a means of membership control. They maintain that the older members who have contributed many years to supporting their unions have enabled the unions to obtain higher wages and better working conditions than would have existed if there had been no unions. Since newcomers to the trade profit by these hard-won gains, the older members consider initiation fees a reimbursement for past services of the union, a method by which the new members share the cost of improved working conditions which they did not assist in procuring. This is evidenced in the practice of some unions of differentiating between the amount of fee charged those joining before a contract with the employer is signed and those joining after union conditions are established.

Historically, high initiation fees have been a means of controlling the intake into the union as well as into the trade. Unions which charge high initiation fees justify them on the grounds that they tend to stabilize employment for their members by acting as a deterrent to large influxes of new workers into the trade during temporary booms; for once new members are accepted, they not only share in the job opportunities during the temporary boom, but also claim rights to jobs when they become scarce. These unions contend that, if the need for extra workers is confined to one locality, their unemployed members elsewhere should be transferred, and that if it is a general but short-time boom the available jobs should be stretched over a longer period for those already in the trade rather than have new members taken in. Unions which charge extremely high initiation fees claim that such fees are seldom if ever actually paid by anyone, but that they are a device for keeping out newcomers.

The 1947 Labor Management Relations Act makes it an unfair labor practice for unions to require members employed under union-shop agreements to pay "excessive" or "discriminatory" initiation fees. The National Labor Relations Board is made the judge of the reasonableness of such fees, the law specifying that "the Board shall consider, among other relevant factors, the practices and customs of labor organizations in the particular industry, and the wages currently paid to the employees affected."

PART THREE

UNIONS AND THE LAW

6

THE COMMON LAW AND LABOR ORGANIZATIONS

Labor unions and their members have the same basic civil rights of freedom of speech and assembly, prohibition against involuntary servitude, and protection of life, liberty and property, that are provided in our Constitution for all our citizens. Similarly, unions and their members are subject to the same regulatory laws pertaining to conspiracy, sedition, violence, racketeering and other criminal acts which apply to all other citizens. In other words, legal protections and restrictions of labor organization activities include not only the laws which are specifically directed toward them, but also the general laws which are applicable alike to members of unions and all other persons.

The legal history of labor unions in this country can be divided into three distinct periods: the 130 years during which organized labor was given few protections but suffered under many judicial restrictions and severe penalties; the fifteen-year period beginning in 1932, when laws were enacted which clearly defined and encouraged the right of self-organization among workers and protected unions against employer discrimination and anti-union activities; and the period since 1947, when laws have been enacted which restrict and regulate many kinds of union activities but nevertheless continue to provide the right for workers to combine for the purpose of collective bargaining.

IMPORTANCE OF JUDICIAL DECISIONS

For many years organized labor was guided and controlled solely by the courts' interpretations and applications of the Constitution and the common laws applying to all citizens. During recent years, in recognition of the peculiar needs and position of wage earners in the modern industrial economy, the federal government and most of the states have enacted laws which pertain particularly to collective bargaining and labor unions.

When applied to specific employer-union situations, both the common law and statutory labor laws are subject to varying interpretations, and judicial decisions throughout the years have shown little unanimity or consistency of opinion. Higher courts have differed from lower courts in interpreting the same case, and the final decisions on many important cases have been by a close margin. Moreover, like all other human institutions, law is dynamic, not fixed for an indefinite period of time. New legislation is enacted and interpretations of existing laws are revised with the changing times, in response to public opinion or by shifts in the court personnel.

Because of these varying and ever-changing decisions by the judicial and administrative agencies throughout the country, as well as the great variety of laws on the statute books of the various states, it is impossible in this brief summary to give a definitive statement of the present legal status of all the various phases of collective bargaining and other union activities. The best that can be done is to indicate some of the broad principles embodied in the major federal statutes and in recent decisions by the United States Supreme Court.

To understand the present legal status of unions and collective bargaining it is necessary to review briefly the developing concepts represented in the court decisions throughout the years. Although some of the earlier decisions have been nullified by recently enacted legislation, many of them represent the latest word on particular issues and may assume importance whenever the appropriate occasion arises, even though they may seem to be dormant at a given time. Furthermore, the recently enacted statutory laws can be understood and appreciated only in the light of the common law that preceded them.

THE DOCTRINE OF CONSPIRACY

Early American law concerning unions and their activities developed out of the English common and statutory laws, which held that the mere existence of combinations of workers was a conspiracy and therefore illegal. During the eighteenth century the British Parliament enacted a series of statutes which forbade groups of workers to enter into combinations to raise their wages or lessen their hours, and condemned offenders "to hard labour or the common goal without bail or mainprize." These Combination Acts were essentially a confirmation of the British common law, which was centuries old.

The essence of the conspiracy doctrine as applied to labor unions was that a number of persons acting in concert or combination possess powers to do wrong which an individual does not possess. In other words, an act which might be lawful for an individual—for example, refusing to work except for a certain wage—may be unlawful if carried out by a number of persons acting in concert. There would also be a crime of conspiracy when a group had agreed to undertake a wrongful act even though the act had not yet been accomplished. The doctrine was further extended to hold that if one or several persons in the combination have committed an illegal act, all the other members are equally responsible even though they had no knowledge of the act.

The conspiracy doctrine was first invoked in this country in 1806 against some Philadelphia shoemakers who, according to the prosecution, ". . . did combine, conspire, confederate and unlawfully agree together that they . . . should not work and labor but at certain prices . . . to the damage, injury and prejudice of the masters employing them . . . did agree that each and every one of them would prevent by threats, menaces and other unlawful means, other workmen from working and laboring. . . ."

The defendants, on the other hand, maintained that ". . . if a single individual has the right to refuse to work for a certain wage, a number can unite for the same object. . . . That a menace is not indictable; that if any employer suffer inconvenience or mischief . . . he has his remedy by civil action in which he may recover damages. . . . That since they did not use physical violence in preventing non-members from working, but only refused themselves to work for the same employer, this was not an offense or crime."

Action was brought under the English common-law doctrine of criminal conspiracy. At that time there was a great deal of contention as to whether any of the English common law should be extended to this country. The Jeffersonian Democrats were strongly opposed to it; but the Federalists, who controlled the courts, were favorably disposed toward English judicial precedent. Conviction followed the judge's charge to the jury, which stated: "A combination of workmen to raise their wages may be considered in a two-fold point of view; one is to benefit themselves . . . the other is to injure those who do not join their society. The rule of law condemns both. If the rule be clear we are bound to conform to it even though we do not comprehend the principles upon which it is founded. We are not to reject it because we do not see the reason of it."

For more than a hundred years after this decision, most courts regarded as criminal conspiracies any combinations of workers which prevented other workers from accepting employment on any terms they might see fit. An exception was a Massachusetts Supreme Court decision in 1842 (Commonwealth *v.* Hunt), which stated: "The manifest intention of this Association is to induce all those engaged in the same occupation to become members of it. Such a purpose is not unlawful. We think that associations may be entered into, the object of which is to adopt measures that may be a tendency to impoverish another, that is, to diminish his gains and profits, and yet, so far from being criminal or unlawful, the object may be highly meritorious and public spirited. . . ." As legal precedent this decision was largely ignored by other judges, although the effect of the conspiracy doctrine was somewhat softened by several state laws enacted during the 1860's, which legalized combinations of workers formed for the purpose of improving working conditions.

RESTRAINT OF TRADE DOCTRINE

Closely allied to the common-law concept of criminal conspiracy was the doctrine of restraint of trade. This doctrine was based on the premise of the natural right of every person to dispose of his own property and labor as he pleased, free from the dictation of others. As applied to employer-labor relations it meant that an employer had a right to buy his labor in the cheapest market, and that each individual laborer was entitled to sell his labor on whatever terms he saw fit or could command. In most labor cases brought before the courts the decision rested upon what the particular court considered to be unlawful coercion by unions to obtain workers' participation in acts directed toward what the courts deemed to be "unreasonable" ends.

The common law of restraint of trade was reinforced by statute with the passage of the Sherman Anti-Trust Act in 1890, in response to popular demand for regulation of monopolies and price fixing. Under this Act the courts were able to impose increasing restrictions on the activities of unions, largely through the legal identification of "trade" and "property" with "good will" and the right to do business. Under this concept, an employer had a right to unhampered access to the commodity and labor market and, therefore, legal protection against boycotts, picketing and other acts of unions which might hinder him from selling his product, or prevent him from getting new employees to take the place of strikers.

COURT DECISIONS UNDER THE SHERMAN ACT

Some of the first cases decided by the courts under the Act had to do with labor disputes. It was invoked in 1895, when Eugene Debs was sentenced to jail for conspiracy in restraint of interstate commerce for his leadership in the strike against the Pullman Company. In the Danbury Hatters' case (1908) the Supreme Court held the individual members of the union responsible to the full amount of their individual property for triple damages to the company because of the union's nationwide boycott. In 1911 the Court held that a nationwide boycott conducted by the American Federation of Labor against the Buck Stove and Range Company was in violation of the Sherman Act, and forbade the AFL officers to speak or write anything in furtherance of the boycott. In essence, these decisions meant that even acts of peaceful persuasion were illegal if they resulted in curtailment of trade and impairment of the "good will" of business.

Organized labor undertook a vigorous campaign to have unions exempted from the provisions of the Sherman Act, and believed it had won with the passage of the Clayton Act in 1914, which it optimistically hailed as "Labor's Magna Charta." The Clayton Act declared that the "labor of a human being is not a commodity or article of commerce," and provided that the anti-trust laws should not be construed to forbid the existence of labor organizations or to restrain their members from carrying out the "legitimate objects" thereof. In actual operation, however, the Clayton Act was construed by the courts as having made no change in the law as previously interpreted.

In the Duplex Printing Company case (1921) the Court held that the Machinists' Union's efforts to force printing companies not to buy Duplex presses was illegal because threats had been used and because the aim was to injure the company. In the American Steel Foundry case and in the Truax case (1921) the Court held that to station more than one picket at each factory gate was unlawful, since this constituted intimidation and violated the constitutional guarantees of liberty and property, although the court explicitly said that the number of permissible pickets depended upon the circumstances in each particular dispute. In the Coronado and Red Jacket Coal cases (1922, 1927) involving the application of the Sherman Act to strikes, the Court held that unions could be sued even though they were unincorporated, and that inasmuch as the union's actions were for the purpose of stopping production of non-union coal they constituted illegal interference with interstate trade.

The Bedford case of 1927 had to do with a secondary boycott, and although the Court's decision was considered at the time to be most severe, it was not far out of line with present statutory law. (See Chapter 7.) In this instance no general boycott was attempted by the union against the firm's products; neither did the union picket nonunion workers. The union's efforts were directed solely toward persuading its own members not to work on nonunion material. The Supreme Court held that this curtailed, or threatened to curtail, the natural flow of interstate commerce, and that even though the ultimate aim was to benefit the union members and no illegal tactics were used, the organization was guilty of conspiracy to restrain trade.

RESTRAINT OF TRADE PRINCIPLE MODIFIED

During more recent years the Supreme Court has tended to restrict the application of the anti-trust laws so far as strikes are concerned. In the Apex case in 1940 the Court recognized that all combinations of workers necessarily restrain trade, since they curtail competition among employees and tend to eliminate wage differences. But they are not thereby unlawful, the Court held. Nor are strikes which obstruct the shipment of goods across state lines in violation of the Sherman Act. The only kind of interference with interstate commerce which the law prohibits is the suppression of competition by monopolizing a supply of goods, controlling the price, or discriminating between purchasers—in other words, interference with trade in a commercial sense where there is an actual or intended or direct effect upon prices and price competition.

Unions are nevertheless subject to the Anti-trust Act when acting in concert with employers to create business monopolies and to control the marketing of goods and services. In the Allen Bradley case (1944) the Supreme Court held that the union as well as the employers had violated the Sherman Act when they banded together to monopolize the entire New York city market for electrical goods by boycotting out-of-city and nonunion products. At present, it is not necessary to invoke the Sherman Act in cases involving employer-union collusion since such collusion is specifically covered in the 1959 Landrum-Griffin Act.

RIGHTS OF LIBERTY AND PROPERTY DOCTRINE

The Fourteenth Amendment to the Constitution[1] provides that "no State shall make or enforce any law which shall abridge the privileges or immunities of citizens of the United States; nor shall any State deprive any person of life, liberty or property, without due process of law, nor deny any person within its jurisdiction the equal protection of the laws."

Two fundamental concepts have influenced the courts when applying this amendment to employer-labor disputes. The first is that the right to engage in business is property, and that employers therefore should be guaranteed protection against abuse not only of their physical property but also of their "good will" and their means of carrying on business. The second is that workers and employers must be treated with formal "equality": As long as the worker is free to quit for any or no reason the employer must be free not to hire him or to fire him for any or no reason. Such a concept completely ignores, of course, the basic economic inequality between employers and workers, and considers a large corporation (which is a combination of capital) to have the same status as an independent owner-employer.

The right to hire and fire at will provided the most direct method of combating labor unions and collective bargaining. It permitted the use of employer blacklists, "yellow-dog" contracts, discriminatory discharges and the hiring of strikebreakers. In recognition of the essential injustice accruing from such unrestrained powers, many states early enacted laws making it a criminal offense for employers to dismiss employees or to discriminate against prospective employees because of union membership. Almost uniformly these state laws were held unconstitutional by the courts prior to the enactment of federal legislation in 1932.

[1] The Fourteenth Amendment was adopted in 1868 to protect the rights of freed Negroes. Its use by the courts in labor cases is an outstanding illustration of a diversion of the original purpose of a statutory law. For fifty years it was used by the courts against union activities and against state laws enacted to regulate minimum wages, hours of work, safety and any improvement of working conditions.

Typical of the reasoning of the Supreme Court was its statement in the Adair decision (1908):

> While . . . the rights of liberty and property guaranteed by the Constitution against deprivation without due process of law, is subject to such reasonable restraints as the common good or the general welfare may require, it is not within the functions of government—at least in the absence of contract between the parties—to compel any person in the course of his business and against his will to accept or retain the personal services of another, or to compel any person against his will, to perform personal services for another. The right of a person to sell his labor upon such terms as he deems proper is, in its essence, the same as the right of the purchaser of labor to prescribe the condition upon which he will accept such labor from the person offering to sell it. . . . In all such particulars the employer and the employee have equality of right, and any legislation that disturbs that equality is an arbitrary interference with the liberty of contract which no government can legally justify in a free land. . . .

"Yellow-dog Contracts"

Before they were made unenforceable in federal courts by statute in 1932, so-called "yellow-dog" contracts were a favorite device to prevent unionism. Although they took various forms, such contracts in substance obligated the employee not to join a union or engage in strikes or other union activities. In turn the employer gave the worker employment either for a definite period of time or "at will." In practice, the yellow-dog contract operated most effectively as a bar to unionization when the injunction was utilized to protect the contract from threatened breach. For example, when in 1917 the United Mine Workers attempted to unionize some nonunion coal mines where the employees had signed such contracts, the Supreme Court enjoined the organizers from soliciting membership. The injunction was based upon the doctrine that action lies against the person who persuades either party to a contract to breach it.

"GOVERNMENT BY INJUNCTION"

Concomitant with the legal identity of *business* with *property* was the use of injunctions in labor disputes. Injunctions were sought by employers primarily to protect their rights to do business

—in other words, to prevent obstruction of the manufacture and sale of their goods and of their access to the labor market. The police and criminal laws provided protection against damage to physical property and violence in labor disputes, but employers sought injunctions to restrain workers from engaging in boycotts, picketing and other acts which interfered with business operations, even though such acts were unattended by violence or physical damage to property.

Theory of Injunctions

The use of injunctions in labor disputes can best be understood by reference to the principles of equity which are supposed to govern the courts in issuing them. Injunctions[2] are orders issued by judges commanding individuals to do or to refrain from doing certain acts. Violation of an injunction constitutes contempt of court, and the judge who grants the injunction has the power and discretion to fine or imprison anyone who violates it. Injunctive relief is supposed to be an extraordinary measure, to be used only when there is "inadequate remedy at law"—that is, when civil action for damages will not provide full redress, either because of the defendant's financial inability to make restitution, or because damage is threatened which would be irreparable owing to the nature of the thing it endangers.

A basic principle of equity is that anyone who seeks injunctive relief must come into court "with clean hands"—that is, he must himself be guiltless of unlawful conduct in connection with the dispute. Another principle is that an injunction should not be granted if it will result in greater loss to the defendant than to the complainant. As originally used, injunctions were served individually and were not binding upon anyone who did not receive a notice.

Distortion of Principles of Equity

The traditional principles guiding the issuance of injunctions were radically changed by the courts when they came to be applied

[2] The injunction originated centuries ago in the British Courts of Equity to supplement and remedy the limitations and the inflexibility of the application of common law, and was supposed to be based on dictates of conscience and natural justice.

to labor disputes. The majority were granted with no notice to those against whom they were directed, and with no hearing at which labor's side of the case could be presented and evidence shown as to whether the employer came before the court "with clean hands." The employers' mere statements were accepted as sufficient,[3] and employers' applications frequently included every possible restriction upon workers' activities that might conceivably be of advantage to themselves. Employers were not required to post bonds or forfeits, and injunctions were granted on trivial pretexts, with no consideration of the *relative losses* to the complainant and defendant that might ensue. Furthermore, they were not always limited to the short period of the strike or boycott; injunctions were sometimes issued which *permanently* restrained unions and workers from engaging in activities that would otherwise have been lawful.

Sometimes an injunction was worded in terms so vague and general that the workers could have no way of knowing in advance whether or not they were violating any of its provisions. This was especially serious because the violation of an injunction entails risks not present under civil and criminal law. Instead of trial by jury with an opportunity to secure change of venue if desired, the violator of an injunction is tried and punished by the same judge who issued the injunction. Many labor injunctions were based on evidence in the form of affidavits, with no witnesses appearing to support the charges, and the accused being neither furnished counsel nor given the opportunity of listening to evidence presented by the accusers.

Probably the greatest travesty of equal rights before the law was the result of the blanket labor injunctions which prohibited lawful as well as unlawful acts and which restrained not only the actual defendants but also "all persons combining and conspiring with them and all other persons whomsover." Such was the famous Debs case in 1895, which provided the pattern for numerous injunctions thereafter. During the Railroad Shopmen's strike in 1922, in-

[3] A study of 118 applications for injunctions presented to federal courts between 1901 and 1928 found that 70 of them were *ex parte,* and in only 12 cases did employers bring records or witnesses to substantiate their statements. (Felix Frankfurter and Nathan Greene, *The Labor Injunction,* The Macmillan Co., New York, 1930).

junctions restrained many specified individuals as well as "all persons acting in aid or in conjunction with them" from "in any manner by letters . . . word of mouth, oral persuasion or suggestion, or through interviews to be published in newspapers or otherwise in any manner whatsoever, encourage, direct or command any person . . . to abandon the employment of said railway companies . . . or to refrain from entering the service of said railway companies. . . ."

"Government by injunction," as the practice was referred to by the representatives of labor, prevailed for almost fifty years. Its use began in the 1880's, but almost half of all such injunctions were issued between 1920 and 1930. During this time organized labor made relief from injunctions its foremost legislative demand. Bills were introduced annually until finally the 1932 federal anti-injunction act was passed by Congress. By this time twelve states had already enacted laws regulating the issuance of injunctions, but these laws had proved ineffective because of the courts' interpretations.

USE OF SPIES AND STRIKEBREAKERS

To the employers there seemed no inconsistency in the courts' protection both of their right to uninterrupted business and of their right, singly and in combination, to keep their employees from participating in union activities. To prevent unions from getting a foothold in their plants, employers engaged spies to report on employees who showed any interest in unions or dissatisfaction with their working conditions. Many "reputable" employers who boasted that their plants were "one big happy family" apparently saw nothing incongruous in the presence of company spies.

Some large companies hired their spies directly, and in some plants the so-called labor relations director was actually the head of the company's espionage system. Most employers used outside services. One of the major functions of some employers' associations was the furnishing of spies and strikebreakers to their members, and a number of detective agencies maintained "industrial departments" which provided spy service to employers on a contract basis, including inside operatives, guards, strikebreakers, and "missionaries" who visited the homes of strikers in order to further back-to-work movements.[4]

Much of the violence that has accompanied strikes and picketing has been caused by the presence of professional strikebreakers, who sometimes were instructed to stir up trouble in order to create a situation which would make it easy for the employer to get an injunction to forbid picketing. Even if they were not under specific instructions to foment violence, the character of the men employed to do such work made it inevitable that violence would occur.[5]

To curtail such activities Pennsylvania enacted a law in 1937 which makes it a misdemeanor for any person, firm or corporation "not directly involved in a labor dispute or lockout" to recruit any persons to take the place of employees in an industry where a strike is in effect. Utah requires every person to register with the State Industrial Commission before starting work for an employer whose employees are on strike. A 1938 New York law makes it unlawful for a detective agency to furnish strikebreakers and strike guards or to engage in industrial espionage. In 1936 federal legislation was en-

[4] The use of private detective agencies for industrial espionage became widespread during World War I and the 1920's. Many companies had continuing contracts with detective agencies to furnish inside operatives, even though no strikes were threatened in their plants. Their duties were described as follows:

"The inside operatives carry on the work of industrial espionage while working for the client employer under assumed names, as ordinary mechanics or worker-men. . . . They do their daily work and draw pay checks like other workmen, and their fellow employees and immediate superiors—often the superintendents themselves—have no inkling that they are spies. But every day they make a report to the detective agency, and this agency in turn reports to the employer. . . . It is an almost invariable practice of the inside operatives to join the union . . . and attend all union meetings and take an active part in all union affairs. . . . They create strife within the union, arouse racial hatreds, and spread suspicion." (E. E. Witte, *The Government in Labor Disputes,* McGraw-Hill Book Co., New York, 1932, pp. 185–186.)

[5] The distinction between a professional strikebreaker and what is commonly called a scab should be kept in mind. The latter word refers to a nonunion employee who continues to work for an employer whom the union has designated as "unfair," or who accepts employment during a labor dispute with the intention of remaining as a permanent employee. A professional strikebreaker is an outsider who has no intention of becoming a permanent employee and usually is not competent to perform the job; his purpose is to fill the job only during the labor dispute.

As required by the Wager-Peyser Act, the U.S. Employment Service does not refer an applicant to a position involving a strike or lockout without first notifying him verbally and in writing of the existence and nature of the dispute.

acted (see Chapter 7) which forbids the importation of strikebreakers across state lines. As a result of the sensational exposures at the LaFollette Committee hearings in 1937, most of the large private detective agencies announced that they were discontinuing their "industrial departments," and there is no doubt that the practice of industrial espionage has greatly lessened within recent years.

7

UNIONS UNDER PRESENT LAWS

The conditions that existed prior to 1932 were the result not of statutory laws favorable to employers, but rather of the absence of laws to offset the inherent advantages held by management and the owners of business. During the 1930's several types of laws were enacted by the federal government which sought to alleviate some of the imbalances in the employer-employee relationship. Thereafter, legislation was passed to limit some of the "protections" given labor, as well as to control the internal operations of labor unions.

THE NORRIS-LAGUARDIA ACT OF 1932

Organized labor received its first substantial and general[1] protection and encouragement from federal legislation with the passage of the Federal Anti-Injunction Act, commonly referred to as the Norris-LaGuardia Act. Of paramount significance was the Act's statement of public policy endorsing workers' right to self-organization:

> Whereas under prevailing economic conditions, developed with the aid of governmental authority for owners of property in the corporate and other forms of ownership association, the individual unorganized worker is commonly helpless to exercise actual liberty of contract and to protect

---

[1] Six years previous to the Norris-LaGuardia Act, the railroad workers had been given legal protection against interference in their self-organization. The 1926 Railroad Act forbade "interference, influence, or coercion exercised by either employers or employees over the self-organization or designation of representatives by the other."

his freedom of labor, and thereby to obtain acceptable terms and conditions of employment, wherefore, though he should be free to decline to associate with his fellows, it is necessary that he have full freedom of association, self-organization, and designation of representatives of his own choosing, to negotiate the terms and conditions of his employment, and that he shall be free from the interference, restraint, or coercion of employers of labor, or their agents, in the designation of such representatives or in self-organization or in other concerted activities for the purpose of collective bargaining, or other mutual aid or protection. . . .

This law offered relief to unions from several approaches: It drastically restricted the use of injunctions by providing that U.S. courts may not issue injunctions against the normal and peaceful activities connected with industrial disputes, and that injunctions can be granted only after open hearings. It outlawed yellow-dog contracts by making unenforceable in federal courts any individual contracts in which the employee promises not to join a labor organization. Also, officers and unions were relieved of liability for unlawful acts committed during labor disputes unless there is clear proof that such acts were authorized.

Through its broad definition of "labor dispute" the 1932 law's limitations on injunctions covered secondary as well as primary strikes and boycotts. It protected from court action any peaceful disputes "regardless of whether or not the disputants stand in the proximate relation of employer and employee" since persons may be participating or interested in a labor dispute if they are "engaged in the same industry, trade, craft or occupation in which the dispute occurs, or [have] a direct or indirect interest therein. . . ." This inclusion of secondary boycotts and strikes within the permissible area of union activities has been drastically curtailed by more recent legislation.

THE WAGNER ACT

The 1935 National Labor Relations Act, sometimes called the Wagner Act, marked the legal turning point in labor-management relations. Based on the premise that inequality of bargaining power existed when workers were not organized and that such inequality was detrimental to the general economic well-being, the Act not only declared the right of workers to organize but provided specific protections and encouragement to collective bargaining. It declared that "employees shall have the right to self-organization, to form, join, or assist labor organizations, to bargain collectively through representatives of their own choosing, and to engage in concerted activities for the purpose of collective bargaining or other mutual aid or protection."

To protect these rights, five unfair labor practices were forbidden by employers:

> They must not interfere with, restrain, or coerce employees in the exercise of their right to self-organization, to form, or join labor organizations, to bargain collectively through representatives of their own choosing.
>
> They must not dominate or interfere with the formation or administration of any labor organization or contribute to the financial or other support of it.
>
> They must not discriminate in hiring, discharge, or any condition of employment to encourage or discourage membership in any labor organization, but they may require union membership under closed-shop agreements signed with unions selected by majority vote.
>
> They must not discharge or otherwise discriminate against employees who file charges or give testimony under the Act.
>
> They must not refuse to bargain collectively with representatives of the employees designated in accordance with the Act.

The Act provided for a nonpartisan board, the National Labor Relations Board, whose duties are twofold: (1) to aid in the free selection of employee representative agencies by holding elections or otherwise determining the choice of the majority of the workers in an appropriate bargaining unit; and (2) to prevent unfair labor practices and to see that employers bargain "in good faith" once the representative agency has been determined.

The legal principle of collective bargaining became firmly established during the twelve years the NLRA was in force, but employers and sections of the general public were not reconciled to many of its implications and concrete effects. They argued that the Wagner Act had tipped the scales too far in favor of labor, and that changes in the law were necessary "to restore equality" between labor and management. The outcome of this bitterly fought struggle between organized employers and organized labor was the Labor-Management Relations Act, enacted over the veto of President Truman by a Republican-controlled Congress.

LABOR-MANAGEMENT RELATIONS ACT OF 1947

In this law, most commonly referred to as the Taft-Hartley Act, the declaration of the rights of employees to organize and to bargain collectively is identical to that contained in the 1935 Act, with one important addition—namely that individual employees "shall also have the right to refrain from any or all such activities" except to the extent that an employee may be bound by a union-shop contract sanctioned by the law. A declaration of rights has meaning only in relation to what employers, unions and employees are allowed or not allowed to do to implement the declared rights. The 1947 law liberalizes some of the practices previously disallowed employers, and also includes a list of unfair labor practices by unions. Through such additions the Taft-Hartley law invoked an entirely different concept of "equality of bargaining power" from that upon which the 1935 law was based.

The sponsors of the 1947 Act justified this shift of focus on the ground that the earlier Act was one-sided in affording "relief to employees and labor organizations for certain undesirable practices on the part of management" but denied "to management any redress for equally undesirable actions on the part of labor organizations." They further held that the government under previous laws and court decisions had been "unable to cope with union practices that injure the national well-being," and that "such practices must be corrected if stable and orderly labor relations are to be achieved."[2]

Organized labor contends, on the other hand, that the "equality of bargaining power" of the Act is specious in that it does not take into account the inherent advantages held by the employer in the bargaining relation—an imbalance which the Wagner Act was designed to rectify—and that the unfair labor provisions as applied to unions serve to weaken the ability of unions to carry on many of

[2] Senate Committee on Labor and Public Welfare, Report No. 105. April 17, 1947.

their "natural" functions and thus, in effect, nullify their basic rights to promote collective bargaining.

UNFAIR LABOR PRACTICES FOR EMPLOYERS

The Taft-Hartley Act lists the same unfair labor practices for employers as does the 1935 law, but with two major differences. The first of these is that the prohibition of employers from interfering with employees' right to organize is qualified by the provision that "the expressing of any views, argument or opinion, or the dissemination thereof, whether in written, printed, graphic or visual form, shall not constitute or be evidence of an unfair labor practice. . . ." Although the National Labor Relations Board had not interpreted the Wagner Act to mean that employers were forbidden to express opinions about unions, it had held that statements made under certain circumstances which were part of a pattern of anti-union conduct might constitute interference or refusal to bargain—for example, an employer's statement just prior to a representation election that he might have to close his plant if the union won the election.

The second and more important change in the listing of unfair practices for employers is the outright ban it places on the signing of closed-shop agreements with unions. This, coupled with another provision in the Act which allows state governments to outlaw union-shop agreements, which are otherwise legal under the federal law, has drastically curtailed the unions' efforts to gain what they call "union security." The ban on closed-shop contracts affects only a few unions, namely those in the building and seasonal trades, where workers are employed for short periods of time by numerous employers and where jobs are completed before elections can be held. In such situations the only practical way to maintain union standards on the job is to require all employees to be union members *before* they are hired. However, if the union refuses to accept a person whom the employer wants to hire, both the applicant and the employer may suffer.

THE "RIGHT TO WORK" AND THE UNION SHOP

Under a union-shop contract the employer may hire anyone he wishes but new employees must join the union within thirty days after employment. The union may not expel any employee, and thus force his discharge, except for nonpayment of dues. Moreover, the Taft-Hartley Act provides that the union may not even ask the employer to sign a union-shop contract until after a majority of his employees have voted in favor of such a provision; and the employer is not legally compelled to agree after such an election. The issue, like wages and other terms of the agreement, is a matter of negotiation and bargaining.

Organized labor voices no serious objections to these legal requirements for union-shop contracts, but it vociferously objects to the Taft-Hartley provision allowing state governments to ban *all* union-shop contracts within their borders, regardless of the wishes of the employer and a majority of his employees, and irrespective of whether the industry is engaged in interstate or local commerce. In these respects the Taft-Hartley provision is unique: It allows state laws to supersede federal legislation in the area of interstate commerce, and it negates a basic principle accepted in all phases of American life, both public and private—namely majority rule.

Thus far nineteen states have enacted laws banning union-shop contracts, almost without exception these are states where the rural, nonindustrial counties dominate the state legislatures. Typically these so-called "right-to-work" laws read:

> No person may be denied employment and employers may not be denied the right to employ any person because of that person's membership or nonmembership in any labor organization.

Proponents of these laws hold that it is the duty of government to protect the inalienable right of an individual to work—a right which is considered as fundamental as his right to quit work—and that even though a majority of the employees designate a bargaining agent, they have no moral right, and should have no legal right, to act for the minority who wish to bargain as individuals. They maintain that to force workers to join and pay dues to a union in order to obtain and hold a job is repugnant to every instinct of liberty, and is a form of human bondage because it infringes upon the individual's right to work under whatever conditions he chooses.

Unions contend that this application of the concept of the inalienable right to work is in fact false: that an inalienable right is one which cannot be taken away, and that no proponent of the ban on union-shop contracts goes so far as to say that jobs should always be guaranteed to those who seek work, or that no one should be dismissed from a job he wishes to retain. Above all unions argue that allowing nonmembers to enjoy the wages and other benefits which union members have fought and paid for is comparable to allowing citizens who voted against a tax measure not to pay these taxes even though they benefit from the services defrayed by the tax levy. Unions argue that the legal protection of the individual's right not to belong to a union which a majority of the employees have voted for, is valid and just only if the laws included a proviso that only union members shall be paid union wages and enjoy the other benefits obtained through collective bargaining.

UNFAIR LABOR PRACTICES FOR UNIONS

Six unfair labor practices for labor organizations are listed, in addition to that of attempting to cause an employer to violate the closed-shop ban or to discriminate against nonunion employees. The following practices are now unlawful for a labor organization or its agents:

1. To restrain or coerce employees from their right *not* to join a union.
2. To require an employer to deal through an employer association for purposes of collective bargaining.
3. To refuse to bargain in good faith, which includes the mandate to file a 60-day notice before the termination or proposed modification of an agreement. During this time no strikes are allowed and meetings with employers must be held at reasonable intervals to discuss the issues.
4. To engage in strikes and boycotts in order (a) to force an employer or self-employed person to join a union; (b) to require any employer to cease using, selling, or transporting the products of another producer, or doing business with another person; (c) to require an employer to bargain with a labor organization which has not been certified by the Labor Board; (d) to require any employer to bargain with a union when another union has already been certified; (e) to force any employer to assign work to one particular union or craft rather than another, unless the employer is failing to comply with a Board certification.
5. To require persons working under union-shop contracts to pay initiation fees which the Labor Board considers "excessive or discriminatory."

6. To cause or attempt to cause an employer to pay an employee for services which are not performed or not to be performed—that is for so-called "featherbedding."

Injunctions

The Taft-Hartley Act specifically sets aside portions of the anti-injunction provisions of the 1932 law by permitting the National Labor Relations Board to seek restraining orders from the federal courts in any unfair labor practices as defined in the Act. Furthermore, it makes it mandatory for the Board to seek injunctions in the case of a secondary strike or boycott, of a strike whose purpose is to force an employer to recognize an uncertified union or to recognize a union other than one already certified, and of a strike to force an employer or self-employed person to join a labor or an employer organization.

Although the injunction provisions of the Taft-Hartley Act reverse many features of the 1932 Act, the 1947 law places some regulations upon the courts which did not exist in the 1920's during the heyday of labor injunctions. When the Board petitions for injunctive relief the courts are authorized to grant temporary restraining orders only, and then only after notice to the persons involved and after both parties have had an opportunity to appear by counsel and present their testimony. However, a five-day restraining order may be granted immediately if the petition alleges that substantial and irreparable injury will be unavoidable without injunctive relief.

In one kind of situation—that is, when a union or a union officer is demanding that the employer make payments in violation of Section 302—an employer may go directly to the court. This section prohibits any "shakedown" of employers by union representatives, and disallows checkoff of union dues except upon the individual authorization of employees.

LABOR-MANAGEMENT REPORTING AND DISCLOSURE ACT OF 1959

While the primary purpose of the LMRD Act (Landrum-Griffin Act) is to eliminate dishonest and undemocratic practices within the labor movement, the law also includes amendments to the Taft-

Hartley Act which affect union activities concerned with picketing and with secondary boycotts.

LEGALITY OF PICKETING

Picketing is the presence of one or more persons at the approach to a work place during a labor dispute for the purpose of (1) informing the public and employees that a strike exists or that the employer is on the union "unfair" list, (2) persuading workers to join or continue the strike or boycott, (3) preventing persons from entering or going to work. Secondary picketing refers to the picketing of an employer not directly involved in the labor dispute but connected through ownership or business dealings with the employer with whom the union is in dispute.

The right to picket stems from the constitutional right of free speech and assembly. If it were based on this right alone, all peaceful picketing would be lawful. But the inherent nature of picketing necessarily causes impingements upon the personal and property rights of others, and the courts are frequently called upon to weigh the relative rights of all the parties concerned, including the general public, and to decide whether or not picketing in a given situation should be restricted or prohibited altogether. Decisions of the various courts are not always consistent. It is probably true that in no other area of labor activity is there so much diversity of legal opinion and practice as there is with respect to picketing. Decisions of the Supreme Court shortly before the passage of the Taft-Hartley Act tended to hold that all peaceful picketing was a lawful expression of the right of free speech, and that the merits of the dispute itself had no bearing upon the rights of workers to advertise their grievances through picketing, although the government had the right to protect innocent third parties.

The Taft-Hartley Act mentions picketing in only one instance, namely in specifically allowing employees to refuse to pass through a picket line of employees of another employer who are engaged in a strike which has been authorized by a certified union. However, the 1947 law inferentially circumscribes the right of peaceful picketing through its provisions outlawing secondary boycotts and its proscription of the use of "restraint or coercion" in connection with jurisdictional and rival union disputes, or with strikes to obtain union-shop contracts.

The 1959 law goes further by limiting all picketing for recognition purposes to a period not to exceed thirty days, during which time the National Labor Relations Board must hold an election to determine whether or not a majority of the employees wish the union to represent them. For the first time, the law specifically distinguishes between "informational" picketing directed toward the general public—which is legally permitted—and picketing intended to influence workers, which it restricts. In its limitations on picketing for purposes of recognition (that is, picketing in connection with an organizational drive), the law specifically allows picketing or other publicity conducted for the sole purpose of advising the public (including consumers) that an employer does not employ members of, or have a contract with, a labor organization.

Secondary Boycotts

As under the Taft-Hartley Act, unions are forbidden to engage in, or to induce, coerce or encourage individuals to engage in secondary strikes and boycotts. Referring to what is popularly called "hot cargo," the 1959 law forbids unions to enter into any agreement, expressed or implied, wherein the employer promises not to handle, use, sell or transport products of any other employer, or to cease doing business with any other employer. The law specifically says, however, that these prohibitions do not apply to agreements in the construction industry concerning the subcontracting of work *at the site* of construction, nor to subcontractors working on the goods or premises of a clothing manufacturer. The two exceptions have no effect on the restrictions against the picketing, for example, of a construction project because the general contractor is using nonunion materials, or the picketing of a retail store which sells clothing manufactured in a nonunion plant.

Rights of Members and Union Elections

The major portion of the 1959 labor law deals with the internal government of unions, and with requirements for reporting financial and other data to the Secretary of Labor. The basic purpose of these regulations is to promote democratic and honest administration of labor unions, the assumption being that public disclosure of practices will serve as a self-corrective measure. In addition, Title I, which is called the Bill of Rights of Members of Labor Organizations, lists not only the basic rights which Congress believed should be assured union members but also the right to bring suit against their union officers when there is reasonable cause for believing there has been a violation of trust.

The Act provides that every union member shall have equal rights with other members in the election of officers; freedom to express views, subject to "reasonable" union rules; a voice concerning proposed increases in dues and assessments; protection against being fined or expelled (except for nonpayment of dues) without a "full and fair hearing"; and full knowledge of the contents of any bargaining agreement affecting his status as an employee.

Elections of union officers must be held at least once every five years by national unions, every four years by joint boards, and every three years by local unions. Officers are defined as being all persons who exercise executive functions, including delegates to conventions and board members. Officers of Nationals may be elected either by secret ballot of the members or by delegates at a convention. Local union officers must be elected directly by secret vote of members. No dues money or employer contributions may be spent to promote the candidacy of any person. No Communist or person convicted of certain stated crimes can serve as an officer until five years after termination of such Party membership or of conviction or imprisonment for any specified crime.

REPORTING REQUIREMENTS

Every labor organization must file with the Secretary of Labor a copy of the union's constitution and by-laws, which shall include such information as the qualifications for and restrictions upon membership; the amounts of dues and assessments to be charged; procedures for authorizing the disbursement of funds; for auditing; for the selection of officers and their removal upon breach of trust; for disciplining members; and for authorizing and ratifying terms of collective bargaining agreements.

Annual financial reports must be filed showing the union's assets and liabilities; all receipts of money and their sources; salaries and other payments to each officer and employee of the union who received more than $10,000; all loans made to any officer or member amounting to more than $250; all loans made to any business enterprise, and the purposes thereof.

Trusteeships

National union constitutions usually permit the National to take over a local when there has been a violation of the union's rules, or when the local officers have been dishonest or have otherwise misbehaved. "Taking over" means installing officers selected by the National rather than elected by local members, and control of all the local's finances and activities. The trusteeship status is supposed to be temporary, lasting only until the matters at issue have been corrected. However, there have been instances in which national officers, in order to perpetuate their power, have continued trusteeships over long periods of time.

Under the 1959 labor law the national unions may assume trusteeships for the following reasons only: to correct corruption and financial malpractice, to assure performance of collective bargaining agreements, and to restore democratic procedures. It is unlawful to count the votes of delegates of the trusteed organization in any convention unless the delegates have been chosen by secret ballot of the members, and it is likewise unlawful to transfer the subordinate union's funds—except for the normal per capita taxes—to the parent organization. A report of all trusteeships, with the reasons for the takeover, must be made to the Secretary of Labor every six months.

Employer Reports

In 1936 the federal government passed a law, strengthened by an amendment in 1938, which makes it a felony for any person "to transport or cause to be transported in interstate or foreign commerce any person who is employed or is to be employed for the purpose of obstructing or interfering by force or threats with (1) peaceful picketing by employees or (2) the exercise by employees of any of the rights of self-organization and collective bargaining." These laws were supposed to eliminate the use of spies and strikebreakers and other overt acts of employers to obstruct unionization of their employees.

During the Senate committee hearings which led to the passage of the 1959 Reporting and Disclosure Act it was revealed that despite the earlier laws, some employers were bribing union agents in order to escape from hiring union members, paying off union agents to get more favorable contract terms, and hiring outside agents to break up the incipient unionization of their employees. Instead of employing spies through detective agencies, as was done during the 1920's, employers now hired suave persons who called themselves "industrial relations consultants."

The 1959 law makes illegal, and requires employers to report annually to the Secretary of Labor, any payments to their own employees, to union officials, and to labor relations consultants for the purpose of persuading and interfering with employees in the exercise of their bargaining and representation rights, and payments made to obtain information on employee or union activities in connection with labor disputes.

FEDERAL *VS.* STATE JURISDICTION

Even though the federal government has assumed jurisdiction over many phases of employer-labor relations, much remains in the hands of the state and local governments, and there is wide divergence among the latter as to the manner in which they exercise their authority in labor matters. Not only do the state laws vary, but on any single day numerous different opinions may be handed down by the various lower courts with respect to similar situations and points at law. Although ultimate decisions rest with the U.S. Supreme Court, relatively few cases are ever processed through the judicial hierarchy, with the result that in a large number of employer-labor disputes, state laws and lower court decisions are binding.

The constitutional basis for federal intervention in labor matters lies in the actual or potential effects which employer-labor disputes have upon interstate commerce. All federal labor laws incorporate such introductory phrases as "affecting the free flow of commerce" or "in industries engaged in interstate commerce and the production of goods for interstate commerce." The Supreme Court has interpreted interstate commerce to include manufacturing plants, any part of whose products are procured from or sold in other states; retail establishments which sell across state lines; mining, and public utilities which supply any service to interstate industries. Even with this broad interpretation, millions of workers are employed in strictly local enterprises and remain outside the jurisdiction of federal labor laws.

State governments rest their claim for jurisdiction over labor activities, especially their outward manifestations, upon the police powers of the state, as well as upon their constitutional right to enact legislation on any subject not expressly denied them by the federal government. The Supreme Court has upheld the states' power to regulate workers' activities which directly affect the public safety and the use of public thoroughfares, as in picketing and other labor demonstrations. But the Supreme Court has also held that any state order which deprives a union or employees of rights specifically guaranteed by federal law will be set aside.

Present federal laws incorporate divergent principles with respect to the extension *versus* the limitations of federal jurisdiction. Both the Taft-Hartley and the Reporting and Disclosure Acts discourage the National Conciliation Service and the National Labor Relations Board from intervening in disputes having a minor effect upon interstate commerce. On the other hand, states are specifically granted the power to outlaw union-shop contracts, even in plants engaged in interstate commerce.

PART FOUR

UNIONS AND EMPLOYERS

8

COLLECTIVE BARGAINING

The primary purpose of labor unions is to negotiate with employers for the purpose of establishing the terms and conditions under which their members shall be employed. The employer-union agreement represents the consummation of these negotiations. A bilaterally signed agreement indicates that civil rights have been introduced into industry and that the personal, one-sided rule of managers has been replaced by rules and terms in whose making all concerned have had a voice.

A mutual agreement entered into by an employer and a union, like other contracts, is an expression of the various rights, duties, and privileges of those covered by the agreement. On the employee side, the contracting party is the union which a majority of the employees have chosen to represent them. While no law requires employers and employees to agree on any particular terms, once they have reached an understanding the union may require the employer to incorporate the terms in a written agreement. The National Labor-Management Relations Act makes it an unfair labor practice for either the union or the employer to refuse to bargain collectively, once the employees' representative agency has been certified, and defines bargaining to mean "the mutual obligation

. . . to meet at reasonable times and confer in good faith with respect to wages, hours, and other terms and conditions of employment, or the negotiation of an agreement, or any question arising thereunder, and the execution of a written contract incorporating any agreement reached if requested by either party. . . ." Such agreements are enforceable in the courts like any other contracts.

The manner in which agreements are negotiated, the variety of subjects covered, and their substantive contents vary greatly between industries and within any industry, for the process and results of collective bargaining are necessarily influenced by many factors—general economic conditions, as well as the situation of a particular employer, his attitude toward the union and collective bargaining, the strength of the union and the ability of its negotiators, and the desires and determination of its members.

Regardless of their specific terms, all employer-union agreements include two fundamental features, namely, the substantive provisions covering work conditions and the status of the union, and the rules of procedure for settling questions or disputes over the interpretation and application of the terms of the agreement. The latter are of major importance because no formalized body of regulations can cover the minutiae of day-to-day work conditions or forestall varying interpretations when applied to specific situations. Furthermore, business is a dynamic process; hence contingencies arise which could not be foreseen at the time the agreement was signed.

THE BARGAINING UNIT

The unit of bargaining has a direct influence on the degree of standardization of wages and working conditions within an industry or area. Whether collective bargaining takes place between individual employers and local unions, or through associations of employers to cover large segments or an entire industry, very largely determines whether the terms of employment are uniform or dissimilar. Standardized wage rates (or other matters involving costs) tend to be what the marginal employer in the industry can afford, and there are advantages and disadvantages to everyone concerned in having a uniform level throughout the industry, or variations based on individual employers' ability to pay.

ATTITUDES ON BARGAINING UNIT

During the early stages of discussion on what became the Taft-Hartley Act, many Congressmen voiced approval of an outright ban on industry-wide bargaining. Later, when these Congressmen discovered that many employers favored bargaining on an industry-wide, or at least a regional basis, the question of prohibition of industry-wide bargaining was dropped. As finally passed, the Taft-Hartley Act makes it an unfair labor practice for a union "to restrain or coerce . . . an employer in the selection of his representatives for the purposes of collective bargaining or the adjustment of grievances." This restriction, in effect, prohibits a union from forcing an employer to bargain through an employers' association if he chooses to bargain separately, but it does not prevent multiple-employer bargaining if the employers so desire.[1]

The policy of a union and of the employers in any industry with respect to the bargaining unit may vary from time to time. Among the factors which affect the union's policy regarding bargaining with an individual employer or on a wider basis are the strength of the union, the number of employers and the degree of centralized control in the industry, the size of the establishments and their proximity to each other, and their relative prosperity. If a few employers are especially prosperous, the union may wish to bargain with them separately and use these agreements as a vanguard for negotiating agreements elsewhere in the industry as conditions warrant.

[1] Congressional desire for legal restrictions against industry-wide bargaining was largely a reaction against the general coal strikes which were taking place at that time; Congress felt that if agreements had to be negotiated separately it would obviate general shutdowns in the industry. Paradoxically, when the first coal agreement after the passage of the Act was being negotiated in 1948, President Lewis of the United Mine Workers refused to allow the Southern Coal Producers Association to participate in the joint conferences with the rest of the industry. Invoking the above cited clause in the Taft-Hartley Act disallowing union coercion of employers in their choice of bargaining agent, the National Labor Relations Board obtained a court injunction compelling the United Mine Workers to bargain with the Southern Producers in order that the industry-wide negotiations could proceed.

The willingness or reluctance of employers to bargain collectively on a wide basis depends largely upon their competitive situation. If labor costs are an important factor in selling costs, the employers who are paying relatively high wages may wish to have the entire competitive market under the same or similar agreements. On the other hand, some employers consider it advantageous to pay better than prevailing rates in order to be able to attract the best workers, and therefore do not welcome standardized wages even though they would entail no advance in their own rates.

In general, unions are more favorable to bargaining on an industry-wide basis than are employers, and the tendency in recent years is in that direction. Unions feel that united action throughout an industry will result in generally higher standards than could be obtained through piecemeal bargaining with individual employers. Some employers, on the other hand, are opposed to industry-wide bargaining in principle and in practice. To them it appears to be one more step away from individual plant control and the intercompany distinctions which promote competition. Many of these same employers, however, have also expressed opposition to a firm's paying higher than the prevailing rates "just because it is more prosperous than its competitors and can afford to do so."

Bargaining with Individual Employers

In spite of the current trends toward wider bargaining units, most of the agreements now in effect are made in the name of a single company and the local union or unions to which its employees belong. If all the employees in a plant belong to a single local union, one agreements results. If, however, the employees are organized into separate unions according to craft or occupation, each union may either sign a separate agreement with the employer or jointly negotiate and sign a single agreement. Joint bargaining on the part of craft unions may strengthen the bargaining power of the individual crafts and from the employer's point of view eliminates the necessity for extended negotiations with several unions, each of which represents only a portion of his employees.

In the case of large corporations with a number of plants, the various local unions may sign jointly with the central office of the corporation. In this way, a single agreement may cover plants in widely separated geographical areas. Even when each local union negotiates separately with each plant management, the substance of the various agreements for all the corporation's plants may be similar. In the case of multiplant corporation agreements, the national office of the union may take a prominent part in the negotiations. Generally the corporation-wide agreement establishes the relationships of the parties, the general wage levels, and the machinery and procedure for further negotiations. Many subjects, including occupational wage rates, are then negotiated locally between the various plant managements and the local unions.

INDUSTRY-WIDE BARGAINING

There are only a few instances of formal industry-wide bargaining in this country, although what approximates it obtains in a number of industries. The most notable is in steel manufacturing, and is an outgrowth of conditions which developed during World War II. Disputes presented to the National War Labor Board were usually settled on an outright industry-wide bases, or for important segments of the industry with the understanding that the remaining companies would also accept the awards. After the end of the Wage Stabilization Program individual dealings with employers were resumed, but it was always understood that terms obtained from the first company would have to be met by all the rest. In 1959 the major unionized companies, having decided it was better for all of them to participate in the initial proceedings, established an industry-wide committee to negotiate contracts with the steelworkers' union.

In anthracite mining a single agreement is signed to cover all mines, and in recent years the equivalent of industry-wide bargaining has existed in bituminous coal mining, where the separate agreements expire on the same date. Once the terms for the most important producing areas have been agreed upon, the other districts proceed to sign agreements with virtually identical general terms but with specific wage rates that are adapted to local conditions.

The traditional bargaining unit in railroad transportation is the individual railroad company or system, with each of the operating crafts (trainmen, engineers, etc.) negotiating separate agreements with the various systems, and the maintenance employees (shop crafts) negotiating joint agreements with each system. Although the agreements continue to be signed by each railroad system, during recent years it has become the practice to negotiate major questions of wages, vacation allowances and general working rules on a national scale.

Bargaining in the airline industry is also on a single-carrier basis, although in 1958 the airline companies entered into a mutual aid pact whereby they agree to compensate a struck company the amount of their net income resulting from strike-diverted traffic. The effect of this "strike insurance" plan is to minimize the unions' ability to pit one employer against another until their terms have been gained throughout the industry.

At one time both the hosiery and the woolen and worsted industries practiced industry-wide bargaining, but in 1954 the hosiery workers' union was forced to give up its long-standing arrangement of a single agreement for all unionized plants because of the competition of Southern, nonunion mills. Likewise, industry-wide bargaining was abandoned in the woolen and worsted industry in 1957 owing to the "contraction in business and product diversification which caused disparate competitive positions among the companies remaining open."

Bargaining for Geographical Areas

When a number of companies in an area who are engaged in the same industry have signed agreements, a frequent development is the formation of an employers' association to represent the unionized firms in that area and industry. This has been the development of collective bargaining relations in the various branches of the clothing industry in the major centers. In this industry, when an agreement is entered into by an association of employers on behalf of its members, the agreement generally specifies that the terms are applicable to all the association's members. Resignation, suspension or expulsion from the association usually does not relieve an employer from his obligation to abide by the agreement.

In the men's and women's clothing, men's hats and millinery, and fur industries, there is highly developed industrial relations machinery in each of the metropolitan areas which are important as producing centers. These unions and employers' associations customarily make use of permanent impartial chairmen to administer the agreement. In addition, joint trade boards, stabilization commissions, and other similar union-management bodies are frequently established to deal with particular problems that arise from time to time. The employers in a given city are usually organized into more than one association within each of the garment industries. The basis of distinction is both the price line of the product and the classification of employers—that is, jobbers, contractors, inside manufacturers.

In longshoring, contracts are usually negotiated on a coast-wide basis. Numerous efforts have been made by the various maritime unions to combine for purposes of bargaining, but union rivalry has prevented any enduring cooperative measures. Allied Printing Trades Councils have been formed in many cities for the purpose of promoting uniform collective bargaining policy among the various printing unions, and to issue joint union labels to employers dealing with member unions.

The pulp and paper industry, though dealing elsewhere on the basis of individual companies, in the Pacific Northwest is combined into the Pacific Coast Association of Pulp and Paper Manufacturers, which deals with the two paper unions jointly. The dominant method of bargaining in the organized section of the lumber industry is through employers' associations in a producing area. For intercity trucking, the Teamsters Union usually negotiates with employers' associations whose operations cover several states; one of the largest is the Midwest Agreement, which covers over-the-road hauling in twelve North Central States.

In many other industries and trades characterized by numerous small establishments within a city, collective bargaining has been conducted with associations of employers in that city. In many cases the associations are formal organizations whose officers have power to bind all the members to the agreed terms of employment. In other cases the employers may unite informally and perhaps only for the duration of the bargaining conferences. In some instances the lack of a continuing employers' association makes no difference in the actual negotiation of the agreement, but considerably complicates its enforcement. Several industries in which the predominant method of dealing is with city-wide associations are brewing, retail trade, baking, printing and publishing, restaurants, local trucking, and barber shops.

The Building Trades

More city-wide association bargaining is found in building construction than in any other single industry. Almost half the building-trades agreements are negotiated by permanent associations of contractors and individual unions. Usually, after the agreement between the union and the association has been consummated, nonassociation contractors are offered agreements containing identical terms, with the exception that some of the joint machinery for settling disputes between the union and association members is of necessity modified. In a few instances, advantages are given to association members, such as a provision that they shall have preference in obtaining union workmen.

A number of building-trades agreements are negotiated by the individual unions with temporary associations of contractors through joint committees appointed for that purpose. Under such circumstances the accepted terms are incorporated either in a single agreement which each employer signs, or in separate identical agreements signed with each employer. Where there is neither a permanent nor a temporary association of employers, the individual building-trades local, often after obtaining tacit acceptance from some of the leading contractors, prepares a contract that is automatically accepted by each unionized firm in the locality. Frequently there is no regular agreement that includes all the usual provisions. Instead, the employers either sign a memorandum or orally give affirmation to pay a specified wage and abide by the working rules of the union.

"Standard" Agreements and Union Labels

In the absence of association bargaining, unions often achieve standardization of wages and working conditions on an industry-wide or market-wide basis by negotiating nearly identical agreements with individual employers. Ordinarily, the individual employers with whom such agreements are negotiated are confined to an industry or trade in a metropolitan area. This is true not only of the retail and service industries but, in some centers, of manufacturers whose products flow into interstate markets.

A degree of uniformity is sometimes effected by having the national union office exercise control over local agreements, such as requiring its approval of them or issuing standard agreements or union-label and "shop-card" agreements. Generally, provisions dealing with apprentices, arbitration, and membership status are standardized and enforced on an industry- or trade-wide scale more often than are provisions regarding wage rates, hours, and working conditions.

The common practice in regard to the approval of local agreements is to have the union constitution require that agreements shall not be considered finally ratified until approved by the national union office. As an incentive toward standardization, some unions make available to their locals printed forms of agreements to be negotiated with local employers. These forms, or "standard" agreements, contain the minimum requirements that have been adopted through convention action (usually appearing in the constitution and by-laws) and have blank spaces in which locally negotiated wage rates, hours, and working conditions may be inserted.

Similarly, the national unions often issue standard union-label agreements that set forth the minimum terms under which employers may use the label. Supplemental agreements establishing local wage rates and working conditions are negotiated. Since the use of the union label is strictly under the control of the national union, a measure of uniformity may be achieved among employers who sign the label agreement.

Local unions in some retail and service trades often secure standardization throughout the city by the use of the union-shop card. To secure a shop card the employer agrees to observe the minimum standards of the national union and, in addition, the local's wage rates, hours, and working rules. Changes in local working conditions are negotiated in joint conferences between the locals and the employers. In the absence of an employers' association, a local may adopt a change by a vote of the membership and merely advise the employers regarding it. The shop-card and union employees may then be withdrawn from employers who do not conform to the new rules.

THE BARGAINING PROCESS

Annual negotiations between employers and unions are most frequent, even though the agreements do not always specify that they are to be in effect for only one year. Many agreements are of indefinite duration but are subject to renegotiation upon notice by either party. Some agreements, including many in the mass-production industries, are negotiated for periods of two or more years without privilege of alteration. Although the longer period may seem to insure greater stability in the employment relationship, if drastic economic changes occur in the meantime, either the employer or the workers may find it difficult to abide by the contract. Numbers of strikes and lockouts have taken place as a result of "frozen" wage rates which were agreed upon some time before a rise or fall in prices and the cost of living occurred.

Regardless of the period the agreement is to remain in effect, most contracts have always required the party which wishes it changed or terminated to notify the other party thirty or sixty days in advance of the expiration date so that new terms can be negotiated without interruption of the contractual relation. The 1947 Labor-Management Relations Act requires the filing of sixty days' notice by either party wishing to terminate or modify an existing agreement, during which time the parties must meet and confer for the purpose of negotiating a new contract. As discussed later, the law also has provisions concerning the settlement of any issues which are not resolved through these conferences of employer and union representatives.

Union Procedure

The effectiveness of a union in negotiating agreements depends considerably on the composition and experience of its bargaining committees. Union negotiations usually are conducted by officers of a local union or of a joint board or district council, although the national representatives may be consulted for advice prior to or during the negotiations, or they may participate directly in the bargaining, especially with the larger employers. These national representatives generally have major responsibility in regional or industry-wide negotiations and in bargaining with a large corporation for an agreement covering many plants.

A union chooses its strongest leaders for the task of negotiating either a new agreement or a renewal. Ordinarily, these leaders are the President and other elected officers, although other union representatives may be put on the negotiating committee, or a special committee may be selected. If the union employs a business agent, he is usually a member of the committee and may play a primary role in negotiations.

When the bargaining involves an employers' association or a multiplant corporation, it is common for each local to recommend the terms it desires to be included in the agreement to a joint conference of representatives from all the locals. These representatives, in consultation with the national union officers, decide the exact nature of the demands to be made, and may elect a negotiating committee. Any agreement reached with the employer is then submitted to the local unions for ratification.

There are several ways in which the members of a union may exercise control over negotiations. First, the members of the negotiating committee are elected or appointed by officers who are themselves elected by the members; second, the demands to be made upon the employer are usually submitted for approval to the members prior to the negotiations; third, the tentative agreement reached with the employer is submitted to the members for ratification at which time the members of the negotiating committee are required to defend the results of their bargaining and explain why any compromises were made. The 1959 Reporting and Disclosure Act requires all unions, local and national, to make copies of bargaining contracts available to all members who request them.

EMPLOYER PROCEDURE

The negotiating machinery on the employer's side depends largely on the size of the company and whether or not the employer is a member of an employer's association. A small owner-employer who is not a member of an association usually bargains directly with union representatives, although he may enlist the aid or advice of his lawyer. Where there are many small employers within a producing area, an employers' association, as already indicated, may function as the bargaining agent for the member employers. Negotiations may be conducted by the secretary and the executive officer of the association, or a special committee of member employers may be appointed. After the agreement has been drafted it may be signed by the executive officer or negotiating committee for the association, or each employer member may affix his signature.

In large companies the negotiating process depends upon the corporate structure. In some instances the plant manager may negotiate final terms, frequently with the aid of the industrial relations director. In other cases, when the agreement is negotiated by the branch manager, it does not become final until it is approved by the corporation's central office. Elsewhere, the central office negotiates directly with the union either one agreement to apply uniformly over all its plants or different agreements for its various plants. Since many companies are highly diversified in the goods they produce, and since many employees are organized on a craft basis, it is not unusual for a single corporation to negotiate annually or biennially with a dozen or more different unions.

OUTSIDE AID

If a controversy arises over the specific terms to be incorporated in the agreement, either party may ask help from the federal or state conciliation service. Since the conciliator has no legal powers of compulsion, his effectiveness is dependent entirely upon the prestige of his office, the assistance he can render by reason of his knowledge of the facts involved, his skill as a negotiator, and the willingness of the parties to compromise or come to terms.

If the conciliator's recommendations are not acceptable to one or both parties, they may decide to submit the issue to an arbitrator for final decision. On the other hand, either party may decide to use its economic strength to obtain its terms, and a strike or lockout may be called. Under such circumstances, the final terms of settlement are dependent largely upon which side is able to hold out longer, although an important factor is the pressure of public opinion, especially in work stoppages which result in inconvenience to the public. For every agreement that has been negotiated after a strike or lockout, thousands have been negotiated peaceably with no stoppage of work.

FACTUAL AIDS TO BARGAINING

The need and use of factual data in determining the terms and conditions of employment are increasing in importance as economic relationship grow more complex and collective bargaining processes become more extensive. Knowledge and mutual acceptance of specific facts remove many areas of conflict between employers and employees and minimize many others. The maximum use of all available data and the diligent search for additional facts indicate mature and rational bargaining.

Knowledge of given facts, however, never automatically resolves all employer-worker differences. Beyond the point where all the parties connected with an enterprise are interested in its maximum prosperity, there remains the basic question of how the gross income of the enterprise shall be distributed. Similarly, although management and workers may agree in principle that standards of efficiency must be maintained, there still exist differences as to the value of specific efficiency methods.

The parties negotiating an agreement must necessarily rely upon various kinds of data. Financial records of the company, economic data on the industry, wages and working conditions prevailing elsewhere, prices and cost of living, and other related matters are taken into consideration to a greater or lesser extent whenever a new agreement is negotiated. The employer in some respects is in an advantageous position with regard to factual data to support his claims. It is difficult if not impossible for the union to know the exact condition of the company's finances. On the other hand, a union that is national in scope can collect data from all its locals and thus be informed about the wages and working conditions throughout the unionized section of the industry. Not all the unions maintain research facilities, but the number who do is increasing and at present research to facilitate collective bargaining is fairly common on the side of both the union and the employer.

9

EMPLOYER-UNION CONTRACTS

An employer-union agreement may be anything from half a dozen typewritten pages to a fifty-page printed booklet, although the length of such agreements is most often between fifteen and twenty pages. The longer contracts include occupational wage listings and detailed work rules, whereas the shorter ones are confined to statements of policy and general provisions, with the specification that other documents such as the company's book of rules and the union's constitution and by-laws are to be observed.

PROVISIONS IN UNION CONTRACTS

Regardless of their length, almost all agreements cover six general areas: (1) the type of union recognition afforded, including check-off or other arrangements for the payment of union dues, and the union activities allowed on company time and premises; (2) basic wages and hours, including overtime rates, job standards and other items affecting earnings; (3) seniority rules applying to layoffs, re-employment, promotions and transfer; (4) work rules, including rest periods, health and safety measures, rules of discipline and procedures for discharge; (5) so-called "fringe benefits" such as paid vacations and holidays, pension and health insurance, and layoff or dismissal pay;[1] and (6) procedures for settling disputes arising during the life of the contract, as well as the date and the procedures to be followed in opening negotiations for a new contract.

[1] Fringe benefits are discussed in Chapter 13.

Depending upon the nature of the business and the strength as well as the desires of the union, contracts may also cover such matters as subcontracting, plant removal, apprentice programs, union participation in decisions concerning technological changes and efficiency programs, profit-sharing and stock options, and provisions concerning special groups such as the physically handicapped, veterans and older workers.

UNION STATUS

One of the first and most important provisions of any agreement is that which outlines the basic relations between the employer and the union, namely, the degree of recognition extended, the membership status of present and newly hired employees, dues collection, the union's use of bulletin boards, and related matters.

Under a closed-shop provision all employees covered by the agreement must be members of the union, and in addition all new employees must be hired through the union or be members of it at the time of employment. In other words, the employer is limited in his new hirings to persons already members of the union. The preferential hiring clause is a modified closed-shop arrangement whereby the employer is committed to show preference to union members in his new hirings; he may hire "from the open market" if there are no union members available, but all new employees must join the union after employment. Closed-shop contracts are now illegal under the Taft-Hartley Act.

A union-shop agreement also requires all permanent employees to be union members, but the employer has complete control over the hiring of new workers; if they do not already belong to the union a probationary period is usually allowed before they are required to join. Under a maintenance-of-membership provision, joining the union is optional, but once an employee joins he must retain his membership for the duration of the agreement. The purpose of this arrangement is to keep employees from dropping their membership as soon as they have gained the improvements included in a new contract. Union-shop agreements are legal under the Taft-Hartley Act in plants where the union has been certified by the National Labor Relations Board, and where the employer is willing to sign such a contract. However, as has already been noted, some states have banned both closed- and union-shop contracts under the permissive clause in the Taft-Hartley Act.

The minimum status afforted by employer-union contracts is that of recognition only, and this is legally required whenever a majority of the employees have shown evidence that they wish the union to represent them. Under this arrangement union membership is optional, although all employees in the bargaining unit are covered by the terms of the agreement. Nonmembers under these circumstances are dubbed "free riders" by union members, since they do not contribute to the financial support of the organization which presumably has improved their wages and working conditions. To circumvent such occurrences, some unions have negotiated so-called "agency shop" contracts whereby nonmember employees must pay a stipulated regular fee for "services performed by the union as the collective bargaining agent." Under such contracts, the union must be willing to accept nonmember employees into full membership whenever they request. Agency shop contracts have received varying treatment by the courts when the question of their legality has been raised.

Closely allied to the matter of union status or degree of recognition is the question of how membership dues shall be collected.[2] The Taft-Hartley Act makes illegal any contract provisions which permit employers automatically to deduct dues from the pay of union members (the so-called "automatic checkoff") but specifies that dues may be deducted upon written authorization by individual employees. Such checkoff authorizations, the law states, "shall not be irrevocable for a period of more than one year or beyond the termination date of the applicable collective agreement, whichever occurs sooner." Since the law went into effect, individual authorization arrangements have become fairly common, having supplanted the former automatic arrangements. If the checkoff is not provided, the agreement may allow union officials access to the plant for the

2 Permission to collect union dues, distribute union literature, and carry on other union activities on company property but outside of work hours—for example, during lunchtime—has been ordered by the National Labor Relations Board under certain circumstances, viz., where plants are located at a distance from cities or where the employees' homes are scattered over wide areas, thus making it difficult for the union to get in contact with its members or prospective members except at their work places.

purpose of collecting dues, or grant the union the right to set up a booth on company premises to collect dues on payday.

WAGE PROVISIONS

The major purpose of labor unions is constantly and persistently to improve the wages of their members. In their pursuit of this never-finished task they follow no inflexible or standardized procedure. Like employers, union leaders are pragmatists and will use any arguments or means which seem appropriate at the time of a given wage negotiation—and each may adopt the arguments of the other at the wage negotiations a year later. During a time of rising prices unions will base their claims for higher wages on increased costs of living and the ability of the employer to pay, while employers will argue that existing labor output does not warrant wage increases and that the suggested increases will advance prices still further. During deflation employers will use the decline in living costs and profits as arguments for decreasing wages, while unions will argue for the necessity of increasing purchasing power and keeping wages in line with advancing technology and productivity.

To obtain a rise in wages on unskilled jobs, union leaders will assert that the existing spread between unskilled and skilled jobs is not justified. Once minimum levels have been raised they may argue that wages on skilled jobs should be increased in order to restore previous differentials. Employers' attitudes toward unskilled and skilled wage differentials are primarily influenced by labor-market conditions and the scarcity of either unskilled or skilled workers. Union wage strategy is complicated by the fact that in a given case the issue may not be entirely a matter of opposition between an employer and *all* of his employees; there may be differences between various membership groups or crafts. Although such differences usually are settled amicably within the union (or among the various unions where the craft organizations exist) before the bargaining with the employer gets under way, some intra-union conflicts over wage policies have resulted in permanent schisms, which have had significant effects upon the wage structure within an industry or plant.

As unionization becomes more extensive throughout an industry, the wage structure tends to follow a more uniform pattern because unions realize that wide differences in rates for comparable work are a constant threat to the maintenance of the higher rates. Collective bargaining, in other words, tends to remove purely fortuitous factors as well as the divergencies caused by the competitive pressures of numerous employers. In seeking uniformity, it is not the purpose or desire of the unions to eliminate competition between employers, but to have competition take place within the realm of efficient management, sales policies and the use of technological improvements, rather than in the wage rates of employees.

Practice varies widely as to the amount of detail concerning wages incorporated in the contracts. For small shops the agreements may include itemized wage lists for each occupation; agreements for larger plants may specify minimum and maximum rates for the major job categories, or merely give a minimum common labor rate with specifications for the determination of all other rates. Where wage-incentive plans exist, the agreements may specify the base or guaranteed rates and outline the conditions under which new production standards and piece rates are to be established.

Other wage provisions concern differential rates for night or hazardous work, call-back pay, guaranteed pay for employees who report at the regular time and find no work to do, pay when transferred to a different job, deductions for damaged work or for equipment used, etc. A number of employer-union contracts, especially in the mass-production industries, provide for automatic increases in the basic wage structure whenever the cost of living rises above a specified percentage. These same agreements, as well as others, may include what is called an "annual improvement factor"—that is, a periodic wage increase based on the estimated percentage rise in productivity in the plant or the industry. These latter provisions are usually limited to agreements which are to be in effect for two or more years, and are a substitute for annual negotiations during which the situation of the moment can be taken into consideration.

Hours Provisions

The level of wages and the length of working hours prevailing in any country are a measure of its workers' standard of living and an indicator of its industrial and political development. In the absence of power machinery and advanced technology the great mass of people not only must subsist on the bare essentials, but must spend most of their waking hours eking out their meager subsistence. In a competitive, capitalistic economy workers are able to obtain their share of the comforts and leisure resulting from improved technology only if they have the political freedom necessary to influence legislation, and the freedom of self-association necessary to bargain effectively with their employers.

Reduction in the daily and weekly hours of work has been a major campaign of labor organizations throughout their history, in this country and elsewhere. In the early nineteenth century the campaign was for a reduction from the 12- and 14-hour day to one of 9 or 10 hours.[3] After the 54-hour week was won there was a half century's struggle to obtain the 48-hour week. Not until the passage of the Fair Labor Standards Act in 1938 did the 40-hour week become prevalent, although many unions had obtained the 8-hour day much earlier.

Using the federal standard as a benchmark, unions have persistently sought further improvements. Almost universally they have obtained overtime rates for hours in excess of eight per day,[4] as well as premium rates for Saturday and Sunday work even though such work does not represent overtime. Most union contracts also provide for special rates for second- and third-shift work, although these rates are usually only 10 or 15 per cent higher than the regular day

[3] In 1840 the normal work week in Massachusetts textile mills was 84 hours; two years later this was reduced to 78 hours for women and to 60 hours for children under 12 years of age. Men continued on the 84-hour schedule until 1850, when their time was also shortened to 72 hours. The 72-hour week prevailed in New York mills until 1867 and in Carolina mills as late as the 1880's. In other occupations, even among the skilled trades, the hours were equally long. Many printers and machinists worked 14 hours a day, 84 hours a week, until almost the middle of the nineteenth century.

[4] The Fair Labor Standards Act provides for the payment of time-and-a-half rates for all hours worked in excess of 40 per week. It says nothing about daily hours. The Walsh-Healey Public Contracts Act provides for a basic 8-hour day and 40-hour week on all contracts entered into by the U.S. government in excess of $2,000. The Adamson Act of 1916 provides a basic 8-hour day in the railroad industry. The hours of employees "whose activities affect the safety of the operation of motor vehicles" engaged in interstate transportation are controlled by the Interstate Commerce Commission.

rates, in contrast to the time-and-a-half or double time paid for overtime and weekend work.

Since the end of World War II organized labor has sought, and in some cases obtained, normal work schedules with less than the federal 40-hour requirement. Many individual unions have passed resolutions favoring the 30-hour week, and the AFL-CIO is officially committed to the 35-hour week with no decrease in wages and with double overtime pay. Organized labor's argument for reductions in normal work schedules is now based, as it was in the past, on the belief that reduced hours are necessary to reduce unemployment—that it is a way to provide jobs for those deprived of employment because of automation and other technological improvements in manufacturing, marketing and transportation. Furthermore, unions contend that there should be no reduction in wages with the shortened hours because maintenance of a high level of purchasing power is necessary for a high level of employment, and any decline in wages would defeat the purpose of reduced hours. Likewise the double overtime penalty, even more than the time-and-a-half rate, will encourage employers to take on new workers during upswings in business rather than have their present employees work longer hours.

Seniority Rules

Since seniority is a measure of a claim to a job, the clauses dealing with seniority are of major importance to both the employer and the employees. Rules governing seniority are a source of contention not only between the employer and the union but among union members themselves, since the rules adopted will determine *which* members are to be laid off when work is slack and whether employee *A* or employee *B* is to be promoted to the better job. Moreover, the "bumping" process required by seniority rules for layoffs frequently involves shifting and demoting many more persons than the number who are actually laid off.

Except for contracts covering workers engaged by any one employer for short periods of time, for example in building construction, practically all contracts at the present time contain detailed rules specifying how seniority is acquired—on a plant-wide, departmental, or occupational basis, or a combination of any of these—as well as how such rights are applied and lost.

Most union agreements provide that layoffs are to be made on the basis of strict seniority, employees with the shortest service record being laid off first, although some specify that the employer may retain a given nucleus of "indispensable" employees regardless of seniority. In order to preserve continuity in the grievance adjustment personnel, many agreements specify that union stewards shall be placed at the top of their respective seniority lists and thus be the last to be laid off.

Re-employment is of course in reverse order to layoff, those with the greatest seniority being the first to be reinstated when work picks up. Some agreements establish a maximum period of layoff—for example, one year—during which seniority rights are retained, although many agreements explicitly or implicitly allow the retention of seniority rights for an indefinite period until such time as the employer is able to offer a suitable job or the employee obtains work elsewhere.

Many agreements which apply straight seniority to reductions in force and re-employment do not recognize an employee's length of service as the sole or primary consideration when promotions are made; in other words, seniority may govern only in the case of employees whose skill and ability are relatively equal. Some agreements, however, go further by providing that the oldest employee in point of service shall be given an opportunity to qualify for a promotional vacancy and that if, after a fair trial, he cannot qualify, the next in line shall be eligible, and so on.

WORK RULES

Work rules necessarily differ for different industries and plants, and there is wide variation in practice as to the amount of detailed instructions included in agreements. A complete outline of the plant's working rules rarely appears, although existing company and union rules may be incorporated by reference to other documents. Agreements may include rules concerning the amount of time allowed for rest periods, the size of work crews and work loads, the distribution of work among employees, and the procedures to be used in time and motion studies. Although some agreements include explicit statements pertaining to the prerogatives of management, in most contracts such matters are implied rather than specifically stated.

Most agreements contain only general provisions concerning safety and sanitation, although a few of them go into much detail, especially in the case of hazardous occupations or where the public safety is at stake. Since state workmen's compensation laws require the reporting of accidents by the employer, agreements do not mention this, although conformity to the law is commonly specified. Some agreements provide for a special safety committee, which may be a joint management-union committee or one composed solely of union members. An increasing number of agreements, particularly those covering "dirty occupations" in which the workers must change from their street clothes, require the furnishing of shower baths, lockers, and dressing rooms. For fear of depriving persons of needed employment, some contracts prohibit physical examinations as a condition of employment, while others provide for appeal to the family doctor in the event of an adverse report from the company physician.

As a safeguard against arbitrary discharge, unions usually insist that the possible causes for discharge be clearly defined in the contract, and that an employee's supervisor must not have the final decision; in other words, an accused employee must be given the opportunity to obtain the intervention of his union and have his case appealed to the highest management authority and perhaps to outside arbitration.

Grievance Adjustment

Important sections in all agreements signed by employers and unions are those which outline the procedural arrangements for the appeal and final adjustment of employee grievances, as well as charges by the union or the employer that the agreement is being violated. Experience with collective bargaining has led to a general acceptance of three essentials for the adjustment of disputes which arise under an employer-union agreement: (1) union-management negotiations, beginning with the foreman in charge of the shop or department where the dispute originates and proceeding up to the highest officials of the company; (2) if such negotiations fail to secure an adjustment, appeal to an impartial outside agency or individual; and (3) restriction on strikes and lockouts until these other means of settling the dispute have been exhausted.

The particular arrangements existing in any plant are influenced by the confidence which the union and the management have in each other and by the personalities involved, as well as the nature and size of the enterprise. Among the items mentioned are the kinds of issues which are subject to grievance procedures, the various procedural steps and the time limits for each, the number of union representatives and their method of selection and how they are to be paid for time spent in handling grievances. Practically all contracts include the provision that there shall be no work stoppage while the grievance is being processed.

EXTENT OF COLLECTIVE BARGAINING

The expansion of collective bargaining roughly parallels the growth of union membership, although the actual number of employees covered by collective agreements is not identical with union membership in three major respects: (1) There are scattered union members working for employers with whom agreements have not yet been negotiated although presumably they will be negotiated whenever a majority of the employees join the union. (2) As indicated above, agreements cover all the employees in the bargaining unit; only under union-shop agreements, in which all employees are required to belong to the union, would coverage be identical with union membership. In other plants agreement coverage would be more extensive than union membership. (3) There are thousands of government employees—federal, state, and municipal, including school teachers—who are union members but who are not working under the usual type of bilateral agreement existing in private industry.

Agreement Coverage

The proportion of all persons in the labor force who are covered by collective bargaining contracts has slightly declined during the past decade. This is a result of the decrease in employment in those

Table 3. Proportion of Wage Earners Under Union Agreements in 1962

Manufacturing Industries

75–100 per cent	50–75 per cent	25–50 per cent	under 25 per cent
Agricultural equipment	Chemicals	Cotton shirts and dresses	(None)
Aircraft	Furniture	Food, except meat packing	
Aluminum	Instruments	Hosiery	
Automobile	Jewelry and silverware	Luggage and handbags	
Brewery	Leather and shoes	Lumber	
Coats and suits	Machinery, except electrical	Textiles	
Dyeing and finishing	Metal products		
Electrical machinery	Millinery and hats		
Fur	Paper and pulp		
Glass and glassware	Printing and publishing		
Meat packing	Steel products		
Ordnance	Tobacco products		
Petroleum and coal products	Woolen and worsted textile		
Railroad equipment			
Rubber			
Shipbuilding			
Steel, basic			
Stone and clay			

Nonmanufacturing Industries

75–100 per cent	50–75 per cent	25–50 per cent	under 25 per cent
Actors and musicians	Bus lines, intercity	Newspaper offices	Agriculture
Airline pilots and mechanics	Technicians, radio and motion picture	Barber shops	Beauty shops
Bus and streetcar, local	Light and power	Cleaning and Dyeing	Clerical
Coal mining	City bus and streetcar lines	Hotels	Laundries
Construction		Taxicabs	Restaurants
Longshoring		Wholesale trade	Retail trade
Maritime			
Metal mining			
Motion-picture production			
Railroads			
Telephone and telegraph			
Trucking			

industries where unions have their greatest strength, and of the inability of unions to attract sufficiently large numbers of employees in those occupations where employment is increasing. The outstanding characteristic of modern industry is the use of fewer persons on unskilled and semiskilled occupations and the greatly increased need for professional, scientific and clerical personnel. At present, our labor force includes more white-collar than blue-collar workers, and thus far collective bargaining has not been sought by many white-collar workers.

The great extension of collective bargaining during the 1930's and the 1940's took place in coal mining and in the mass-production industries—steel, automobile, rubber, meat-packing and shipbuilding—which have experienced vast technological changes, with resulting declines in employment of machine tenders and those who work with their hands. Although the proportion of plants covered by union contracts has not declined in these industries, the number of workers has done so because of the smaller numbers employed on the production lines. As automation is extended there will probably be further declines in the proportion of production workers to the total labor force.

At present, approximately one out of three persons in nonagricultural pursuits is employed under union contracts. As a measure of collective bargaining coverage this figure is misleading, however, since "total labor force" includes not only those who are unemployed but domestic workers, the millions of self-employed business and professional persons (lawyers, doctors, etc.), and all unpaid family workers and all those managers and supervisors who are not eligible for union membership. A more accurate measure of contract coverage is the proportion of employed "production" workers—i.e., those who operate and tend machines and work primarily with their hands.

In manufacturing as a whole, approximately two-thirds of all production employees are under the terms of union contracts. The percentage varies among the several industries—from over 80 per cent in petroleum products, primary metals, transportation equipment, ordnance and rubber, to only 30 per cent in textiles. Unionization also varies geographically. In the North Central states more than three-fourths of the production workers are covered by union contracts, as compared with less than one-half in the Southern states.

In the service trades, unionization is prevalent in the large cities and almost absent in the small communities. Thus, most of the barbers, taxicab and bus drivers, and hotel and restaurant workers are employed under union contracts in the metropolitan centers, but the proportion of the total so employed throughout the country is comparatively low because of the absence of collective bargaining in the small cities and rural areas. Almost 60 per cent of the employees in wholesale trade and 40 per cent in retail trade in eighty metropolitan centers are covered by union contracts, but scarcely any in the rural and small-town areas are employed under terms of union contracts.

10

EMPLOYER-LABOR DISPUTES

So long as free men and women engage in economic undertakings, there will always be disputes between employers and employees. A complete absence of disputes for any period of time would indicate a condition of absolute dominance of one group and abject servility of the other, a situation which makes for stagnation rather than progress. Likewise, the total elimination of interunion controversies could be attained only by stifling natural, and in some instances desirable, expressions of group rivalry.

The presence of a dispute does not mean that a work stoppage exists or that it must necessarily take place. It is sometimes argued that if a dispute can be settled after a strike or lockout occurs it could just as well have been settled without a stoppage; that work stoppages are therefore wasteful and unnecessary. This may be true in some cases, but the fact is that in many instances different terms of settlement are obtained following a work stoppage than would have been effected without the stoppage. It is the prospect and the hope of obtaining more favorable terms which induce workers (or an employer in the case of a lockout) to undergo the hardships and inconveniences of a cessation of work.

Moreover, the knowledge that a work stoppage can or may take place materially affects the nature of the bargaining relationship. Indeed, it can be said that the essence of collective bargaining is absent if the parties involved do not have the right or ability to use the economic pressure of a work stoppage. The possibility of the use of a strike or lockout as a last resort has been expressed as "an ever-present and controlling factor in the realistic processes of collective bargaining. Those processes lose all color of reality if the workers have not the right to reject the management's offer and quit, or if management has not the right to refuse the workers' terms and close the plant. It is the overhanging pressure of this right to strike or to lockout that keeps the parties at the bargaining table and fixes the boundaries of stubbornness in the bargaining conferences. It sets the limit upon the aggressive and emotional conduct of the negotiations and dominates the situation in the final moments of responsible decision. Unless the negotiating parties are faced with this possibility of a strike or a lockout, and are forced to examine and accept the consequences of their own decision, they are free from the responsibility that makes genuine collective bargaining possible and produces, through it, creative results. Thus, for the ordinary labor dispute, the possibility of a strike or lockout is, in the last analysis, the most potent instrument of persuasion."[1]

SIGNIFICANCE OF STRIKE ACTION

To concede that the potential of a strike or lockout is a necessary condition for genuine collective bargaining does not imply that all work stoppages which have taken place were necessary or that stoppages should under all circumstances be allowed to take place. Work stoppages may be costly and sometimes disastrous to the parties who engage in them; they may seriously inconvenience and sometimes jeopardize the health and safety of the general public. The settlement of labor disputes before work stoppages occur is the goal of government, employers, and unions alike, and various methods for their prevention are now being utilized and many more are proposed from time to time. Short of an absolute ban on all strikes and lockouts which can be imposed only by a police state or totalitarian government, there is no one panacea for dealing with work stoppages resulting from labor-management disputes.

Because of the relatively strong bargaining position which the employer usually has in the employment relationship, most stoppages take the form of strikes rather than lockouts.[2] Most generally

[1] *Strikes and Democratic Government,* The Twentieth Century Fund, New York, 1947, pp. 13–14.

[2] Technically, the distinction between a strike and a lockout depends on the party which actually initiates the stoppage, but in actual experience it is fre-

it is the employees who must take overt action to obtain new terms of employment or to protect existing standards. The employer needs only to announce that he will not raise his wages or intends to reduce them, and his proposals will *automatically go into effect* unless his employees protest. Work stoppages due to employer-labor disputes, therefore, are conceived of and generally referred to as strikes.

STRIKES *vs.* OTHER FORMS OF PROTEST

A strike is an evidence of discontent and an expression of protest; it represents the final act by which workers seek to better their condition or mitigate a worsening of conditions. While a strike indicates dissatisfaction, it is also a manifestation of hope. Workers driven to the point of despair, either because of fear of retaliation or because of the general hopelessness of their economic situation, seldom indulge in such overt acts as strikes. Their protests must necessarily take the form of sabotage or of a listless slowing down on the job.

A strike is a temporary stoppage of work for specific reasons, entered into with the expectation that work will be resumed when a settlement of the grievances is effected. So far as the intentions and attitude of the strikers are concerned, they look upon themselves as continuing to retain the status of employees of the company against which they are striking, with vested interests in their individual jobs and with the right to return to their jobs when they have reached a mutual agreement over the matters in dispute or, if unsuccessful, when they are willing to return to work on the terms offered by the employer.

The employer, on the other hand, may decide not to re-employ any or all of the strikers, even after the dispute is settled. He may

---

quently impossible to make a distinction. For example, an employer says he cannot operate a plant unless wages are reduced. The workers refuse to accept the reduction and the plant shuts down and reopens a month later at the reduced wage. Here the employer sought to enforce terms upon the workers, who at first refused to accept them. On the other hand, a union may announce certain terms which it says must be adopted as a condition of continued work by its members; work ceases when the employer refuses to accept those terms. In both cases, the workers would claim that these stoppages were lockouts, whereas employers would probably call them strikes.

have employed a sufficient number of qualified persons to enable him to continue operations during the dispute and thus have no vacancies when the participants in the unsuccessful strike apply for reinstatement. Or the employer may refuse to reinstate large numbers of the strikers in order to break up the union, in which case he might ask for a representation election in which the new employees, unsympathetic to the union, would be the voters. This latter tactic was made illegal by the 1959 Reporting and Disclosure Act in the case of economic strikes—those over wages, hours and related matters. The law now says that even though these strikers are not reinstated to their jobs they are privileged to vote in any representation election held within twelve months after the commencement of the strike.

A stoppage is effected either by walking out, not reporting for work at the usual or expected time, or reporting for duty but refusing to perform any work ("sit-down"). Restriction of output or sabotage sometimes approximates a "sit-down" strike but cannot be identified as one unless the participants openly state that their action is done for specific reasons, and will be concluded if and when their grievances have been adjusted. Some unions which follow the practice of not allowing their members to work after the expiration of a contract and before a new one has been concluded ("no contract—no work"), maintain that such interruptions are not strikes. However, these stoppages are due to the inability of the union and employer to reach an agreement and therefore can be interpreted as strikes resulting from disputes over the terms of employment.

KINDS OF WORK STOPPAGES

Work stoppages due to industrial disputes can be classified into four general categories, depending upon the relationship of the parties involved and the purpose for engaging in the stoppage: (1) a sympathetic strike in which the purpose is to broaden the group pressure upon the employer whose employees are on strike; (2) a secondary strike in which union members refuse to work on materials produced under nonunion conditions or in a struck plant; (3) jurisdictional and rival union strikes which are due to disputes between two or more unions; (4) a strike or lockout which is the result of a dispute between an employer and his employees. A large majority of work stoppages result from disputes between individual employers and their own employees, and take place when one party makes definite demands on the other.

SYMPATHETIC STRIKES

In a sympathetic strike the dispute is not primarily one between an employer and *his own* employees; it is called for the purpose of demonstrating the solidarity of workers and broadening the group pressure upon the employer against whom there is a strike for specific cause. In some sympathetic strike situations the employer or employers involved may not be responsible in any way for the dissatisfactions which brought about the primary stoppage. In other cases, however, the workers' willingness to participate in the sympathetic action may be induced by the feeling that there is a tacit understanding among the several employers with regard to the issues involved in the primary dispute; that should the original strike fail their own work conditions will also be adversely affected.

Sympathetic strikes have never been common in this country. Since they may involve suspension of a no-strike provision in employer-union contracts, they are resorted to only in extreme cases when the union or union standards appear to be in jeopardy throughout the trade. If a sympathetic strike becomes so widespread as to include all or a large majority of the workers in different industries, it is referred to as a "general strike." Not more than a half-dozen general strikes have taken place throughout the history of this country, and all of them have been confined to single cities where they have been called in protest against some action taken by city authorities with respect to the conduct of the original strike.

In this respect American experience thus far differs from that of some other countries where general strikes have occurred which included workers in all the industries throughout the country. A notable example is the one which took place in Great Britain in 1926 in which all organized workers, including government employees, quit work in sympathy with the striking coal miners. French and Italian labor unions, especially those dominated by Communists, have called a number of nation-wide strikes to which large numbers of workers have responded.

Secondary Strikes

The distinction between a sympathetic and a secondary strike lies in the degree of the business relations between the employers involved. In a secondary strike there is a direct and immediate business connection between the two employers, or between the primary employer and several secondary employers. In the most common situation the second employer is using materials or equipment manufactured at a plant whose employees are on strike or in a nonunion plant which the union is trying to organize. In other words, a union is in conflict with an employer, and workers elsewhere refuse to work on, transport or sell the goods produced in his plant.

The refusal to handle certain goods may result in a complete work stoppage at the second employer's place of business. Frequently the protest results in a boycott only, since the second employer may substitute another manufacturer's materials or give his employees other work to do until the dispute with the primary employer is settled. The secondary strike or boycott may involve a retailer who is selling goods manufactured under conditions in dispute; a trucking firm delivering such goods ("hot cargo"); or a building contractor who is using materials manufactured in a struck plant or who is subcontracting part of his construction work to a nonunion contractor.

From the earliest days of labor organizations, unions have considered it their natural right to be able to extend their area of pressure to employers who have business relations with, and are presumably profiting from such relations, an employer with whom the same or another union has a dispute. Outside the building trades, unions have exercised this form of protest only rarely—that is, when the dispute with the primary employer had been unusually prolonged and bitter. Secondary stoppages have been more frequent in the construction industry since it is a cardinal rule of the building trades unions that their members should not work alongside nonunion workers. Very infrequently, however, have building trades unions engaged in boycotts against materials or equipment used in the construction.

Public opinion has generally looked with disfavor upon secondary strikes and boycotts, both because of the extent of pressure they make possible for unions and because of their seeming unfairness in causing hardship to employers who are not directly involved in the dispute. As has already been indicated, secondary strikes were specifically legalized in the 1932 Norris-LaGuardia Act but are now outlawed under the Taft-Hartley and Landrum-Griffin Acts, although the courts have not yet definitively resolved many issues connected with these disputes. Secondary strikes and boycotts continue to take place, sometimes frankly as a known illegal act but frequently with the expectation that the courts will interpret the given case not to be in violation of the law.

RIVAL UNION AND JURISDICTIONAL DISPUTES

Where there are two or more unions functioning in the same trade or industry, a dispute may arise as to which union shall represent the workers as their bargaining agent. This may result in a work stoppage if members of one of the unions seek to have their union displace a union which has already been recognized by the employer. While the immediate issue causing the stoppage of work appears to be the rivalry of two factions of workers, the employer is nevertheless an integral factor in the situation. The very fact that there are two rival unions fighting for the allegiance of his employees generally signifies the discontent of one group of workers with the terms which their union has obtained from him, and the hope that the other union can secure better terms.

Present laws covering workers engaged in interstate commerce forbid workers to force an employer to recognize a union if he is already dealing with another union that has been certified as the result of a valid election during the preceding twelve months. After this period of time any rival union may set up its picket lines, but any party involved in the dispute—the employer, the established union or the second union—may demand an immediate election under the auspices of the National Labor Relations Board.

A jurisdictional strike represents another situation in which the dispute is not primarily one between an employer and his employees. In the usual jurisdictional dispute the employer is passive, the quarrel being solely between two or more labor organizations. However, the employer has a stake in the outcome because of possible differences in wage scales and other work standards demanded by the contending unions.

In a jurisdictional dispute, the issue is which one of two or more unions has a right to claim jurisdiction over a particular class of work or kind of job. Unlike a representation dispute between dual organizations, the dispute is not over which union a majority of a given group of employees wish to have represent them. In fact, no workers may actually be employed on the job when the dispute arises, or those who happen to be at work may have to leave if the contending union wins the strike and decides to give the jobs to its own members.

Jurisdictional disputes are by-products of the continual changes in machinery, methods, and materials that take place in a dynamic industrial economy. Each such change causes the elimination of certain kinds of occupations or types of jobs and the substitution of others. Conflicts arise when a union seeks to continue its jurisdiction over the function performed, regardless of the new materials or processes which may be introduced, or when a new process arouses a desire for a new craft autonomy. Because of their potentially disruptive results to the labor movement, and because organized labor realizes they are the least defensible in the eyes of the public, the AFL-CIO has sought various means to resolve jurisdictional disputes before stoppages take place.

UNION RULES CONCERNING STRIKES

Practically every union constitution contains some statement regarding the calling and conduct of strikes. In general, the purpose of such clauses is to minimize hasty and ill-advised action and to provide financial aid and insure maximum success once a strike is called. In considering the purpose and character of strike clauses in union constitutions it should be remembered that any organization's formally adopted rules may not be adhered to by all its members at all times. Just as individuals may ignore or violate laws, so members of unions may on occasion engage in strikes contrary to their unions' regulations. Such stoppages the unions themselves call "illegal" and fines may be imposed upon members who instigate them.

RULES FOR CALLING A STRIKE

In order to call a strike, the majority of unions require a two-thirds affirmative vote of the membership affected, and sanction by the National President or General Executive Board. Most stipulate that the vote shall be by secret ballot at a special meeting of the members, which has been announced a given number of days in advance. In the building trades and some other unions, the local business agent is sometimes given authority to call "job" or "shop" strikes when in his opinion the agreement is being violated. But if such strikes will affect the members of other unions as well as his own, approval of the local or district trades council or joint board is required.

Although almost all unions require the sanction of the National President or General Executive Board, in practice this permission is usually effective only so far as financial aid is sought and obtained from the National. Some unions specifically limit the permission requirement to strikes which the national union is to finance, and in such cases the local's vote to call a strike is final if the membership does not expect to receive strike benefits or other aid from its national office. On the other hand, the members of some unions are absolutely forbidden to engage in any strike without approval from the national office; otherwise they may be suspended.

When it is anticipated that the union will have difficulty in its negotiations for a new contract, a strike vote of members may be taken but no date set. The vote authorizes the President to call a strike if and when he deems it advisable during the course of the negotiations. The purpose of such a membership vote is obvious; it strengthens the bargaining hand of the union negotiators by its evidence that the rank-and-file members are serious in their demands and that they expect their negotiators to obtain a favorable or at least a compromise settlement.

Unions usually require only a majority vote for the termination of a strike. As with the calling of a strike, the authority of the general officers to end one varies in the different unions. In some instances the National President has the power to call off a strike whenever in his judgment it is to the best interests of the union to do so. More generally the termination of a strike is dependent on the vote of those immediately involved, although the influence of the national officers usually has considerable weight. In all cases, so far as the continuance of strike benefits is concerned, the national officers have the final word.

Strike Benefits

The calling of a strike is a serious matter to the workers and union concerned, for it means loss of earnings and union dues and perhaps substantial cash outlays from the union treasury. Although the unions' ability to pay strike benefits when needed varies greatly, practically all of them seek to maintain a reserve to finance strikes, which is most commonly called the "defense fund."

The amounts in these defense funds naturally fluctuate, depending both upon the provision made for maintaining them and upon the necessity for withdrawals at any particular time. Some union constitutions specify that a certain portion of the regular dues shall be regularly deposited in the defense fund, while others specify a minimum amount which shall be maintained; if the fund falls below the specified amount, the treasurer is authorized to levy special assessments. In the case of a prolonged strike by a local which the national union considers important to union security or expansion, the national office may levy a special assessment upon the members of the locals not involved in the stoppage. The justification for such general assessments is based on the conviction that the welfare of the union and all its members is at stake in the outcome of the dispute.

SETTLEMENT OF DISPUTES UNDER EMPLOYER-UNION AGREEMENTS

The signing of an agreement by an employer and a union automatically removes some of the major causes of conflict—the matter of union recognition has been settled and the questions of basic wages, hours, and working rules have been agreed upon. Although the establishment of such a contractual relationship does not entirely remove the possibility of disputes, they should not develop into strikes and lockouts if the agreement also provides adequate adjustment machinery, and if all parties are willing to use the specified procedures.

NEGOTIATING PROCEDURE

Under collective bargaining agreements the most common procedure is for the employees in a shop, or in each department of a large plant, to elect one of their group to serve as the shop chairman or steward who acts as their representative in the initial handling of a grievance. In large plants there are shop committees composed of the stewards elected from the various departments. Under the terms of many agreements, the stewards and members of the shop committees are placed at the top of the seniority list of the plant or department in which they work. This serves as an inducement to assume the responsibilities of a stewardship, removes fear of discriminatory dismissal because of action taken in connection with the work of a steward, and safeguards continuity in grievance adjustment personnel.

In the building-trades and a few other unions, the shop chairman or steward performs a less important function. He may handle some negotiations with the foreman, but the major burden of enforcing the agreement provisions falls upon the business agent. Although the steward is responsible for securing compliance with the terms of the agreement on a particular job, the business agent has this responsibility for all the employers in the same industry throughout the city. The business agent is a paid, full-time officer elected by the members of the local or appointed by a designated union official. He is not an employee of any of the workplaces covered by the union agreement, but he usually has a knowledge of the industry through previous employment.

The employee's immediate supervisor is ordinarily the first negotiator on behalf of the employer in dispute negotiations with the union. In small establishments, the owner himself may handle the initial negotiations; in large industrial concerns the foreman, department superintendent, division superintendent, and plant manager are in turn responsible for dealing with the union representatives. Personnel or labor relations officers, where these are employed, usually take an active part when appeal is taken beyond the foreman.

In a number of industries, agreements are made with associations of employers which are city-wide or regional in scope. Although these associations are at times established solely for the purpose of negotiating new agreements, they may also serve as enforcement agencies; in this case the association officials help to settle disputes which arise between the union and any employer who is a member of the association. These association officials are elected by the member firms and, like business agents of the union, are experienced in the industry and familiar with its problems.

Initial Steps in Appeal Procedure

Shall an aggrieved employee take his complaint directly to his foreman or to his union steward? If the latter, how much responsibility shall the steward assume in deciding the validity of the grievance, that is, whether or not the complaint shall be presented to the foreman? Must the decision negotiated by the steward and the foreman be accepted as final by the employee? These questions have aroused a great deal of controversy between managers and unions.

Management usually prefers to have an aggrieved employee take his complaint directly to his foreman, maintaining that this procedure preserves a healthy personal relation between workers and their foremen, that it is less time consuming, and that stewards tend to magnify troubles and make unimportant differences become "issues." The attitudes of individual workers differ, depending upon how adequate they feel they are to handle their own grievances, their personal relationship with their foreman and with their steward. If an employee has a "stand-in" with his foreman, or for some reason does not like or trust his steward, he naturally prefers to deal directly with his foreman. On the other hand, a large proportion of employee grievances involves some action or decision of the foreman, and few employees have the desire or the courage to argue with their "boss" about something he has done or not done.

In general, unions want their stewards to participate and to assume the deciding role in all the negotiations of employees with their supervisors because they feel that such day-to-day personal service increases loyalty to the union. Moreover, unions claim that by having all complaints channeled through the stewards there is more uniformity in decisions throughout the plant, and there is less likelihood of partiality or discrimination on the part of the foremen.

The Taft-Hartley Act specifically allows individual employees or groups of employees to take up their grievances with their employer and to have such grievances adjusted without the intervention of the union representative "as long as the adjustment is not inconsistent with the terms of a collective-bargaining contract." However, the law provides that the union representative shall be given an opportunity to be present during the process of adjustment.

ARBITRATION UNDER UNION AGREEMENTS

Most disputes arising while agreements are in effect are adjusted at some stage in the union-management negotiation process, and only occasionally do they have to be referred to an "outsider" for final settlement. Nevertheless, the great majority of employer-union agreements make provision for the arbitration of disputes arising over the interpretation or application of the agreement in the event the parties to the dispute are unable to settle the matter.

As a rule, unadjusted disputes may be referred to arbitration upon the request of either the employer or the union; in practice, this insures automatic arbitration whenever a dispute is not mutually resolved. Under the terms of a few agreements, both parties must agree to have the matter referred to arbitration; this means that the party satisfied with the *status quo* is able to prevent recourse to arbitration. Since it is usually the union that is seeking redress, under the latter type of arbitration referral the union must either decide to accept the management's decision or resort to economic pressure and call a strike.

The most common form of outside reference is through the selection of an impartial chairman by a committee on which both sides are equally represented. Some agreements do not leave the selection of an arbitrator until a dispute gets to the stage of arbitration, but specify an individual who is to act as arbitrator as needed throughout the life of the agreement. The arbitrators hold hearings, take testimony, and occasionally make independent investigations of the facts. In order to avoid unnecessary delays, a time limit is generally set for each step in the process—the selection of arbitrators, the conduct of hearings, and the rendering of decisions. The decision of the arbitrator is final and binding on both parties and is based on his interpretation of the contract terms—not his judgment as to what is right or wrong in the situation.

FEDERAL AGENCIES FOR SETTLING DISPUTES

Most disputes arise over the terms to be included in new agreements—that is, wages, hours, and working conditions—as well as over the question of union status. For the final determination of such issues there are usually no prearranged contractual procedures because these matters involve the essence of collective bargaining. When collective bargaining fails or threatens to fail, government agencies are widely utilized on a voluntary basis. If the dispute threatens a stoppage which would affect the public health and safety there are special procedures established by law.

Present government agencies for the adjustment of labor disputes are of two general types: (1) mediation and conciliation agencies, which have no legal power to compel acceptance of their recommendations and which may not even have a legal right to intervene if the parties to the dispute do not request their assistance; and (2) boards and commissions, which are empowered to administer and enforce specific laws concerning employer-employee relations and working conditions.

Federal Mediation and Conciliation Service

The 1913 law which established the U.S. Department of Labor provided among other things that "the Secretary of Labor shall have the power to act as mediator and to appoint commissioners of conciliation in labor disputes whenever in his judgment the interests of industrial peace may require it to be done." Pursuant to this law the Federal Conciliation Service was established which functioned as an arm of the Secretary of Labor until the passage of the 1947 Labor Management Relations Act, which established a Federal Mediation and Conciliation Service independent of the Department of Labor and under a director appointed by the President.

Government conciliators are engaged in efforts to settle questions in dispute before strikes and lockouts occur, or to bring the latter to a speedy settlement if they have already begun. The Conciliation Service may enter a case at the request of either party to the dispute, or at the request of some representative of the public, such as a mayor, governor, or congressman. It may also intervene upon its own motion, but this is done only in the more serious disputes when it is believed that the public interest warrants. Government conciliators have no power of coercion or means to enforce their recommendations, although parties to a dispute are required by law to participate fully and promptly in conferences called by the Service.

A conciliator has no set formula of procedure when he is called in to help settle a dispute. Whenever possible, he tries to get the parties concerned to discuss their differences in conference, in which case he acts as a conciliator. Sometimes, especially during the early stages, either or both parties may refuse to meet together. He then acts as a mediator, holding separate conferences with the respective sides, adjusting the minor points of misunderstandings or differences, and getting each side to agree upon what major points can or shall be further negotiated. If either or both sides still refuse to discuss these major points together, the conciliator may draft a plan of settlement independently and submit it to the parties as a recommendation, or he may obtain the approval of both sides to have the matter arbitrated. He may be asked to select an arbitrator, or the parties may request him to serve as arbitrator. As an arbitrator, his decisions are final and must be accepted by both parties in accordance with their voluntary agreement to accept such arbitration.

NATIONAL MEDIATION BOARD

Labor relations for the railroad and air transport at the present time are governed by amendments to the 1926 Railway Labor Act. These created a three-man National Mediation Board appointed by the President, and a National Railroad Adjustment Board consisting of eighteen carrier (employer) representatives and eighteen union representatives. The Adjustment Board, with headquarters in Chicago, is divided into four separate divisions, each of which has jurisdiction over a distinct class of employees, namely, train and yard service, shop crafts, and so forth.

In this arrangement for handling labor relations on the railroads, a clear distinction is made with respect to the basic differences in the character of labor disputes, that is, those over the interpretation and application of existing agreements, and those over the terms of a new agreement.

The Adjustment Board handles disputes "growing out of grievances or out of the interpretation or application of agreements concerning rates of pay, rules, or working conditions." Its decisions may be enforced by civil suits in federal district courts. If the bipartisan board is unable to agree, it must appoint a referee; if it cannot agree in a selection, the National Mediation Board appoints the referee.

The National Mediation Board intervenes in the other two classes of disputes. By holding elections or by other means it certifies who shall represent the workers in their collective bargaining. On request of either party to a dispute involving changes in pay, rules or working conditions, or on its own motion in cases of emergency, it intervenes and through mediation attempts to bring about an agreement. If its mediating efforts fail, the Board endeavors to induce the parties to submit their controversy to arbitration, the arbitration board to be selected by the parties concerned. If they cannot agree on the selection, the Board is authorized to name the members of the arbitration board.

If arbitration is refused by either party and the dispute should "threaten substantially to interrupt interstate commerce to a degree such as to deprive any section of the country of essential transportation service," the Board is required to notify the President, who may appoint an emergency board to investigate the facts and report thereon within thirty days. During this time no change, except by agreement, may be made by the parties to the controversy in the conditions out of which the dispute arose. The law does not require compliance with the recommendations of the emergency board, although the publication of the findings makes it difficult for either party not to follow its suggestions.

The National Labor Relations Board

The activities of the National Labor Relations Board concern all employers and workers engaged in interstate commerce except those covered by the National (Railroad and Airline) Mediation Board.

The Labor Relations Board functions in two general areas: It conducts employee elections to determine which union, if any, shall be certified as the bargaining agent; and it enforces the unfair labor practice provisions in the 1947 Taft-Hartley and the 1959 Reporting and Disclosure Acts.

Any group of employees, a union or an employer may petition the Board to hold an election to determine what union, if any, shall represent the employees as their bargaining agent. The Board determines the appropriate bargaining unit (craft, industrial or modification of either) and, if no election has been held within the past twelve months, conducts a secret ballot with the results being determined by a majority of the votes cast. If two or more unions are contending, a run-off election may be necessary. The Board also has the duty of holding elections to determine whether or not a union shall be *decertified* at the close of a contract period, whenever an employer or group of employees assert that the existing bargaining agent no longer represents a majority of the employees.

Incidental to the unfair labor practices, the Board must determine when a union's initiation fees are excessive; whether or not an employee has been "coerced" to join or not to join a union; whether or not a discharged employee under a union-shop contract has been expelled from the union for reasons other than for failure to pay dues; whether or not an employee has been discharged "for cause" so as to make him ineligible to receive back pay; whether or not a given group of employees are justified in refusing to pass a picket line. In jurisdictional disputes the Board is empowered to make decisions when the parties concerned are not able to reach mutually satisfactory settlements within ten days after the filing of charges. Upon complaint of a secondary strike or boycott the Board is required to seek injunctive relief if it finds that such a strike or boycott actually exists.

To secure compliance with its determinations the Board may petition the appropriate Circuit Court of Appeals, and the court is in turn authorized to grant such temporary relief or restraining order as it deems proper, and to make a decree enforcing, modifying or setting aside the Board's order in whole or in part. In like manner, any person aggrieved by a final order of the Board may obtain a similar review by filing in the appropriate Court of Appeals. All decisions of the Circuit Courts, of course, are subject to appeal to the U.S. Supreme Court.

Fact-finding Boards

Under a democratic, free-enterprise system there is no way to force employers or employees to come to terms and to settle their disputes without work stoppages. Compulsory arbitration is tantamount to government fixing of wages, prices and profits, and this is contradictory to the essence of free competition. Nevertheless, when there are work stoppages large enough to close down vital industries, the government must take some action in the public interest. During the two world wars Congress enacted emergency measures which gave the President the power to forbid or terminate strikes when he deemed it advisable. At present, the handling of disputes where stoppages endanger the national interest are covered by the Railroad Labor Act (see page 167) and the Taft-Hartley Act. Both provide for fact-finding boards appointed by the President.

According to the Taft-Hartley Act, threatened stoppages affecting "an entire industry or a substantial part thereof," which would "imperil the national health or safety," can be outlawed for as long as four and one-half months. At any time within the required sixty-day notice of a threatened strike the President may appoint a board of inquiry to investigate the issues and may apply for an injunction against the threatened strike. While the strike is held up, the parties must make an effort to settle their differences with the assistance of the Mediation Service. The President may reconvene his board of inquiry which, by the close of the second sixty-day period, must submit a new report giving the current status, including the last terms offered by the employer. Thereupon, within fifteen days the National Labor Relations Board must conduct an election to determine whether or not a majority of the employees wish to accept the employer's last offer. If a majority vote unfavorably, the injunction is lifted and the President refers the case to Congress "for consideration and appropriate action."

Thus far no disputes have been referred to Congress. Although there have been a number of so-called "emergency" disputes, the parties involved have invariably yielded to public opinion and the pressure of the various government agencies.

11

UNION-MANAGEMENT COOPERATION

Industrial peace, when based upon a foundation of collective bargaining, is a manifestation of employer-union cooperation because it involves a willingness to accept compromises and mutually to work out solutions to problems as they arise. Union-management cooperation can, however, mean something beyond the mere attainment of industrial peace. The term is commonly used to refer to specific programs of joint effort toward a concrete goal, such as to increase plant efficiency and reduce costs, or to improve the quality of the product or service rendered to customers, as well as to promote the sale and use of the employer's products.

Many employers and unions are satisfied with the achievement of harmonious relations and do not seek or even desire to enter into any further joint efforts. They believe that management and the union each has its peculiar functions, which tend to be weakened through joint action beyond negotiations over work conditions and the observance of the terms of these negotiations. Contract observance in itself is no easy matter, especially for union officials. Top management has absolute control over its supervisory staff; it has merely to pass the word down the line as to what should or should not be done. Labor unions and their officers must depend upon the loyalty of many persons to abide by decisions which some of them may not even have agreed upon when adopted. Management personnel, in contrast to union officials, are not dependent upon popular elections to hold their jobs.

POTENTIAL PITFALLS IN COOPERATION

Union-management cooperation carried to its extreme limits could lead to a corporate society in which the general economy would be divided along vertical lines between industrial blocks instead of along the horizontal lines of competition between employers and employees. Such an arrangement was embodied in the original plans of Italian fascism, which provided for a hierarchy of joint associations of capital and labor (both called corporations) headed by a national council of corporations. The philosophy of Italian fascism was a fusion of syndicalism and nationalism, although the former soon gave way to the latter. Nationalism maintained that the sovereignty of the state left no room for class struggle: that there should be solidarity of capital and labor. In practice, it required the dissolution of free trade unions and the substitution of government decrees for collective bargaining contracts.

In present-day Communist countries the theory of what their leaders term union-management cooperation is a pillar of the industrial structure, but its operation involves a perversion of the function and character of trade unions as conceived under democratic governments. The union in a Soviet country, instead of being a representative and defender of the employees, becomes an instrument of the government to *enforce duties* on workers. The workers' organizations cooperate with management in the administration of all measures for increased efficiency, whether it be incentive systems and work loads, or the personal deportment of employees. The unions are represented on the labor courts in each plant, which discipline employees who fail to meet their quotas or who are absent or tardy.

Cooperation in Democracies

Union-management cooperation can take various forms and by necessity must fit into the political-economic system within which both unions and management operate. Even in democracies, the role of unions is different in a government-owned-and-operated industry from that in private, competitive industry such as prevails in the

United States. Under our industrial system there are potential pitfalls in union-management cooperation as well as possibilities for constructive accomplishments. So long as a cooperative endeavor is confined to methods for improving internal plant efficiency and achieving lower prices, the result can be beneficial to everybody—the employer, the employees and the public. If, to promote the success of the enterprise or business, cooperation extends into areas of controlling competition, fixing prices or retarding innovations, the result can be detrimental to the public interest and may be in violation of the anti-trust laws.

For example, unions have cooperated with the coal and railroad industries in opposing the installation of oil pipelines and the development of the St. Lawrence Waterway. There have been instances in the construction industry where local unions have joined with employers in boycotting materials from other areas in order to promote "home" industries, even though such materials were produced under union conditions elsewhere. The unions in some industries have joined with the employers in seeking high protective tariffs and government subsidies. In some instances employers have accepted unionization of their plants for the primary purpose of obtaining union support in their efforts to forestall or discourage competition of one kind or another.

JOINT DETERMINATION OF PLANT POLICIES

The ultimate test of any employer or union policy, or of their collective agreement on policy, is whether in the long run it helps or hinders the production of goods and services which can be sold in a competitive market. However, in most instances the impact of a policy or work rule cannot be immediately and conclusively determined. It cannot be proved that a specific condition has caused a business to decline or to progress; it cannot always be foreseen whether or not a certain work rule will promote or hinder maximum employment. In every unionized plant the employer and the union are daily faced with the problem of defining the wavering line separating constructive cooperation from encroachment upon responsibilities which each regards as part of its peculiar function.

Many employers who have accepted the principle of collective bargaining so far as wages and related matters are concerned, are opposed to having work rules and plant policies established through the process of union-management negotiation. They contend that employers cannot properly carry on their managerial functions if they are deprived of the right to make decisions and enforce policies necessary for the efficient conduct of the business. They regard these functions as "management prerogatives" which cannot be shared by unions if the business is to operate successfully.

The issue has its philosophical as well as its practical aspects. One doctrine to which most employers adhere holds that management has the natural right to retain all the authority to run its business as it sees fit except with regard to the specific matters which it has relinquished to management-union negotiations. According to this concept, collective bargaining is a retreat from the pre-existing natural and moral rights of employers, and therefore management must exercise caution and not yield too much to joint negotiations.

In contrast is the concept that management operates as a trustee for all those affected by the enterprise—those who furnish the capital, those who furnish the labor, and those who buy its products. Accordingly, collective bargaining is a *way* of managing the labor aspects of a business enterprise and not a concession on the part of the owners or managers of capital; joint negotiations do not imply a retreat from employers' inviolate rights but only a change from former or customary procedures. Implied in this theory is the expectation and hope that the balancing leverage of collective negotiations will serve in the long run to promote the interests of owners, workers and consumers.

Determination of Work Rules

In specific terms, those who believe that collective bargaining represents a negative influence on good management maintain that the employer should have the sole right to control the hiring and firing and the assignment of the work force, to establish job and quality standards, and to determine such matters as the processes and equipment to be used, the inventories and reserve funds to be maintained, the location of plants and the subcontracting of work. Unions, on the other hand, argue that all these activities affect job and working conditions; that the workers have a stake in their outcome and should therefore have a voice in their determination. For example, plant relocation and subcontracting not only affect the job security of people already on the job, but influence general wages throughout the industry. If branch plants are established in low-wage areas, or if work is subcontracted to non-unionized plants, those employed in higher-wage union plants may eventually lose their jobs because of competitive costs, and working standards throughout the industry will inevitably decline.

To most employers, union participation in the determination of plant policy is synonymous with restrictive work rules, which place arbitrary limits on the amount of individual output, require the employment of excess workers, or cause duplication of work and featherbedding of all kinds. Although union-imposed rules may be for reasons of health and safety, unions admit that sometimes their purpose is to prolong the jobs of their members. Job security is naturally the chief concern of the millions of persons who have nothing to rely upon but their daily wages, and the expectation that the union will protect their jobs is a primary inducement for workers to join unions. From the short-term point of view, there is a sharp divergence of interests between management and those managed, and it is only natural that each should want to protect and promote its own interests. However, artificial protection of jobs results in ephemeral benefits since the industry or the plant sooner or later is bound to lose out in the competitive struggle. The human problem involved is the willingness of both parties to work out solutions which will cause a minimum of hardship before disaster overtakes both of them.

SENIORITY AND JOB ASSIGNMENT

The "right person on the right job" is a cornerstone of successful business which management contends is impaired by strict application of seniority rules. Not only may persons of lesser competence be assigned or retained, management asserts, but the general effect of the seniority criterion offers little inducement for individuals to attain their maximum efficiency. When job security and promotions are primarily dependent upon the mechanical operation of seniority rules, ambition to excel is minimized, with a consequent leveling influence throughout the work force. Unions and workers argue that seniority rules have the opposite effect—that the feeling of security and fair play engendered by seniority rules improves morale and encourages good performance. Furthermore, they contend, even though an employer (or his foreman) does not consciously practice discrimination, human judgment is fallible, and in the absence of fixed rules, employees who are good self-advertisers rather than good workers are likely to receive preferential treatment.

Employers concede that seniority rules tend to reduce labor turnover and that this may compensate in part for their disadvantages. Young persons of steady work habits are attracted to jobs where they are assured of steady progress up the promotional ladder, and are not prone to change jobs after they have accumulated seniority standing. On the other hand, an ambitious, above-the-average person may be impatient with the slow operation of promotion by seniority, and a business which needs persons of this caliber may find it difficult to attract them.

Promotion and job assignment policies offer one of the most challenging areas for possible union-management cooperation. Unions as well as employers are aware that some jobs must be filled on the basis of individual fitness and qualification alone; union members give evidence of this in their choice of union leaders. Much of the contention disappears when employees' suspicion of discrimination and favoritism is removed. Under such circumstances it has not been too difficult for employers and unions to agree to exempt certain specified jobs from seniority coverage, or to arrange for joint conferences on assignments to nonroutine jobs. Such conferences offer the most constructive arrangement for supervisory jobs, for no matter how well qualified a person may be technically for a foremanship he cannot succeed if his subordinates "are against him."

Cooperation for Industrial Efficiency

Joint efforts on the part of the union and the employer to devise and administer programs for the improvement of the business enterprise represent the highest degree of cooperative effort. The object may be to eliminate waste, to improve the quality of production, to increase output, to reduce costs and to modernize equipment. It may also involve the loan of union funds to a company, the sponsoring of a sales and advertising campaign, or the establishment of a jointly financed stabilization program.

Although there have been a number of experiments with such cooperative programs throughout the years, relatively few have survived for more than a brief period. Some were allowed to lapse when the conditions which occasioned their establishment changed; some did so because of the waning enthusiasm of their promoters, and some as a result of suspicion on the part of the employees that their union was "selling out" to the employer. Others were allowed to lapse when the employer became dissatisfied with the union's "interference" in management. The rarity of union-management programs is understandable when one considers the conditions necessary for their establishment and continued success.

It is a characteristic of human beings, individually and collectively, not to change accustomed ways so long as existing conditions are reasonably comfortable. New patterns of thinking and action are usually the result of a shock produced by a change in the environmental situation, and in response to a felt need for coping with new or worsening conditions. A joint employer-union program for improving plant efficiency necessitates radical changes in customary habits of thinking on the part of both the employer and employees. Traditional suspicions must be supplanted by mutual trust; feelings of superiority and inferiority must give way to a belief and confidence that all concerned have the ability to make a constructive contribution to the program. This is not easy for either side, and is not likely to take place unless both are faced with an extreme crisis.

The infrequency of union-management programs is attributable to several factors. One is that the employer must share with the union certain executive functions which he long has exercised without restriction. Many employers regard this as a reflection upon their administrative ability and do not believe that labor is capable of making any worth-while contribution in the managerial field. Another is that workers and union leaders fear that cooperation for more efficient production methods will lead to layoffs, and to increases in the work loads of those who are retained. Although they realize that over a period of years the economic welfare of employees depends on the profit status of the company, they believe that the union's function should be to protect workers from speed-up and unemployment rather than to participate in programs which might bring about these situations.

RECENT EXAMPLES OF COOPERATION

From time to time a number of local unions have entered into joint programs with their employers to improve plant efficiency or to promote sales. Usually these have been undertaken during a time of stress, when the individual employer's competitive position was in jeopardy and the employees faced the loss of their jobs. There are also instances of joint efforts on a wider scale, between a national union and an entire or a major section of the industry. For example, in 1956 the Hatters' Union embarked on a three-year program, involving expenditures of six million dollars, for loans to employers, purchase of stock and building mortgages, and for advertising campaigns. It was the union's effort to bolster the industry and save the jobs of its members.

On the premise that improved technology pays off in the long run, the Lithographers' Union has recently spent a million dollars, matched by the employers, for research to hasten automation. In the New York dress industry there have been a number of cooperative programs to improve efficiency in the making and the marketing of women's clothing, such as the employment of an impartial chairman to establish standards of shop efficiency—with power to fine employers who failed to adopt the suggestions—as well as the promotion of fashions and sales. Various joint boards of the men's clothing union have upon occasion made loans to their employers to finance expansion and installation of improved equipment.

The 1959 Packinghouse Workers agreement with the Armour Company established an automation committee headed by an impartial chairman to study the conditions of the thousands of former employees who had lost their jobs because of automation and the closing of several Armour plants. Solutions were not found, but the committee meetings provided "new channels for the employer-union relationship over and above contract administration." Recent agreements negotiated by the steelworkers provide for a continuing joint Human Relations Committee to study problems of employment stabilization, subcontracting, overtime scheduling, work assignments and job classifications.

In contrast to plans which call for outlays of union funds is the recently established program covering the Pacific Coast longshoremen, whereby the workers receive payments as a *quid pro quo* for the union's abandonment of certain work rules. Employer-employee relations in the West Coast longshoring industry have been stormy ever since the general strike of 1934, which was followed by the union's gradually assuming control of practically all hiring and work rules. After some years the union began to realize that the shipping industry was losing business to the railroad and trucking industries, with a consequent loss of jobs greater than the union could compensate for through its featherbedding rules.

As the result of prolonged negotiations a five-and-a-half-year agreement was signed in 1960 between the Pacific Maritime Association and the Longshoremen's and Warehousemen's Union, by which the employers regained much of their freedom to manage efficiently, with the right to introduce labor-saving machinery, eliminate multiple handling of cargo, etc. In return, the employers agreed to pay a total of five million dollars a year to be used for guaranteed minimum wages for all registered longshoremen, payment of almost $8,000 to each registered longshoreman when he is sixty-five years old and has twenty-five years' service, and monthly payments to those with twenty-five years' service who retire between the ages of sixty-two and sixty-five. This agreement is an outstanding example of a method of dealing with the problem of restrictive working rules through the encouragement of early retirement to reduce the work force in line with available jobs, as well as of income security for those continuing on the job.

PROBLEMS ATTENDANT UPON JOINT ACTION

It can be assumed that neither the employer nor the union will ever undertake a cooperative program unless each expects to gain from it. In those programs initiated by unions, the motive has been the protection of jobs and work standards of union members, rather than increasing business profits. Even though the programs themselves are concerned with improving efficiency this is considered as a means toward job and union security rather than an end in itself. When the employer enters into cooperative programs it is usually a last-minute effort to stave off plant closure or bankruptcy.

Employer-union cooperation in the determination of plant policies presents unique problems in the art of management—the age-old problem of democracy translated into terms of modern industrial conditions. The entire history of unionism has been a step-by-step admission of workers into the area once held to be the sole prerogative of management. Under the simplest form of collective bargaining, wages and at least a few job rules are negotiated instead of being fixed by management alone. For some years after collective bargaining *per se* was given legal protection, many employers maintained that pension and other welfare activities when financed entirely by the employer were not subject to collective bargaining, but in 1948 the U.S. Supreme Court held that such activities were within the area of legal obligation to bargain. In several later cases the same Court held that an employer's intent to subcontract existing work is a mandatory subject for collective bargaining, and that an employer must bargain with the union before he gives individual workers merit increases; also that the union has a right to obtain full information from the employer on merit-rating increases and promotions even though the contract gives the employer control over administering the merit-rating system.

The problem of cooperative action is not simple or easy for either employers or unions. Management is charged with the duty and responsibility of obtaining maximum efficiency, and at the same time it is deprived of its sole competence over functions which it considers necessary for efficient operation. Unions are charged with the responsibility of protecting the jobs of their members and improving their conditions of work, but cooperation with management might result in lower wages and loss of jobs—at least in the short run. Management and union responsibilities are not always compatible, and when employers and unions attempt to cooperate a *modus operandi* must be worked out—one based upon a frank acceptance of these divergent interests, but also with an equally frank recognition that the ultimate well-being of all concerned, including the general public, is dependent upon efficient operation of the enterprise.

PART FIVE

OFF-THE-JOB ACTIVITIES

12

POLITICAL AND EDUCATIONAL ACTIVITIES

The major function of labor unions is to improve the job conditions of its members through collective bargaining with employers. Job conditions are also affected by government action, and collective bargaining itself is influenced by laws which define its allowable procedures and areas of operation. Beyond the government and the employers is the general public, whose opinions in the long run will decide what kinds of laws and employer-union relations will prevail.

Necessarily, then, unions must concern themselves with government affairs and with the persons to be chosen to run the government. They must also be concerned with what the general public thinks about what they are doing and, more especially, with the opinion of the great masses of workers upon whose loyalty the unions' survival depends. Organized labor's political, educational and public relations activities are vital parts of its program. Although they are constantly undergoing changes, a knowledge of their general nature and the historical reasons for their adoption is important to an understanding of unionism.

POLITICAL POLICIES

Unlike most European labor movements, organized labor in the United States has never put major reliance upon political action to attain its goals. For many years the AFL actually opposed legislation on hours and minimum wages (except for special groups such as minors and women), on the grounds that working conditions could best be improved by the organized efforts of the workers themselves through bargaining with their employers. This attitude changed somewhat during the great depression of the early 1930's when labor, like other sectors of the economy, was forced to realize that under extremely dire circumstances only a people's government could save them from utter collapse. Although organized labor during the past thirty years has actively sought the enactment of specific legislation and the election of candidates favorable to such legislation, it has never seriously considered the establishment of a labor party.

Background

From the date of its formation up until the 1940's, the American Federation of Labor followed a nonpartisan political policy of supporting its friends and opposing its enemies regardless of their party affiliations. This nonpartisanship was based on the belief that (1) partisan politics might create dissention among its members and turn their attention away from trade union matters; (2) neutrality was more effective for obtaining political concessions, since so long as no slate of candidates was automatically assured of labor's endorsement, competing candidates must bid for union members' support; (3) labor should not run the risk of identifying itself with any particular party because it would lose all its political influence whenever that party was defeated.

From its inception the CIO adopted a policy of vigorous activity in political affairs. In 1936 various CIO unions, joined by several AFL nationals, established a Labor's Non-Partisan League which campaigned for the re-election of the New Deal administration, and eight years later its Political Action Committe carried on a program which is generally conceded to have been a major influence in the election of Roosevelt for his fourth term.

The passage of the Taft-Hartley Act in 1947 caused all branches of the labor movement to reconsider their former policies with respect to political activity. Although the law placed severe restrictions on the kind of political activities unions could engage in, its initial effect was a display of intensified vigor. The AFL, taking an unprecedented step, established Labor's League for Political Education in order, as its founders stated, "to serve most effectively the interests of the workers of the nation and adequately to meet the challenge presented by predatory and vested interests" and to gain "the restoration of the rights of labor as heretofore enjoyed and the realization of a more sound and equitable labor relations policy. . . ." Railway Labor's Political League was also organized and, with the already functioning CIO Political Action Committee, the entire labor movement was galvanized into action.

Spurred by labor and liberal forces within the party, the 1948 Democratic national convention adopted a platform which unequivocally committed the party to a continuation of the New Deal philosophy. This clear-cut break with its conservative wing enabled organized labor, as never before, to look to the Democratic party as its means for political action. Its campaign hopes were dashed, however, when labor was unable to get a sufficient number of "friendly" congressmen elected to carry out the "Fair Deal" which President Truman had personally espoused.

In 1952, the first time in its seventy-one-years history,[1] an AFL convention formally endorsed a presidential candidate, namely the Democratic nominee Adlai Stevenson, who went on record as favor-

[1] Upon a few occasions AFL officials had endorsed particular presidential candidates. Samuel Gompers, first and long-time President of the AFL, actively participated in the Democratic party campaign in 1908 after he was repulsed by the Republicans in his efforts to obtain relief from the courts' use of the Sherman Anti-Trust Act and injunctions in labor disputes. He continued to support the Democratic party, although less actively, until 1924 when, in protest against the conservative platform and candidate this party had chosen, he persuaded the AFL Executive Council to endorse a new third party—the Progressive party, which also received the official support of the railroad brotherhoods in that election. Prior to this, in 1919–1922, a number of AFL state federations in the Middle West had identified themselves with the Farmer-Labor party, which was successful in a number of state and local elections.

ing the repeal of the Taft-Hartley Act. By 1960 the two branches of the labor movement were united all the way down to the local level, and union political activity was greatly intensified. The united AFL-CIO formally endorsed the Democratic national ticket, giving as its reasons the "sharp and clear" contrast between the two platforms as well as the records of the candidates.

COMMITTEE ON POLITICAL EDUCATION

The Taft-Hartley Act makes it unlawful for any labor organization (or corporation) to make a contribution or expenditure in connection with the election of any candidate for national office, including primaries, political conventions and caucuses. According to the wording of the law, direct union contributions to a political party or a nominee are unquestionably outlawed.[2] The meaning of "expenditures in connection with an election" is far from obvious, and the definitive interpretation by the courts on this point has yet to be made. The highest court has ruled that unions may use their regular periodicals to endorse candidates. Some lower courts have ruled that regular union funds may not be used to purchase radio time or advertising space in a newspaper for the purpose of promoting or defeating candidates for federal office.

Since the passage of the law AFL–CIO unions have relied solely upon individual voluntary contributions from their members, urging them to give "a buck a year." This money is used for "educational" and "get-out-the-vote" campaigns administered through the Committee on Political Education. COPE seeks to inform union members and their friends about the issues in all national, state and local elections, as well as the records of the candidates for office, and above all to get union members to the polls. This last activity is of crucial importance.

[2] When the law was passed the Republican legislators undoubtedly had in mind the half-million dollar contribution of the United Mine Workers to President Roosevelt's campaign in 1936. (See note 5, Chapter 2.) The law does not forbid donations to political committees whose activities are confined to a single state. Donors can legally contribute unlimited amounts to numerous state committees established on behalf of their preferred candidates. The Senate subcommittee on the 1956 general election campaigns found that members of twelve wealthy families contributed a total of $1,010,526 to the Republican party and its candidates and $107,109 to the Democrats.

HANDICAPS TO EFFECTIVE POLITICAL ACTION

Union members and their families comprise at least a third of the electorate of the country, and a substantial number of nonunion workers undoubtedly agree with union members on many political and legislative issues. However, organized labor has seldom been able to "deliver the vote" which its numerical strength would seem to make possible. The reasons for this are varied. Some are due to the political behavior patterns of the members themselves, but others are the results of conditions beyond the immediate control of union members.

An obvious reason is the lack of political solidarity among the membership, as well as the union leaders. Traditionally in this country, workers have not been inclined to vote according to their economic interests alone. Inherited political party loyalties frequently take precedence over other considerations on election day. Appeals based on cultural or national origins tend to dilute the voting strength of a group whose composition is as diverse as is that of organized labor in this country.

The chief handicap to labor's effective political influence is the failure or inability of many union members to vote at all.[3] This is attributable, in part, to the mobility of the working population. In their quest for new or better jobs, large numbers of workers change their places of residence each year. Legal residence requirements, the feeling of not belonging in the new community, ignorance of local political issues and candidates, all cause millions of workers to remain away from the polls at every election.

Even if workers cast ballots in proportionately equal numbers to the population at large, industrial wage earners would be politically disadvantaged because of our prevailing electoral systems which favor rural, nonindustrial areas, with the result that legislation sponsored by labor is frequently defeated by legislators who have little need to concern themselves about labor's reaction.

[3] In 1960 it was estimated that working people made up 37 per cent of the voting-age population but that they comprised only 26 per cent of those who voted. In contrast, the professional and executive group made up 18 per cent of the potential voting population but constituted 26 per cent of all those who voted.

THE LABOR PRESS

Like a democratic government, labor unions are dependent upon an informed and loyal membership for their survival and progress. With their sprawling membership of diverse cultural and educational backgrounds, unions must ever keep their members conscious of their common core of interests and the way by which their unions can best further these interests. Even though scattered over thousands of miles, members must have a sense of unity and a feeling of loyalty and confidence in their organizations and leaders. They must know the reasons for their unions' actions and policies, for no union officers can long pursue a course of action, whatever its merits, which does not have the support of the rank-and-file members.

Moreover, leadership must be developed from within the ranks of the membership if unions are to be organizations *of* workers as well as *for* workers. In the latter respect labor organizations are more like democratic political organizations than economic enterprises such as business corporations, whose managers and supervisors are hired rather than elected. Some unions employ a limited number of professional persons such as lawyers and economists as advisers, but policy and administrative functions are zealously retained by "card" members of the unions.

To meet these needs unions have always considered their educational activities to be one of their major tasks. Such activities are directed toward three major objectives: First, to keep their members informed about their unions' internal and external affairs and about general economic and political conditions which affect workers; second, to present and interpret workers' attitudes and problems to the general public; third, to provide union leaders and potential leaders with the factual and theoretical knowledge which will aid them in administering their unions' internal activities and in their dealings with employers and the public, including government agencies.

Unions have always relied upon their own publications to keep their members informed about union activities and general matters affecting workers' interests. A few of the union journals are "trade" papers in that they are confined almost entirely to the news within their own organizations. Most of them cover a much wider field, placing major emphasis on the broader interests of labor such as the progress and difficulties of the general labor movement, and the economic and political issues which affect members and workers generally. Since union papers naturally discuss matters from labor's point of view and in relation to what they consider to be in the general interest of wage earners, these papers frequently present a different interpretation and selection of news and events from that given in the daily press.

AFL-CIO PUBLICATIONS

The American Federationist, the official monthly magazine of the AFL–CIO, is a 24-to-34-page glossy-paper journal which appears on some public newsstands, since it is designed for reading by the general public as well as by union members. It describes itself as labor's journal of opinion, and contains illustrated articles on subjects directly and indirectly related to the interests of workers, including labor news from foreign countries. It also contains specific items about collective bargaining contracts recently negotiated and internal shop problems which are issues in employer-union dealings.

The *Free Trade Union News* is a monthly bulletin, published by the AFL–CIO Department of International Affairs, which contains material about labor in foreign countries and labor's role in international affairs. Also the AFL–CIO publishes a Spanish-language clipsheet, *Noticiero Obrero Norteamericano,* designed to give information about U.S. labor to Spanish-speaking members in this country and those interested in labor matters in South America.

COPE Memo is a four-page bulletin, published every two weeks by the Committee on Political Education, which deals exclusively with political campaign news and legislation affecting labor's interests. The Industrial Union Department of the AFL–CIO publishes the *IUD Digest,* a quarterly magazine which includes articles by eminent persons inside and outside the labor movement. Its special appeal is to the intellectual and liberal groups interested in labor and social problems.

In addition to the regularly published periodicals are the pamphlets issued from time to time on particular subjects. Some are designed to induce nonmembers to join the union; some are to instruct new members on union and labor matters and to encourage their continued loyalty; some are prepared especially for the use of shop stewards and organizers; many are quite exhaustive discussions of complex economic problems. Recently published titles suggest the variety of subjects covered: *Labor Looks at Automation; Your Rights Under Fair Employment Practice Laws; Progress and Productivity; Why Unions?; How To Run a Union Meeting; American and Soviet Economy—Contrast and Comparison; Federal Taxes—Problems and Solutions; 20 Ideas for Steward Meetings; Clean, Democratic Trade Unions;* and *Union Political Activity.*

Audio-visual Materials

Like many other organizations, labor unions are turning more and more to ear and eye media as educational aids. Their central offices are producing an increasing number of sound slide films, film strips, sound motion picture films and recordings, which are rented to local unions and to other groups interested in labor. The latest catalogue of films issued by the AFL–CIO Department of Education lists several hundred titles, the various films running anywhere from 10 to 45 minutes. They are classified under the general headings of "Building Unionism," "Union Training," "Civil Liberties and Civil Rights," "Farmer-Labor Cooperation," "International Problems," "Political Education," "General Welfare," and "Special Use" (the last including films prepared by individual unions dealing with their specific activities and problems).

National and Local Union Journals

The most widely distributed publications are the journals issued by the national unions. Since most unions include the subscription price as a part of their dues assessments they are received regularly by all their members. There is great variety among the various union journals in format, size, and content. Most are issued monthly although a few are issued weekly or fortnightly. Some are in the form of illustrated magazines, some are in newspaper style, while others, especially those of the smaller unions, are four- or eight-page pamphlets. A number of the craft union journals devote considerable space to the technical problems and new processes within their trades, thus serving to promote the skills of their members. To encourage family reading, most of them have sports and comic sections and columns devoted to household matters.

Almost every city and county central organization issues some kind of weekly paper for the members of those local unions affiliated with it. These papers serve as clearinghouses for their member locals, promote unified action on common problems within the community, and keep their readers informed on local labor matters. They also include items from the general labor press and thus are important media for reaching the rank-and-file members throughout the country. Most of them carry paid advertising to help cover the cost of publication. In addition to the local central organizations, some of the state federations issue weekly newspapers or monthly journals which are concerned primarily with federal and state legislation, workers' education, and the activities of their affiliated organizations.

PUBLIC RELATIONS

In spite of the extensive press activities of unions, many persons inside and outside the labor movement feel that much remains to be done by way of informing the general public concerning the policies and problems of labor organizations. Discounting deliberate partisan bias and personal prejudices, a great deal of the misunderstanding about unions is due to the simple fact of being uninformed, and organized labor faces a serious challenge in getting its story across to the public through the ordinary channels of communication—the schools, press, radio and television.

During recent years an increasing number of colleges have introduced labor courses into their curriculums, and a number of the larger universities have established departments or centers for teaching and research in employer-labor relations. At best, however, these reach only a small segment of the general population. Relatively few secondary schools offer studies on labor unions and labor problems, although most of the youth attending these schools will enter industry as wage earners and will have to face the question of their personal relation to labor unions. The omission stems largely from the composition of the teaching staffs and administrative boards of the schools. Few elementary and high-school teachers have had any opportunity or need to learn about the problems of industrial wage earners through personal experience; only a handful have acquired vicarious familiarity through the college classroom. Similarly, the boards of education which determine the kinds of courses offered and the textbooks used, are composed largely of men and women whose background and experience have given them little intimate awareness of the impact of economic forces on the great mass of industrial workers.

Newspapers and broadcasting systems, as business enterprises, are naturally attuned to the attitudes of employers, as well as economically dependent upon the good will of other business enterprises. Although radio and television advertising is ostensibly for the purpose of publicizing commodities, in the ears of the listeners it also becomes good-will propaganda for the company furnishing the program. The millions of listeners to a corporation-sponsored symphony hour unconsciously grow to feel that the company's internal affairs and employee relations must be as happy as the program is enjoyable! The "corporate image" resulting from the public's viewing of a corporation-sponsored television program is quite different from the "union image" resulting from the public's witnessing of a strike. Yet the purposes of the advertising and the strike are similar—one to improve the economic situation of the company and its stockholders and the other to improve the economic conditions of the union's members.

By the very nature of their position in the economic system, employees' efforts to obtain improvements almost always result in public inconvenience. The longtime effects of a work stoppage may be good or bad, but the public's attitude is influenced by the immediate hardships. To a large segment of the general public, unions are synonymous with work stoppages and other visible activities interfering with the smooth operation of business; their usefulness as an economic leverage is not so clearly visible or easily understood.

Some unions in the past assumed a defeatist attitude and made no attempt to "sell" themselves beyond their own actual and potential membership. Within recent years organized labor has taken a more positive stand by undertaking programs to explain its policies and problems and to counteract misrepresentation. Union leaders are showing an increased willingness to talk to groups of students and adults, and to participate in public forums. Although the AFL–CIO has no elaborate public relations program comparable to those of many large corporations and business associations, it sponsors coast-to-coast news telecasts in which the commentator presents the general news of the day in a manner similar to that of other commentators, and the "commercial" time is used to publicize labor's activities.

TRAINING FOR JOB SKILLS

Organized labor has always been vitally concerned with programs to further educational opportunities for both youth and adults. It was largely through the efforts of early workingmen's associations that a tax-supported school system was established in this country during the first half of the nineteenth century. With the general adoption of public education, organized labor has been concerned with extending its benefits to an ever-widening group. To that end it has opposed child labor and favored compulsory school attendance, and has sponsored evening classes in the public schools for employed adults. The enactment in 1917 of the Smith-Hughes Act for vocational training under a system of federal grants-in-aid to the states was a culmination of a decade's effort on the part of organized labor. During recent years labor has actively supported the general principle of providing federal support for equalizing educational opportunities throughout the country and for raising substandard levels in the poorer states and in rural areas. While labor believes that the control of education must be left to local communities, it is convinced that federal financial assistance is necessary to obtain adequate educational standards throughout the country.

In addition to supporting efforts for the improvement of the public school system, organized labor conducts, or participates in, various kinds of educational programs designed especially for its own members. These are of two general types—vocational programs for the training of apprentices and improving the skills of older workers, and so-called "workers' education" which is concerned with providing a better understanding of economics and labor problems and the development of proficiencies in the conduct of union activities.

Apprentice Training

Most of the craft unions in the metal, printing and building trades have always considered the training of apprentices one of their major functions. There are several reasons why these unions have been willing to assume this responsibility instead of relying upon the employers for the training of new workers. The unions' ability to guarantee employers a sufficient supply of competent, skilled workers has helped them in their collective bargaining; by establishing fixed training rules and procedures, the unions are able to maintain those skill and job standards which they consider of prime importance; formal apprenticeship provides a means to guide the intake of workers into the trades.

While apprentice training programs rely chiefly upon learning on the job, all formal training systems include supplementary classroom or other off-the-job instruction. In former years a number of the unions undertook classroom instruction for their apprentices but this was seldom satisfactory because of lack of equipment and competent instructors. With the development of vocational schools as a part of the public-school system, the classroom and laboratory training of apprentices has been largely taken over by the vocational schools which work in close cooperation with the local unions and employers.

To stimulate and promote apprenticeship under acceptable standards and under the safeguards and protections of formal indenture agreements, a Federal Committee on Apprentice Training composed of union, employer and government representatives, was established in 1934 to guide the work of the Federal Bureau of Apprenticeship and Training. Most of the states have established joint apprenticeship councils and many cities have joint local committees to develop and supervise the local programs, using the federal standards as a guide. Thus the unions actively participate in most of the apprentice training programs at all levels.

ADVANCED TRAINING

Owing to ever-changing processes and improvements in machinery and materials, completion of the best kind of apprentice training is no guarantee of continued competency, and those unions which have assumed the responsibility of providing skilled workmen for employers have had to face the problem of keeping the skills of their journeymen members up to date. Most commonly this has been accomplished by arrangements with individual employers whereby journeymen versed in old methods are given an opportunity to learn to operate the new machines after they are installed in the plant. In a number of instances unions have undertaken or promoted more formal programs. The Brotherhood of Electrical Workers has sponsored a program for the training of members in the operation and maintenance of electronic equipment by arrangements with the Engineering College of Marquette University. In 1951 the St. Louis Plumbers and Steamfitters' local obtained an agreement from the contractors whereby the latter contributed the equivalent of 5 per cent of their payrolls to support a school for steamfitters to learn new techniques of their trade. The printing unions provide an outstanding example of continuing programs for advanced training and technical research. The Training Center of the Typographical Union at Colorado Springs offers specialized courses for skilled craftsmen in the operation of the most modern machinery and processes in composing and mailing room work. Members taking courses at the ITU headquarters are expected to teach the new methods to other members in their own locals. The Printing Pressmen's Union owns and operates what is probably the largest technical trade school for printing in the world. This school conducts correspondence courses for apprentices and provides facilities for journeymen members who wish to qualify for better positions by learning the most modern letterpress and offset processes. The union's journal, *The American Pressman,* which is printed at the school, is a model of good printing and contains a great deal of technical information designed to improve the skill and knowledge of its readers.

WORKERS' EDUCATION PROGRAMS

"Workers' education" as commonly used is not a generic term but has a specific connotation. It is a special kind of adult education designed to give workers a better understanding of their status, problems, rights and responsibilities as workers, as union members, as consumers and as citizens. Workers' education places emphasis upon group advancement and the solution of group problems, and thus differs from vocational and professional education, which is primarily training for individual advancement.

An important phase of workers' education consists of the programs especially designed to train members for positions of leadership in their organizations. Such training requires a special type of curriculum which no institution of higher learning is offering today. The nature of the work of union leaders has changed from that of simple propagandist to that of a highly complicated and responsible profession. Union leaders must know how to interpret and utilize the studies of industrial engineers, the opinions of lawyers, the knowledge of sociologists, actuaries and economists. They must be familiar with the whole area of collective bargaining, the impact of technological changes, union intra- and extra-communication, government legislation, community activities, foreign policy and international labor affairs. They must have an understanding of organized labor's larger aims and purposes.

Content of Workers' Education

Workers' education is inextricably bound up with that of the labor movement, and as the labor movement has assumed an increasingly expanded role, workers' education has likewise broadened its approach to cover the wider interests of workers and their group activities. While it seeks to prepare organized labor to take its place in industrial society and to participate in every aspect of social and political life, it nevertheless stresses workers' actual and concrete needs as trade unionists. The hub of its program is collective bargaining—the skills needed and the milieu in which it takes place, the judicious use of collective power, its significance for workers and its relation to our democratic processes.

Specifically, the content of workers' education programs is built around a core of economics and political science, labor history and the philosophy of the labor movement, union administration, collective bargaining, and such tool subjects as parliamentary law, English, and public speaking. The subjects are not taught, however, in the customary academic manner. Instead of formal lectures, the workshop and discussion methods are used in the classroom. Whatever the title of the course, the subject is approached from the actual experience of the worker-students, being directed toward giving them a background for deeper understanding of their situation and problems, rather than merely extending their knowledge.

Increasingly, workers' education programs have become more functional, built around an interpretation of specialized problems or "burning issues," and closely interrelated with programs for action. A study of labor legislation, for instance, will be focused on the specific effects of pending or recently enacted legislation and what organized labor should do about it. A course on race relations will deal with the realities of race discrimination in the shop and how prejudices can be dealt with on the job and in the immediate community. The study of collective bargaining will begin with a particular industry and union situation and from there proceed to the study of wage theories and general economic principles. All programs are extremely fluid, being continuously adapted to the particular group's needs at any given time.

GROUPS SERVED

Workers' education programs are designed for both rank-and-file members and for union leaders or potential leaders. For members generally, it serves the twofold purpose of increasing their bonds of loyalty to the union and helping to make them intelligent, informed trade unionists. After a union is well established, the enthusiasm incident to getting recognized is likely to wane and the rank-and-file member tends to accept his union as his "hired agent" for getting him better wages and coming to his aid when he is in difficulty with his employer. The mere act of attending classes in the union hall, or elsewhere under the aegis of the union, brings members closer to their union and strengthens ties of group loyalty.

Sustained loyalty is dependent upon more than emotional enthusiasm, and it is the purpose of workers' educational programs to give members an understanding of the history of the labor union movement, of the unions' present legal and economic status, and a close understanding of the member's own union. This is especially important for younger persons now entering industry, who have not personally experienced the struggles of getting organized in the face of overwhelming difficulties. A few unions require all new members to take "orientation" courses, on the theory that just as one cannot be a good and loyal citizen without knowing something of the history and ideals of one's country, so one cannot be a good trade-union member without knowing something of the history, ideals and struggles of the labor movement.

Major emphasis is directed toward union leaders—leaders at all levels from shop stewards, local officers and staffs on up to the national organizers. There are programs built around the immediate problems of shop stewards and committeemen whose major responsibilities have to do with handling employee grievances, job evaluation, work loads and plant rules. For union officers and staff there are courses of study in the techniques of collective bargaining, on how to conduct union meetings and make them more interesting, on how to improve union bookkeeping and on newswriting and reporting. Other programs deal with such matters as economics, the operations of the industries in which the unions function, and national and international affairs.

Sponsorship of Programs

Workers' education is sponsored by various groups and is conducted in many different ways. Most of the programs are developed by the unions themselves, although many utilize the services of outside instructors. At least thirty national unions, as well as many of the state federations and a few of the larger locals, have full-time directors of education. The AFL–CIO Department of Education, with headquarters in Washington, helps to promote and guide the programs, especially through furnishing the necessary teaching materials and instructional staff.

The programs that reach the largest number of members are the evening courses held at union headquarters or in the classrooms of local colleges and universities. The United Automobile Workers have recently established an educational center in Detroit for their leaders and staff representatives; the Ladies' Garment Workers and the paper industry unions have conducted evening and weekend programs for their national and local officers, as have many locals of other national unions.

Some workers' education programs are sponsored jointly by numbers of state federations—for example, the eleven-state Southern Labor School and the eight-state Rocky Mountain School. These schools conduct each year a number of institutes, lasting from two to five days, in various strategic cities in their areas. Some are advanced institutes for state and city central body officers; others are designed for local union officers. The courses offered at a recent advanced institute of the Southern Labor School are typical: Southern Economic and Social Problems; Problems of Unemployment; Relations of State and Local Central Bodies with National Legislation; Higher Education in the South; Labor's Image in the Schools; Problems of Local Central Bodies; and Social Welfare.

UNIVERSITY PARTICIPATION

An outstanding development in workers' education has been the programs conducted through the extension divisions of a number of the state universities. These programs reflect the new status that labor has come to occupy, and the new recognition by tax-supported universities of their responsibilities to serve all groups in the community. State universities in this country traditionally have been concerned with providing educational services to businessmen and farmers to aid in the solution of their individual and collective problems. Although the purpose of a School for Workers may be considered parallel to that of a School of Agriculture or a School of Commerce, recognition of the similarity has come only recently.[4] Currently, more than twenty universities throughout the country have full-time staffs and year-round service for labor groups, and

[4] The Pioneer was the University of Wisconsin, where a Summer School for Women Workers was started in 1925 and became coeducational in 1928. The earliest extension service in workers' education was inaugurated in 1931 at Rutgers University in New Jersey.

many other colleges and universities render limited services such as occasional evening classes and one- or two-day institutes.

Several universities conduct resident summer schools consisting of one- or two-week sessions for each group. Those attending live in the college dormitories, enjoy the recreational and cultural facilities of the campus, and have the opportunity for informal "bull sessions" among themselves and with the faculty. Each summer institute is planned in cooperation with a particular union, or with several unions whose members are interested in the same problems. Teaching staffs are drawn both from the universities' regular faculties and from the outside. Tuition charges are moderate, and some unions provide scholarships to enable their members to attend.

University cooperation is not limited to summer schools and evening classes. For example, the Communications Workers recently launched a leadership training program beginning with ten weeks of intensive study at the University of Chicago, including courses in anthropology, sociology, psychology, economics, labor law and history, accounting and political science. This university session is followed by another fourteen weeks at the union headquarters in Washington, working alongside experienced staff people in organizing projects and with collective bargaining problems.

To meet the needs of the labor movement for staffs well grounded in traditional social science subjects, the National Institute of Labor Education, with financial help from the Fund for Adult Education, sponsored three ten-week residential study institutes during the summers of 1961 and 1962. They were held at the University of California (Berkeley), Cornell University and Michigan State University, and the program centered around four core subjects: Economic Problems of the 1960's; American Government and Politics; Man and Society; and History and Philosophy of the American Labor Movement. The program was supplemented by seminars and evening sessions on such subjects as Trade Unions and the Public Interest; The Defense of a Free Society; Civil Liberties and Civil Order; The Organization of Business and Industry; The Welfare State; Government Regulation of Unions; The Impact of Improved Technology.

13

WELFARE PROGRAMS

Unions are interested in all matters that affect the well-being and economic security of their members. High on the list of such activities have been health and old-age insurance programs. Others have been directed toward furnishing members with better housing, recreational and credit facilities. Some activities which were actively sponsored at one time have been discontinued because of disappearing need; others have been abandoned because of lack of success. Among the latter are the producers' cooperatives and banking enterprises.

COOPERATIVE ACTIVITIES

Producers' Cooperatives

When workers first began to organize, in the middle of the nineteenth century, many of them considered trade unions to be merely a first step on the road toward self-employment through cooperative or worker-controlled factories and other producing activities. The Knights of Labor was founded upon the ideal of a society composed of cooperative enterprises in which there would be no hired labor, but in which producing units would be owned and managed by those engaged in them—industrial workers, farmers, clerks and technicians.

The failure of the Knights of Labor experiments and the conviction that such ambitions not only were futile but were diverting the energies of organized workers from more practical and near-at-hand achievements were major factors in the establishment of the American Federation of Labor. By the turn of the twentieth century the American labor movement had formally renounced the principle of an industrial society composed of self-governing or cooperative workshops. However, a number of unions upon particular occasions have taken over bankrupt and other businesses and managed them on a cooperative basis. As late as 1937 there were at least twenty-seven such producers' cooperatives—chiefly small print shops and laundries and plants engaged in making cigar, clothing and shoes—which had been taken over by unions for the practical and immediate purpose of providing jobs to members who were left stranded after private owners had gone bankrupt or had locked them out during a labor dispute. Practically all of these ventures have been abandoned during recent years.

Labor Banking

Years after most labor unions had abandoned any aspirations they might have had for widespread, cooperatively owned manufacturing enterprises, a number of them enthusiastically embarked on banking and other financial ventures. While there had been some discussion for a number of years at AFL and various union conventions concerning the question of labor-owned-and-operated banks, it was not until the antiunion campaigns following World War I that any such banks were actually established.

In 1920 the Association of Machinists took over a majority of the stock of a bank in Washington, D.C., and the Locomotive Engineers initiated their ambitious investment and banking program by founding a bank in Cleveland, Ohio.[1] Union after union followed, some by purchasing the controlling interest in already established banks and others by founding entirely new banks. In 1926, which saw the peak of union banking activities, various national and local unions, state federations and city centrals owned thirty-six banks with total

[1] During the following six years the Locomotive Engineers owned and controlled fourteen banks, a holding company, an investment company, six security corporations, a realty and mortgage company, an insurance company and several "thrift" companies, besides having an interest in a Wall Street bank and another in Florida. They also started a real estate development in Florida covering 50,000 acres, and including three hotels. All these enterprises had failed or been abandoned by 1930 at a great loss to the union and individual members.

resources of over $126 million. A few years later most of these were liquidated. Currently there are two labor banks in operation, both owned by the Amalgamated Clothing Workers.

The motives for embarking on these banking activities were varied: to provide a means for investing union funds; to pay higher interest rates to member depositors and make more generous loans to member borrowers than commercial banks were making; to protect the labor movement by withdrawing the funds of unions and their members from banks which were participating in antiunion campaigns; and to render financial assistance through loans to "fair" employers and others who were friendly toward organized labor.

The reasons for their failure were equally varied: selection of persons to run the banks who had had too limited banking experience; interference of union officials who served on the boards of directors; losses from character loans to members who frequently considered they had a right to obtain loans upon the asking; skepticism and indifference of rank-and-file members who refused to deposit their savings in their union banks. Also, a number of the unions were finding that their banking enterprises were causing disruption and factional disputes between unions: In order to protect their investments, some of the banks had faced the embarrassing situation of having to cooperate with and even take over nonunion businesses, thus finding themselves competing with concerns paying union wages.

Unions generally have concluded that their banking adventures were a mistake. A typical comment upon final liquidation was that of the Railway Clerks: "We learned the lesson at not too great a cost, that the proper business of a labor union is to promote the welfare of working people through processes of collective bargaining."

CONSUMERS' COOPERATIVES

Although consumers' cooperatives in this country have never had as wide an appeal as they have had in Great Britain, Sweden and some other countries, the American labor movement has endorsed the principle of such undertakings and some unions have been actively engaged in them. First among the reasons for such participation, of course, is the desire to make wages go further through the lower prices made possible through cooperative enterprises. Beyond this purely economic motive is the belief shared by all "cooperators" that the cooperative movement is a force for democracy and a salutary competitor to monopolies and big business.

While some union members belong to consumers' cooperatives and serve on their boards of directors, few cooperatives in this country are confined to union members. The predominant attitude of union leaders is that cooperatives should not be restricted to union members; that one of the important benefits to be derived from such activities is the opportunity they offer for union members to mix with other groups in a common endeavor to serve the entire community.

Cooperative Housing

Several unions during recent years have embarked upon cooperative housing projects. Although the primary purpose is to provide modern housing at the lowest possible cost to their members, a second motive is the opportunity for investment of union funds. Unions whose members are concentrated in a few urban centers are most inclined to sponsor cooperative housing projects. Thus the Amalgamated Clothing Workers is sponsor of four projects in the Greater New York City area, and the Ladies Garment Workers Union is sponsor of the huge Cooperative Village on the east side of New York City—all of these being apartment houses. Quite different are the single-family dwellings of Sunnyhills in Milpitas, California, sponsored by the United Automobile Workers. In line with the anti-discrimination policy of the UAW these homes are sold to and occupied by both Negro and white families.

These union-sponsored housing companies are cooperative organizations; the union lends its name and occasionally acts as a financial guarantor but it does not own any stock. Control and ownership rest entirely with the tenant-cooperators and each tenant-member has one vote regardless of the number of shares of stock owned or size of unit occupied. Membership is limited, so far as is possible, to wage earners and families of moderate income, but is not confined to the union's own members. The "open membership" principle is maintained for two reasons: first, because there is less financial risk when the investors are not limited to persons engaged in a single industry; and second, a broader and more interesting social life is afforded when the tenants are employed in a variety of occupations.

COMMUNITY SERVICE ACTIVITIES

One of the most significant aspects of labor's new status is the quiet change that has taken place with respect to labor's participation in local community services. In earlier days the labor movement remained aloof from social welfare activities, considering them a form of charity whereby the well-to-do, in a paternalistic manner, soothed their consciences by "helping the deserving poor." The aloofness was mutual, since community service agencies did not feel it necessary or desirable to have labor participation, and if labor had sought to participate most local boards and staffs would probably have objected. Workers were asked for contributions through their employers, but the policies and programs of the services were determined by the large donors and their paid staffs.

The change has taken form in two concrete ways: the method by which workers' financial contributions are made, and worker representation on community service boards. In the past, fund-raising among workers was largely a "shakedown" affair whereby a foreman brought pressure upon the workers to make donations which were then announced as coming from the company. Today the unions conduct the fund-raising drives in the plants and share the credit for the money raised.

On the Community Fund staffs of most of the cities there are now one or more union persons helping on the fund-raising and the planning of the programs. Throughout the country there are thousands of union members serving on the local boards of the various agencies—the Scouts, the family service and public assistance agencies, the Red Cross, and many others.

Union cooperation in community services has many by-products for both union members and the community. It provides an opportunity, in some places the sole opportunity, for union members and citizens from other walks of life to learn to know each other and to discuss matters outside the controversial area of employer-employee relations. Through the mutual exchange of viewpoints, the needs and attitudes of the recipients of community services can be presented first-hand so that programs are no longer planned unilaterally by the "substantial" donors on their preconceived notions of what is good for the recipients. For the union member who hitherto has felt isolated from the mainstream of community life, participation in the programs affords him the broadening experience of learning about his community and the social and economic problems of groups outside his own work place.

UNION-FINANCED BENEFIT PROGRAMS

Many of the early trade unions established in the latter part of the nineteenth century were expressly organized for the purpose of providing various types of benefits for their members, as well as for collective bargaining purposes. In the absence of any governmental social insurance, or even any group insurance plans which later were provided by private insurance companies, it was natural for workers to seek some arrangements which would provide a modicum of financial assistance against those inevitable contingencies which result in loss of wages and hardship to their families. Until the passage of social security legislation, union organizers frequently found that the benefit features of their unions were their best selling points when seeking to extend membership.

Organized labor actively participated in the promotion of federal and state pensions and unemployment insurance programs, and since the enactment of the Railroad Retirement Act and the Federal Social Security Act in 1935, labor has sought to have these acts liberalized and expanded to cover additional groups of workers and types of benefits. During recent years an increasing number of unions have succeeded in having disability and retirement benefit plans included in their contracts with employers. Despite these outside programs, some of the older unions continue the benefit activities which they assumed many years ago; in most cases this means supplementary income to their members in addition to social security and employer-financed plans.

DEATH BENEFITS

A popular form of union benefit activity is the death allotment made directly from the union treasury. Most commonly this is a lump sum payment of $100 or $200 which is primarily intended for burial expenses. In some cases the allotments are more generous, and a few unions provide additional allotments of several hundred dollars for the immediate assistance of the dependents of deceased members. Instead of direct death allotments, or supplementary to them, a number of unions provide group insurance, usually covering life and permanent disability. Many of these policies are written by the Union Labor Life Insurance Company which was established in 1925 by the American Federation of Labor. It is probable that the various unions through their treasuries and through their group insurance policies distribute considerably more than $20 million a year in death benefits.

OLD AGE AND DISABILITY BENEFITS

Benefit and insurance programs of the national and local unions are financed either through the per capita tax (regular dues) or by special assessments. Those which maintain costly benefit programs usually specify in their constitutions the exact portion of the per capita tax that is to be used for benefit purposes, and keep these funds separate from their general administration funds. The benefit programs of several unions cover only a portion of their members, usually the skilled craftsmen whose dues are much higher than those of nonbeneficial members.

Beneficial members of the Carpenters' Union who have had thirty years' continuous membership in the Brotherhood, are sixty-five years of age and unable to provide for themselves, receive a monthly pension. The Bricklayers' old-age relief system provides payments to members of twenty or more years' standing who have reached the age of sixty-five. Members of the Bridge and Structural Iron Workers' Union who have been engaged in structural work for at least twenty-five years, are covered by a pension program after reaching the age of sixty-five. The Brotherhood of Electrical Workers maintains a pension program for its Class A members who have been members for at least twenty years.

The Brotherhood of Railroad Trainmen, through its Insurance Department, provides sickness, accident, disability and death benefits, as well as medical care for tubercular members. The Pressmen's Union pays weekly benefits to its incapacitated members who have been in good standing for at least twenty years. Any member with twenty-five years' membership in the Typographical Union is entitled to an old-age pension upon reaching the age of sixty. Should a member at any time in his career become incapacitated he is eligible to enter the Printers' Home[2] for treatment and rehabilitation. Also he may enter the Home upon retirement and live there for as long as he chooses, with no charge.

The weekly cash benefits provided by union-financed programs are moderate, most not more than $10 a week. An exception is the Typographical Union's pension, which pays $22 a week and is financed by a 2½ per cent assessment on members' wages.

BENEFITS PROVIDED BY COLLECTIVE BARGAINING

So-called "fringe benefits" have become a major issue in collective bargaining, frequently superseding wages as a point of contention and cause for industrial disputes. For the most part, union demands for fringe benefits in their collective agreements are a countermove prompted by their inability to have the government social security programs liberalized and extended. Whatever their particular form, fringe benefits consist of monetary payments other than direct pay for work performed.

Traditionally, wage earners have been remunerated only for time actually spent on the job. Most generally the rate of pay is on an hourly basis, as distinguished from a weekly or monthly salary, so that even a few moments or hours of lost time is reflected in take-home pay. Likewise, wage-earners' pay has customarily made no provision for extended absences from the job, whether as a result

[2] In Colorado Springs the International Typographical Union maintains on spacious grounds a complex of buildings which include the union's national headquarters building, a training center, a home for the aged and a modern hospital and tuberculosis sanatorium.

of layoffs, of an employee's inability to work owing to sickness or old age, or the desire or need for a vacation from the job.

PAY DURING SLACK WORK PERIODS

One of the first demands made by unions after they became effective bargaining agents was for remuneration for short periods of time lost through no fault of the employees. Most union contracts, for example, now require payment of wages for a specified number of hours ("call pay") to an employee who reports for work at the usual time and finds he has no work to do. Some unions have been able to obtain pay for more extended periods of unemployment. The current Automobile Workers' agreements provide that in a scheduled short work week, employees are to receive 65 per cent of their regular wages for the difference between forty and the hours actually worked. For time lost during unscheduled shortened work weeks resulting from mechanical difficulties, stock shortages, and the like, employees are paid at 50 per cent of the regular wage. In cases of permanent layoff, severance pay up to a maximum of 1,500 hours' wages is provided, the individual amount varying according to length of service with the company. Most of the agreements negotiated by the Steelworkers' and the Aluminum Workers' unions provide that if work is once started in any week, workers shall be guaranteed thirty-two hours' pay at regular wages.

Supplemental Unemployment Benefits[3] plans, which were first negotiated by the Automobile and Steelworkers' unions in 1955, have been extended to other industries, although they have not yet become widespread. Most of the SUB plans now in effect provide a maximum of around $40 a week for fifty-two weeks, with individual payments varying according to an employee's earned credits, his seniority and, in some instances, the number of his dependents. The 1962 Steelworkers' agreements provide a maximum of $43.50 a week while state benefits are paid, and $66 a week thereafter.

[3] They are called Supplementary Unemployment Benefits (SUB) because payments are in addition or supplemental to those provided under state unemployment compensation programs. However, some states have ruled that government payments are not due so long as workers receive payments from company programs which amount to as much as, or more than, they would be entitled to under unemployment compensation.

Paid Sick Leave

Only a small proportion of the workers in the United States receive compensation when absent from work because of sickness. Several states (Rhode Island, California, New Jersey and New York) have laws making provision for weekly benefits to employees unable to work because of sickness, on terms similar to those states' unemployment compensation programs. In 1947 sickness benefits were incorporated in the Railroad Unemployment Insurance Act, with payments on the same basis as for unemployment due to lack of work.

About 20 per cent of all employees covered by union contracts now receive pay for a limited number of days—anywhere from two to twenty a year—if absent from work because of sickness. Some of the agreements provide for full pay, some for half pay; and the majority require at least one year's service before becoming eligible for sick leave reimbursement.

Paid Leisure Time

Traditionally, the American economy has been oriented toward work more than toward leisure. Gradually, a productive economy and a changing climate of public opinion have made more leisure time possible, although until the middle of the 1930's the right to annual vacations and to the observance of national holidays with no loss of income was an almost exclusive privilege of managers and supervisors and some other white-collar workers. Even though most factories and other business establishments closed down on holidays, wage earners were compelled to take this time off with loss of pay. The taking of an annual vacation, stimulated by the widespread use of automobiles, had become a national custom some years before wage-earners' vacations ceased to be payless.

One of the major objectives of unions after they gained widespread recognition was to obtain paid vacations for production workers. The obvious fairness of their demands impelled most employers to grant the unions' demands with comparatively mild resistance. Workers have probably never gained any other benefit of comparable proportion so quickly and peacefully or with less government assistance. At present more than 90 per cent of all workers covered by collective agreements are eligible for paid vacations and a substantial number are entitled to as much as three or four weeks' paid vacation after specified lengths of service.

Unions had been able to negotiate a few agreements providing for paid national and religious holidays during the 1930's, but they

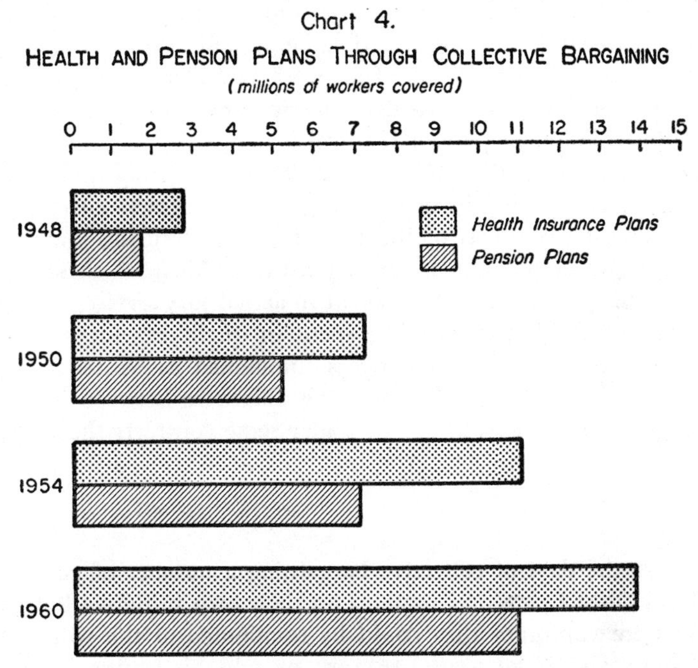

SOURCE: *Monthly Labor Review*, U.S. Department of Labor, March, 1962

One of the outstanding postwar developments in industrial relations has been the growth of collectively bargained health insurance and pension plans. By 1960 health insurance plans covered 80 per cent, and pension plans 60 per cent, of all workers employed under union contracts.

were greatly aided during World War II when the National War Labor Board frequently granted paid holidays in lieu of wage increases. Thereafter unions sought to extend the practice, and to increase the number of days for which pay is granted. Almost all employees now working under union contracts are paid for at least six holidays a year; three-fourths of such employees are entitled to seven or more paid holidays. Holidays immediately preceding Christmas and New Year's have become increasingly popular, and the Friday after Thanksgiving has become a recognized holiday in some agreements.

Paid Leave for Non-leisure Purposes

An increasing number of employer-union contracts provide leave with pay to employees who lose time because of death in the family. At present, about one-fourth of all workers under contracts receive some pay for death leave, usually a maximum of three days although some provide longer periods if travel is necessary.

Pay leave for civic duties, such as time for voting and serving on juries, is specified in nearly half of the contracts currently in force—almost two-thirds of the total in manufacturing and about one-third in nonmanufacturing agreements. Most of these agreements limit paid leave to time spent in actual jury service, although some also provide pay for time spent in qualifying for jury duty and some grant pay to employees summoned as witnesses. Most commonly, the employees receive the difference between jury fees and their regular pay, although under some contracts the jury fee is not deducted.

Pensions

Before the days of collective bargaining a number of employers had established pension programs on their own initiative but since these were voluntary they could be terminated at the will of the employer, and if he went bankrupt or sold his business the employees had no legal claim to pension rights. The termination of such a plan meant not only that the present employees were deprived of the prospect of old-age benefits but that monthly payments ceased abruptly for those already on the pension rolls. Although most of these private plans became a casualty of the great depression of the 1930's, some were later incorporated, with modifications, into union-negotiated plans.

For many reasons organized labor had never looked with favor upon private pension plans (almost all of them were in nonunion plants), and welcomed the government social security program when it was established in 1935. However, social security pensions, although they have been liberalized from time to time, have never been sufficient to cover the costs of even a modest standard of living, and when organized labor during the post-World War II era tried and failed to obtain more adequate social security legislation, unions immediately made pensions and other welfare plans a dominant issue in collective bargaining. The struggle was crucial, and the results had far-reaching effects upon all workers, both members and nonmembers of unions. It raised the sights on what should be considered reasonably adequate old-age benefits and it decisively turned the tide against old-age assistance based on a means test, a system that had been gaining support in Congress and elsewhere as an alternative to an extension of insurance programs.

Within a little more than a decade after the start of their drive, unions were able to have pension programs included in almost 80 per cent of their agreements in manufacturing industries and in about half in nonmanufacturing industries.[4] At first most of the plans provided for joint financing by the employers and employees; but employee contributions have gradually been eliminated and at present at least three-fourths of the plans are financed entirely by employers. In large companies the programs cover the single employer and are usually administered by the employer in accordance with the terms of the negotiated agreement. In industries characterized by intermittent, seasonal or casual employment, or by many small employers within a locality, the plans are usually multi-employer and administered by joint boards of representatives of the employers and the union.[5]

[4] The railroad unions do not seek negotiated pension plans but rely upon the Federal Railroad Employees Retirement Insurance program, which is more generous than the social security program. Also government workers are covered by government sponsored plans rather than union negotiated arrangements.

[5] The Labor-Management Relations and the Welfare and Pension Plans Disclosure Acts permit employers to make payments to union-established trust funds, provided that the basis on which payments are to be made is specified in the agreement, that employees and employers are equally represented on the administrative board and that there is provision for a neutral person to resolve any deadlock between the partisan representatives. Employer contributions must be made to a trust fund which provides that the funds shall not be used for any other purpose. Administrators are required to report the names of each person performing the specified administrative functions, including maintaining of records, determining eligibility, processing claims, and determining investment policy.

Through the years benefit formulas have been liberalized, and most of the plans now include provisions for disability and voluntary retirement before the normal age of sixty-five. Usually the benefits are reduced in the event of early voluntary retirement, but many provide for full benefits when early retirement is made necessary because of permanent disability. To encourage early retirement, the 1962 Steelworkers' agreements provide for a 10 per cent reduction in retirement credits for every quarter of a year's work after age sixty-five. The formulas for computing individual benefits vary: some are based on both earnings and length of service; some are geared to credited service only; and in some, for example in the mining, water transportation and clothing industries, the benefits are uniform for all retired persons who have met minimum service requirements.

Under the earliest of the negotiated plans, employees lost their pension rights whenever they changed jobs, although some latitude for changing jobs within the industry was provided under multi-employer plans. To overcome this weakness, at least three-fourths of all plans negotiated during recent years include vesting provisions —that is, a guarantee to the worker of a right or equity, based on all or a part of the employer's contribution made in his behalf, should his employment be terminated before he attains eligibility for retirement benefits.

The benefits specified in many of the early plans included payments under Social Security—that is, the company plans paid the difference between the individual's government pension and the amount specified in the agreement. Most pension programs now being negotiated, however, are independent of Social Security, which means that those retiring receive any increases which might be provided by changes in the Social Security law. The amount of the benefits provided under the various negotiated plans varies greatly, ranging from $10 a month to more than $150. On the average, the monthly payments of employees with thirty years' service amounts to from $75 to $85 a month, exclusive of Social Security.

Death and Survivors' Benefits

Under a majority of the negotiated plans now in effect, pension payments stop upon the death of the pensioner, although some specify that if the worker dies before receiving a guaranteed number of payments, the remaining payments are to be given his widow. Continued payments for retirees' survivors are becoming more common. For example, the 1961 Automobile Workers' agreements provide for survivor benefits equal to 45 per cent of the basic benefits.

Most agreements provide for separate group life insurance policies, most commonly for $1,000, with convertibility privileges upon retirement. Upon death, many pension plans also provide for lump sum payments to the worker's beneficiary.

MEDICAL BENEFITS

The high cost of sickness is a major concern of workers as it is of everyone else. In the absence of government health insurance, unions have sought and obtained health insurance through collective bargaining. At present at least 80 per cent of all workers employed under union contracts are covered by sickness insurance of more or less adequacy. A large majority are financed entirely by the employers for coverage of active workers, but many plans provide joint financing for dependents and retired workers.

The most prevalent feature of all the negotiated sickness insurance programs is the payment of fixed amounts per day for hospital care, including specified fees for various types of surgery. Many of the plans allow payments to doctors on hospital calls only, although an increasing number provide for a limited number of out-of-hospital visits from doctors. Almost all plans limit payments to specified maximums for single disability periods or during twelve-month periods. The maximums range from a total of $100 to $2,500; almost half have maximums of from $200 to $500. Payments usually begin with the first day of treatment in accident cases, and with the fourth of fifth day in cases of illness.

Two health and welfare programs will be described here to illustrate the variety of activities included in an increasing number of the programs now being negotiated. In the coal mining industry there are two separate funds, one for the anthracite and one for the bituminous coal miners. In the men's clothing industry there are separate programs for each branch of the industry (suits and coats, cotton garments, neckware, etc.) with varying amounts of benefits.

Coal Miners' Welfare and Retirement Program

Because coal mining is extremely hazardous and also because it is performed in isolated communities, distant from normal medical facilities, special medical arrangements for miners and their families have always been necessary. The customary arrangement was for coal companies to employ "company" doctors and maintain first-aid centers. However, the costs of these medical services were not borne by the company alone; there was a forced checkoff of miners' wages to pay for a portion, and in some cases all of the expenses, even though the miners had no voice in the selection of the doctors or administration of the programs.

This compulsory checkoff for company-managed medical services was always a major grievance of the miners, but it was not until 1946 that a change was effected. According to the contract negotiated that year by the United Mine Workers, a Welfare and Retirement Fund was established for the payment of disability, retirement and death benefits, financed by a 5-cent levy on each ton of coal produced. This levy was gradually raised to 40 cents per ton of bituminous coal and 70 cents per ton of anthracite. Benefits include retirement pensions, disability grants, death benefits, hospital and medical care.

One of the unique features of the program consists of the preventive and rehabilitation medical services. From the Anthracite Welfare Fund a substantial grant was made to the Jefferson Medical College in Philadelphia for a five-year program of research and treatment of silicosis and other occupational diseases. Miners disabled as a result of accidents are being sent to the Institute of Rehabilitation of the New York University Medical Center. Other disabled miners are being sent to California rehabilitation centers at the Fund's expense.[6] The hospital and medical program is carried out through ten regional offices strategically located in the coal mining areas. Physicians and hospitals are cooperating to provide

[6] When the Fund was started, the medical staff reported that more than 400 miners were paralyzed from the waist down as a result of mine accidents that had literally broken them in two and severed their spinal cords. Many of these men had lain in hill cabins or in small mining camps without medical care for more than twenty-five years. (Report of United Mine Workers Welfare and Retirement Fund, May 1, 1949.)

high standards of medical and hospital care at costs as reasonable as is possible under any system for care of comparable quality.

Even though the coal levies have been increased, the Fund has not been able to maintain the level of benefits originally conceived. In 1961, for instance, total receipts from royalties and income from Fund investments amounted to almost $117 million, while the expenditures were over $133 million. It was necessary in 1958 to reduce the pensions of the anthracite workers from $100 per month to $50 and in 1961 to reduce the pensions of bituminous miners to $75. Hospital benefits are no longer provided to miners after one year of unemployment, and the eligibility requirements for all hospital and medical care have had to be tightened.

AMALGAMATED CLOTHING WORKERS

Amalgamated's social insurance program is financed by employer contributions based on a stated percentage of payrolls and is administered jointly by employers and the union. Because of the mobility of the workers from shop to shop, the program is on an industry-wide basis: that is, each fund's share is prorated for members who move from one branch of the industry to another.

Life insurance payments under the various funds range from $500 to $5,000. Some of the disability benefits are a fixed $27 per week; others specify one-half of the weekly wage with a minimum of $20 or $26. Maximum periods of coverage range from thirteen to twenty-six weeks for sickness plus an equal number of weeks' benefits for accidents in any twelve-month period. Hospital payments range from $9 to $24 a day for periods of from thirty-one to sixty days lost owing to sickness, plus an equal number of days lost owing to accidents. Maximum surgical costs allowed under the various funds range from $200 to $300, and most of the funds provide coverage for hospital care of dependents. Amalgamated's retirement pensions range from $27 to $50 a month for members with at least twenty years' employment in the industry who are sixty-five years of age, although many of the funds allow optional retirement at sixty-two.

Joint boards of the Amalgamated Clothing workers have established medical centers in New York, Philadelphia and Chicago which are almost entirely financed by the welfare funds established under their contracts. Participating members pay a nominal annual fee for which they and their wives receive free preventive and remedial medical and dental services, including X-rays, and prescription medicines at cost. The Sidney Hillman Center in New York provides retired members with facilities for the pursuit of individual hobbies as well as for group recreation.

14

INTERNATIONAL ACTIVITIES

Organized workers of every country have always felt the need for establishing common bonds with workers' organizations in other lands. Throughout the years, this consciousness of similar needs and common problems has found expression in various kinds of movements. The forms of coordinated action which have been pursued at various times have been motivated by different goals, and even where there has been agreement as to final goal there have been sharp divisions as to methods for attaining the ultimate goal. Of utmost significance is the fact that at all times the associated efforts of workers' groups have been colored, and upon occasion decisively influenced, by the political situation within and among their governments.

The impetus for international coordinated action by workers has been the same as for organized action on the national level, namely, the insecurities resulting from competitive trade and the desire of workers to procure a greater share of the benefits from technological advancement. International labor movements[1] are, in one sense, a natural concomitant to international trade. When workers of one country have been able to obtain better wages and hours only to find their achievement is a Pyrrhic victory because of competition from low-wage foreign countries, they are forced to realize that no

[1] In this chapter the term "international" refers to movements and organizations embracing labor unions of most or all continents. As has been indicated, although many American unions have "International" attached to their names, this simply means that they have members in Canada, and possibly Puerto Rico and the Canal Zone, as well as the United States.

one group can advance far beyond all others. Inevitably there is a desire to join hands for mutual protection and advancement. Similarly, industrial workers everywhere have found a common cause in the unemployment and other insecurities arising from our competitive economic life. Cyclical depressions are world-wide, and in their search for remedies workers have felt the need for international cooperation.

FOREIGN RELATIONS OF THE AFL

Leaders of the American Federation of Labor were always convinced of the desirability of an international organization of all trade unions, but they looked askance at the socialistic tendencies prevalent among many of the European labor movements during the early twentieth century. As early as 1893, Samuel Gompers sought to enlist the British trade unions into forming an international movement which would be entirely distinct from the socialists' so-called Second International.[2] The effort failed, although the practice was established of carrying on mutual correspondence and exchange of fraternal delegates between Great Britain and this country.

When World War I broke out, all formal international labor organizations were dissolved although ties were never completely severed. Within a month after the signing of the Peace Treaty at Versailles an international congress of trade unions was attended by delegates from fourteen countries, including Gompers and others from the AFL. After stormy sessions over the question of war guilt and discussions of organizational structure, a constitution was finally adopted and the International Federation of Trade Unions was established, with headquarters in Amsterdam.

Even though the IFTU debarred all organizations which had

[2] Karl Marx was a leader of the First International (1864–1876). Although he toned down the expressions in his Communist Manifesto in order to persuade diverse groups to unite, internal dissension over Marxist policies caused the organization to dissolve. The Second International (1889–1914), composed of the dominant labor movements of western Europe, was largely socialistic but purged of Marx's revolutionary doctrines. It collapsed at the outbreak of World War I. The Third International, called the Comintern, was organized in Moscow in 1919. The Soviet authorities dissolved the Comintern in 1943 in return for military aid and as a gesture to Western public opinion.

affiliations with the Moscow-controlled Third International (Comintern), it was dominated by its socialist members. Because of this, and of the fear that the new organization was destroying the autonomy of its constituent national organizations, the AFL withdrew in 1921. During subsequent years there were repeated efforts toward reconciliation, but the American labor movement followed the general isolationist tendencies of our government during the 1920's, drifting away from European affairs but seeking to build up closer relations with labor in Latin America.[3] With the spread of Fascism and Communism during the 1930's the American Federation of Labor was more inclined to be sympathetic with the middle course which the IFTU was trying to pursue, and in 1937 it reaffiliated. Active participation was just getting under way when World War II broke out, and the International Federation of Trade Unions, the first cooperative association of free trade unions throughout the world, became a casualty of war.

WORLD WAR II AFTERMATH

A year before the end of World War II the American Federation of Labor took steps to revive the International Federation of Trade Unions, including the offer of a substantial fund to help finance its rebuilding. The British Trade Union Congress, the most influential labor movement in international circles, had other plans. The British took the position that the "unity built up in the

[3] Early in the 1920's Samuel Gompers was instrumental in organizing the Pan-American Federation of Labor, which actually was a Mexican-American cooperative endeavor. But the AFL found it difficult to overcome South American hostility resulting from the United States "dollar diplomacy." Also the growing radicalism of Mexican labor, as well as differences over Mexican immigration into this country which the AFL wanted to restrict, caused the AFL to lose interest in its inter-American connections and the Pan-American Federation ceased to exist within a few years. During the 1930's the AFL attempted to renew relations, especially with the Confederacion Regional Obrera Mexicana (CROM), but by that time the bulk of Mexican organized workers had become affiliated with the more radical Confederacion de Trabajadores de Mexico (CTM), organized by Lombardo Toledano. In 1948 Toledano was expelled and the CTM dropped its Communist connections. Toledano later became the leader of the Latin-American Workers' Confederation (CTAL) which handled Moscow's trade union activities throughout Latin American until in 1962 it was replaced by a new Cuban Communist-led organization, the Labor Confederation of the Workers of Latin America.

furnace of war [should not] be thrown aside in the days of peace" and that labor should "fight for unity between all states despite differences of social systems."[4] Accordingly, they called for a conference which would include Soviet and other Communist trade unions.

The British urgently sought the cooperation of the American Federation of Labor but the AFL emphatically declined to participate. The Congress of Industrial Organizations accepted, mainly because its members felt, as did many other people during the closing months of the war, that it was possible to work with Communists without being dominated by them.

World Federation of Trade Unions

In September, 1945, delegates from fifty-six countries met in Paris, where a new World Federation of Trade Unions was established. Before the adoption of the constitution there were heated debates as to the objectives, structure and program of the new body. The British insisted that it should be composed of bona fide trade unions whose autonomy should be guaranteed; also that the new organization should not be drawn into "the maze of politics," as some of the delegates seemed to want to have happen, but should "carry on practical day-to-day trade union work . . . and . . . secure practical results for the individual members of our unions."[5] The constitution finally adopted seemed to fulfill that purpose and to give fair representation to all national bodies, although the Russians, claiming a membership of over 27 million in their Trade Union Council, were given five delegates as against three each for Great Britain, France and the United States, and one each for the smaller countries.

The great hope for world-wide labor cooperation was soon shattered. Within a few months after the formation of the World Federation of Trade Unions it became evident that its Communist members, including not only the Russian but also the French and Italian Communists, were seeking to convert it into a successor of

[4] Address of Arthur Horner, delegate from the British Trade Union Congress to the 1944 AFL convention.

[5] *Monthly Labor Review*, January, 1946, p. 48.

the Third International. The struggle between the opposing forces came to a head with the inauguration of the European Economic Recovery Program which the Communist groups, in adherence to the Soviet foreign policy, insisted upon opposing. Through their affiliation in the WFTU, the anti-Communist trade unions throughout Europe were thus forced to condemn and oppose by overt action, such as refusal to unload goods from the United States, the aid which was essential to the very life of their members. And while condemning the Marshall Plan, the Communists forced the WFTU to keep silent as the Soviet Union extended its iron curtain into eastern Europe and converted the trade union movements in these countries into instruments of Soviet policy.

INTERNATIONAL CONFEDERATION OF FREE TRADE UNIONS

Thoroughly disillusioned by the spring of 1948, the British Trade Union Congress and the CIO took steps to break relations with the World Federation of Trade Unions. They were assisted by the AFL in a very vital way, namely, by a reversal of its policy of insisting that any international organization must be composed solely of representatives from the "dominant" labor movement in each country—in other words, their acceptance of a policy of sharing representation with the CIO.

This decision for unified action by the two branches of American labor served as a catalyst for united action by all "free" trade union movements throughout the world. In December, 1949, delegates from fifty countries, representing about 50 million workers, met in London and established the International Confederation of Free Trade Unions. Charter members of the new organization included the AFL and the CIO, the national trade union centers of Great Britain, Canada, the Scandinavian countries, Switzerland and Western Germany, and the non-Communist centers of France and Italy, as well as unions from the Middle and Far East, including Japan and India, and several from Latin America.

The ringing manifesto which was adopted by the ICFTU is significant in its worker-class appeal—minus the revolutionary call to arms of the Communist Manifesto. It opens and closes with the following rally call:

MANIFESTO OF ICFTU—LONDON, DECEMBER, 1949

BREAD: economic security and social justice for all!
FREEDOM: through economic and political democracy!
PEACE: with liberty, justice and dignity for all!

Workers of all countries, races, creeds—workers in factory, field and office, and all other groups—unite within the ranks of the International Confederation of Free Trade Unions! Unite with us to achieve a world in which men can be both free and secure and in which peoples of all nations may live in peace with each other! For these things we fight! These things we will win!

. . . . .

Together we can conquer poverty and exploitation and create a world of abundance and security.
Together we can destroy tyranny and oppression and create a world of freedom and human dignity.
Together we can defeat the forces of war and aggression and create a world of peace and justice.

The International Confederation of Free Trade Unions is committed by its constitution to support "the right of all peoples to full national freedom and self-government," and to "champion the cause of human freedom, oppose and combat totalitarianism and aggression in any form." Its aims are to assist workers throughout the world in developing trade unions, especially in underdeveloped countries, such unions to be free from domination by employers, governments or political parties, and to be genuine bargaining instruments deriving their authority from their members; to raise living standards and improve working conditions everywhere; to encourage development of resources and freer exchange of products throughout the world; to eliminate forced labor; to represent the free trade union movements in all international agencies which perform functions affecting working people; to exchange information and foster education and publicity to increase workers' understanding of national and international problems; to support all measures that are necessary for assuring the defense of world democracy and the freedom of nations against any totalitarian aggression.

REGIONAL CENTERS

The ICFTU is the first international trade union organization which has succeeded in creating regional organizations exclusively administered and guided by unionists from the regions themselves. This regional structure recognizes that although the ICFTU and its affiliates have a common goal, each region has its own problems arising from differences in trade-union development and the economic and political conditions within the region. The first two regional offices to be established were those in Brussels for Europe and in Mexico City for the Western Hemisphere. In 1951 the Asian regional organization was established with headquarters at New Delhi, and in 1957 the African with headquarters near Lagos, Nigeria. Membership coverage of the various regions in 1962 was as follows: African (AFRO), 38 countries with 1½ million members; Asian (ARO), 15 countries with 6 million members; Inter-American (ORIT), 35 countries and territories with 21 million members; European (ERO), 18 countries with 28½ million members.

From the outset the ICFTU has taken the view that one of its principal tasks is to help the trade unions in the economically underdeveloped areas to train the leaders they need for putting their movements on a sound and enduring basis. In 1952 a residential training college for Asian trade unionists was established at Calcutta, and in 1958 an African college was opened in Uganda. Both of these cater to English-speaking workers. For French-speaking Africa a residential college has recently been established on the Ivory Coast, and there is another in Mexico for Spanish-speaking workers in the Western Hemisphere. The general plan of these institutes is to provide two- or three-month courses for around twenty members at a time. Although they are sponsored by the regional organizations, the Confederation gives financial assistance, provides faculty members and helps with over-all planning.

TRADE SECRETARIATS

Trade secretariats are international organizations of national unions whose jurisdictions cover particular trades or industries. For example, the International Transport Workers Federation, the largest existing Secretariat, is composed of national unions of maritime, railroad, and motor vehicle workers of various countries; the International Federation of Metal Workers, the second largest, includes national unions having jurisdiction in the metal and steel industries, including automobile and other fabricating industries. The function of trade secretariats is to provide regular interchange of information and personal contacts among the various national union leaders and, through periodic regional meetings, among rank-and-file workers of different countries who are engaged in the same trade; to formulate standards and policies as guides for national union action; to represent the interests of their affiliated unions on intergovernmental bodies.

Trade secretariats were the first effective form of international cooperation among organized workers, some of them having been established before the turn of the century. Also, most of them have functioned continuously through the vicissitudes of the several general international labor movements. In 1962 there were twenty-two trade secretariats affiliated with the ICFTU, and American unions were assuming an active role in most of them. The Machinists, the Automobile and Steelworkers and others are active in the Metal Workers' Secretariat; the United Mine Workers are affiliated with the Miners' International Federation; the American railroad brotherhoods and maritime unions are influential members of the Transport Workers Federation.

THE INTERNATIONAL LABOR ORGANIZATION

Entirely different in structure and operation from the international organizations described above is the International Labor Organization, commonly referred to as the ILO. The ILO is an offshoot of the Versailles Peace Treaty of 1919 but its roots were planted many years before World War I. Early in the nineteenth century humanitarians like Robert Owen were convinced that the conditions of industrial workers in any one country could be permanently improved only by the international cooperation of all governments; that, conversely, under conditions of international trade, work standards in all countries tend toward the lowest level existing in any one country. These humanitarians, it will be noted, looked toward government action for redress and gradual improvement through parliamentary means, in contrast to class struggle or efforts of worker groups alone. Under a political democracy, the parliamentary process involved joint participation by all classes, employers as well as workers, and the elected representatives of the general public.

The numerous proposals for international cooperation did not come to fruition until 1900, when the International Association for Labor Legislation was established at Brussels. During subsequent years this Association "ratified" several important "conventions,"[6] such as one prohibiting night work for women. The United States government made annual contributions toward the support of the Association, and the American Association for Labor Legislation, a private organization, took an active part in its program.

"International labor" was one of the foremost subjects discussed at the Paris Peace Conference in 1919. The collapse of the Central Powers was threatening to bring with it a collapse of capitalist society, at least in the defeated nations, and there was no knowing where the contagion of revolution might end. Behind all of this ferment and uncertainty lay the ominous threat of a Bolshevist Russia. Faced with this world situation, the Conference unanimously adopted a resolution that began, "Conditions of labor exist involving such injustice, hardship and privation to large numbers of people as to produce unrest so great that the peace and harmony of the world are imperiled," and included provisions for an International Labor Organization in Part XIII of the Treaty of Versailles.

Samuel Gompers, President of the AFL, served as chairman of the commission which drafted the proposals submitted to the Peace Conference and made arrangements for the first conference to meet in Washington in October, 1919. He, like President Wilson with respect to the League of Nations, fully expected that the United States would assume a prominent role in the new world organization. But when the Washington conference was held, the United

[6] These conventions, or treaties, actually had no legal status until they were enacted into law by the respective governments, but the ratification by an international organization with prestige carried a great deal of moral weight toward their adoption.

States Senate had failed to ratify the Versailles Treaty and the American Federation of Labor was in the anomalous position of being an onlooker at a conference which it had sponsored, and which was held in the same city as its own headquarters. During the subsequent fifteen years of United States isolationism, American labor remained aloof from active participation in the ILO although friendly relations were maintained.

All this was changed in 1934 when Congress, at President Roosevelt's recommendation, authorized this government to become a member. The same year, the Soviet Union, the other large nation outside the ILO, also became a member. This expanded participation was soon interrupted by international tensions; and one by one, Germany, Spain, Italy, Japan and the Soviet Union left the ILO. Nevertheless, the ILO carried on, and was the only League of Nations agency to survive. Headquarters were moved from Geneva to Montreal for the duration of the war. After the war, the ILO became a specialized agency of the United Nations and moved back to its Geneva headquarters. At the Philadelphia conference (1944) when postwar plans were discussed, the ILO reaffirmed its basic principles, declaring that "poverty anywhere constitutes a danger to prosperity everywhere; war against want must be carried on with unrelenting vigor within each nation, and by continuous and concerted international effort"; that ILO activities "are fully applicable to all peoples everywhere and that, while the manner of their application must be determined with due regard to the stage of social and economic development reached by each people, their progressive application to peoples who are still dependent, as well as those who have already achieved self-government, is a matter of concern to the whole civilized world."

Method of Operation

The uniqueness of the ILO is its tripartite system of representation. At the General Conference, which meets at least once each year, each member government has four voting delegates of whom two are representatives of the government, one of employers, and one of workers. The Governing Body of forty persons, which is elected by the General Conference, is also on the 2:1:1 representation basis. Delegates vote as individuals and not by national units.

Thus the employers' or the workers' representatives may vote for or against a motion contrary to the votes of their government representatives. This permits voting by horizontal class interests of employers *versus* workers and, in theory, the government delegate votes could be the deciding factor. In actual practice, there is much splitting of votes among each of the three groups; seldom if ever do all the government delegates, all the employer or all the worker delegates, vote as a block.

The General Conference serves as a world forum for the discussion of social problems and all questions pertaining to employment and the welfare of workers. If two-thirds of the delegates vote for a proposal it becomes an international "convention" (or a "recommendation" when the matter is not considered appropriate or suitable for a convention) which the member delegates are under obligation to refer to their respective governments for enactment into law or other appropriate action. The Conference has no final legislative powers; it is not a "super-government." The conventions and recommendations adopted are not binding upon its member governments merely by virtue of their having been adopted by the Conference, any more than international treaties concluded by diplomatic procedure are binding without ratification. But the adoption of conventions by the Conference does place all members under obligation to take action such as will maximize the probability of ratification by their respective governments.

When ratified and applied, conventions constitute codes of fair international competition; they afford protection for workers employed in countries other than their own; they resolve conflicts of laws and conflicts of jurisdiction in regard to the application of social legislation; they create rights of an international character, such as the pension rights of migrant workers, which could not be effectively established by action of any one country; they make possible reforms on a world-wide basis by establishing minimum standards which are binding everywhere.

PROBLEMS

Like the United Nations, the International Labor Office is faced with the dual problems of assimilating large numbers of new members and trying to find a *modus operandi* between the two opposing forces of democracy and communism. During the past fifteen years the ILO membership has increased from 52 to 102 members; more than half of the new members are African states. The addition of the African and Asian states has caused a marked shift in the power structure of the ILO, as well as in its policies and programs.

Colonialism and racial issues have come to the fore, and action taken may not reflect the judgment of the delegates from western Europe and America who formerly had the deciding vote. For example, at the 1961 conference the new African nations pressed for the expulsion of the Republic of South Africa because of its racial policies. The delegates from most of the older nations favored a vote of censure but not expulsion, since the ILO constitution has no provision for expelling members. Nevertheless, the African delegates succeeded (by a majority of one) in having a resolution passed calling for the withdrawal of South Africa until such time as it abandons its apartheid policy.

Since Russia rejoined the ILO in 1954 there has been constant friction between the representatives of the East and the West. The Soviet delegates have sought to use the conference as a forum for propaganda against colonialism. The Western delegates, while not defending colonialism, have sought to keep the record balanced and free from exaggerated statements. Even more serious is the problem of representation from countries where industry is owned and managed by the government. The tripartite arrangement of government, employer and worker delegates, each free to vote as he pleases, becomes an anomaly under a system where the worker and the employer delegates must always vote with their governments. Employer delegates from the democracies have refused to recognize their designated counterparts from the Communist countries, and as a consequence the tripartite committee statements of position during the past several years have included the votes of employer members from the free nations only.

In the general conference, the Soviet bloc has not been able to muster a majority vote. This was made evident at the 1961 conference, which passed a resolution calling on all countries to adopt as a major goal of social and economic policy, the objective of "full, productive, and freely chosen employment." The U.S.S.R. delegates naturally opposed a resolution including the phrase "freely chosen," but the free trade unions made it plain that they were not merely concerned with *full* employment but equally with *productive* and *freely chosen* employment. In other words, they refused to underwrite forced labor masquerading as full employment.

FOREIGN ACTIVITIES OF AMERICAN UNIONS

Probably no private sector of our society expends more energy and money on international programs than does the American labor movement. Most of the activities are frankly motivated by reasons of self-interest: a realization that high standards of living cannot be maintained in a few sections of the world alone, and that democracy must display itself as a dynamic, expanding force if it is to survive anywhere. On the other hand, many activities sponsored and financed by American labor unions are purely humanitarian—for example the generous contributions made from time to time for famine relief and health programs in Asia, Africa and South America.

POSTWAR EUROPE

When American and allied occupation authorities were faced with the problem of establishing democratic regimes in the defeated totalitarian countries and in rehabilitating war-torn Europe, they immediately became aware of the need for organized labor's cooperation. American military authorities who previously had given little thought to the role of labor unions in their own country, were brought face to face with the fact that a free trade union movement is an indispensable pillar of any democratic, industrial society. Realizing this, they saw that one of their first and most urgent problems was finding a way to bring about the reconstruction of labor organizations in the defeated countries which would be in harmony with the democratic political and social structure they were seeking to get established.

The prewar totalitarian governments of Germany, Italy, and Japan had taken over their labor movements and made them instruments of their governments. "Recalcitrant" union leaders had been liquidated or forced into hiding. The military occupation authorities naturally were unacquainted with former union leaders who could be trusted with the task of winning over the millions of disillusioned and perplexed workers of these countries. United States labor leaders (as well as those of Great Britain) were able to step into the breach since they had maintained contact with the trade unionists in the European anti-Fascist underground.

European labor, always more socialistically inclined than workers in the United States, was prone to regard the U.S. recovery program as an instrument of American capitalistic imperialism—a device to extend "dollar diplomacy" and gain economic and perhaps political control over war-stricken, bankrupt nations. Such suspicions were intensified by the aggressive propaganda from the Kremlin, with the result that the Marshall Plan was jeopardized before it got under way. (There were in fact a few instances where dock workers in France and Italy refused to unload Marshall-Plan goods.)

In an effort to allay this distrust and to gain the confidence of the working masses, the Economic Cooperation Administration established a Labor Division with headquarters in Paris, and appointed American union leaders to serve as labor advisers in each of the countries participating in the recovery program. In carrying out their duties, the U.S. labor representatives sought always to serve as a link between the government authorities and the labor movements within each of the assisted countries. Coming from the ranks of workers, they were in a strategic position which enabled them to interpret the many ramifications of the recovery program in a way which the European workers could understand, thereby gaining their cooperation. Also the labor representatives bent every effort to see that the benefits from the program were distributed equally among all segments of the economies; in this, however, they felt they were only partially successful.

Current Activities

The international activities of American labor are channeled through several courses: cooperation in U.S. government programs; participation in the work of the international labor organizations such as those described above; and programs conducted independently by the AFL–CIO and various individual unions. These programs are costly, and they are paid for by American wage-earners, either through their regular union dues or through voluntary special assessments and gifts. Annual payments by the AFL–CIO to the International Confederation of Free Trade Unions and the Inter-American Regional Organization amount to about $400,000, and nearly all the national unions belong to one or more international trade secretariats which they help support. These are regular payments, originating for the most part from membership dues.

The ICFTU maintains a Solidarity Fund which supports much of its educational, organizing and benevolent activities throughout the world. In 1961 the AFL–CIO contributed to this fund almost $700,000 collected by special assessments, and individual unions made additional contributions. The United Automobile Workers, for instance, have established what they call their "Free World Labor Fund," which comes from the interest from the union's $40-million strike reserves, to help support the Solidarity Fund, as well as the International Metalworkers Federation (an ICFTU affiliate) and other activities in foreign countries.

Officers of the AFL–CIO serve on various committees of the United Nations, and in conjunction with the New York Central Labor Council they have established a Friendship Office in New York, where trade unionists on United Nations delegations from other countries can meet and exchange views. The AFL–CIO staff in Washington and members of unions in other industrial areas spend a great deal of time serving as hosts to visiting delegates from all over the world. Some of these delegates are sent by their governments, some by their unions, and some are chosen and financed by American unions. The purpose of these visits is to show the foreign visitors how free trade unions function in a political democracy.[7] On the other hand, many U.S. unions have financed trips

[7] One observer has reported:

". . . the members of these visiting teams have learned to appreciate and to understand our American way of life and have become, in their own countries, articulate in explanation of the cultural, social and economic values they have been surprised to discover here, their previous impressions of this country having been limited largely to their judgment of the Hollywood motion picture and the allegations of the Communist line. Now this is not to say that they have em-

abroad for certain of their members so they can see working conditions and observe how unions operate in foreign lands, and bring back information about them.

At present, the U.S. labor movement is especially concerned with conditions in South America, where labor unions must frequently struggle not only against Communist infiltration but against political dictatorships, which either suppress labor organizations altogether or regiment them into alliances in order to cultivate among the masses of people the notion that everything workers get comes as the munificent gift of the political dictator. In addition to supporting the U.S. government's efforts to improve the economic well-being of the people of Latin America, the AFL–CIO is active in promoting and developing free labor movements in each country. In this, the AFL–CIO works closely with the Inter-American Regional Organization of Workers (ORIT), the Western Hemisphere branch of the ICFTU. The AFL–CIO takes an active part in all the meetings of ORIT's committees and general conventions, supports its organizational and special projects, makes donations to ORIT's affiliates in times of strikes and other emergencies, and supplies personnel for special missions of many kinds.

In 1962 the AFL–CIO established the American Institute for Free Labor Development, whose aim is to demonstrate that "the pluralistic, democratic society has the best means of carrying forward the powerful historic changes sweeping through the southern half of the world; means which are vitally superior to those of the totalitarian society."[8] Its immediate program is the bringing of from 100 to 120 Latin Americans each year to this country for three months' intensive training on the techniques of union organization and administration. Upon completing the course, the

---

braced without qualification, or even approved, every facet of our national life—to the exclusion of values they consider important in their own—but it does mean that now they have come to understand our society, can explain it effectively and honestly, and are thus in a position to refute the falsehoods so avidly spread by the propaganda machine of the Soviet Union. . . ."

[8] *Aims, Objectives and Program,* American Institute for Free Labor Development, Washington 6, D.C., May, 1962. The board of Trustees of this Institute is composed of U.S. and Latin American representatives of labor, industry and the public, and it is also supported by interested individuals and by groups other than the AFL-CIO.

graduates are supported for nine months after their return home in order that they may devote their full time to building up democratic trade union movements in their respective countries. The Institute aims to create a leadership based not on the concept of the class struggle, but on the constructive role labor can play in cooperation with other segments of society, including management, toward raising living standards throughout Latin America.

GLOSSARY OF LABOR TERMS

The following glossary contains definitions and explanations of terms pertaining to labor and labor unions. While many of these terms have a wider application, this glossary is limited to explaining their usage in connection with working conditions, unions and collective bargaining.

ACCIDENT RATE. A measure of frequency of industrial injuries, the standard formula being the total number of disabling injuries per one million employee-hours worked.

ACCELERATING PREMIUM. A form of incentive wage system which provides increasingly larger percentage premiums at progressively higher levels of production. (See Incentive Wages)

ADAMSON ACT. Act passed in 1916 which establishes the 8-hour day as a basis for computing wages of railway employees.

AGENCY SHOP. The provision in a union-management contract which requires employees who do not become union members to pay a specified assessment to the union for collective bargaining services.

ANNUAL WAGES. Sometimes used in a general sense to refer to total earnings received during a year; more particularly used in connection with plans whereby workers are guaranteed a minimum amount of wages or employment each year. (See Guaranteed Employment)

AGREEMENT. (See Collective Agreement)

ALLOWED TIME. Under incentive wage systems, the number of minutes allowed for tool care, personal needs, and fatigue, added to operating time in establishing job standards or "task" as a basis for determining piece rates or incentive bonuses. (See also "Dead Time")

ANTI-KICKBACK LAW. A federal law enacted in 1934 which imposes a penalty on any employer (or agent of the employer) who by force, intimidation, threat or dismissal, or any other means induces any person employed on public construction work, or on work financed in whole or in part by federal funds, to give back any part of his compensation.

ANTI-LABOR LEGISLATION. Federal and state laws and municipal ordinances which organized labor considers inimical to the interests of wage earners; more especially, legislation which seeks to restrict the activities and status of labor unions.

ANTI-STRIKEBREAKING ACT (BYRNES ACT). A federal law passed in 1936 which prohibits the interstate transportation of "any person who is employed or is to be employed for the purpose of obstructing or interfering by force or threats with the peaceful picketing by employees during a labor controversy, or the exercise by employees of any of the rights of self-organization or collective bargaining." (See Strikebreakers)

APPRENTICE. A young person training for a skilled trade through a comprehensive program of graduated experience on the job combined with individual or classroom instruction. (See also Learner)

APPRENTICE RATE. A formally established schedule of wage rates, usually graduated in such a manner as to permit the achievement of the minimum journeyman rate at the end of the apprenticeship period.

ARBITRATION. The process of referring disputes between employers and employees (or between two rival unions) to the decision of impartial adjudicators. (See Compulsory Arbitration, Impartial Chairman, Umpire)

AREA AGREEMENT. An employer-union agreement which covers all or most of the establishments and workers in a given industry within a geographical region, usually more extensive than a city or metropolitan center. (See also Association Agreement, Master Agreement, Standard Agreement)

ASSESSMENT. A monthly, annual or single charge levied by the union on each of its members for a special purpose not covered by regular dues. Rules regarding the levying of assessments are found in union constitutions and by-laws.

ASSOCIATION AGREEMENT. An agreement negotiated and signed by an employers' association, on behalf of its members, with a union or a joint board representing several unions. An association agreement may cover all or most of the employers within an industry throughout the country or in a single city or locality. (See also Area, Master, Standard Agreement)

ATTRITION. Reduction of work force through natural causes such as death, retirement and resignation.

AUTOMATIC CHECKOFF. (See Checkoff)

AUTOMATIC WAGE ADJUSTMENT. A plan whereby wage rates are raised or lowered according to an established formula in response to other specified changes such as changes in the cost of living, prevailing wages, business profits, or prices. Usually refers to wage levels throughout the plant, although it may refer to a system of increasing employees' wages according to their individual service records or adjustments in piece rates. (See also Longevity Pay, Permissive Wage Adjustment)

AUTOMATIC WAGE PROGRESSION. A plan by which wage rates of workers in jobs with established rate ranges are increased automatically at set time intervals until the maximum rate for the job is reached. Some plans combine automatic progression up to a specified point (for example, the midpoint) within the range, with discretionary increases up to the maximum based on merit or other factors. (See also Merit Increase)

AUTOMATION. Broadly, all technological improvements in production methods. More specifically, the use of electronic devices that automatically control the operation of machines, including conveyors and other equipment which link together the different operations into a continuous flow.

BACK PAY. Wages due an employee for past services, usually representing the difference between money already received and a higher amount resulting from a change in wage rates following an arbitrator's decision, enforcement of a legal minimum, or adjustment of piece rates. (See also Hold-back Pay)

BACKTRACKING. (See Bumping)

BARGAINING UNIT. A group of employees who voluntarily unite, or by decision of a government agency such as the NLRB are deemed to be an "appropriate" unit for bargaining collectively with their employer (or employers). Such units may be composed of workers in a single craft, or include all or most workers in an entire plant or numerous plants within an area or entire industry.

BASE RATE. Under incentive wage systems, the rate for the established task or job standard, production beyond standard bringing extra pay. Base rate is also used to denote the "regular" rate on timework, that is, the established rate per hour for the job exclusive of extras resulting from merit or service increases, overtime or shift differentials, etc. (See "Standard Time," Piecework, Incentive Wages, Wages)

BIDDING. System of having vacant jobs posted on bulletin boards or otherwise circularized, with present employees having the privilege of applying on basis of their seniority.

BLACKLIST. A list of names of union leaders and members secretly maintained and exchanged by employers and employers' associations for the purpose of keeping such persons from obtaining employment.

BLUE-COLLAR WORKERS. Craftsmen and foremen, operatives and nonfarm laborers engaged in production and transportation. While some blue-collar jobs are highly skilled, preparation is usually through on-the-job training rather than higher academic education. (See White-collar Worker)

BONUS. Any payment in addition to regular or base wages. It may be in the form of a Christmas bonus or other annual allotment or it may consist of higher rates paid for nightwork, overtime, hazardous work, etc. Also used in connection with incentive wage systems to designate amounts earned in excess of base or guaranteed rates. (See Premium Pay, Penalty Rates, Shift Differentials, and Overtime)

BOOTLEG WAGES. The wages above those at the prevailing rate or the union scale which an employer may pay in a tight labor market to hold or attract employees. May also refer to wages below or above the legal or union rate.

BOYCOTT. A concerted effort to withhold and to induce others to withhold the purchase of goods or services produced in a nonunion plant or by an employer accused of objectionable labor practices. It was first used by the tenant farmers of an Irish landlord named Boycott and was later adopted by both British and American organized labor movements as a weapon in labor disputes.

BROKEN TIME. (See Split Shift)

BROTHERHOOD. A title used by some of the older international and national unions, especially the railroad unions, which were originally established primarily as fraternal and benefit organizations.

BUMPING. During layoffs, the displacing of junior employees by workers of longer service; sometimes referred to as "backtracking."

BUSINESS AGENT. A person employed by a local union to assist in negotiating agreements with the employer, help settle grievances, and see that both employers and members observe the terms of the agreement. (See Steward)

CALL-BACK PAY. Extra rate paid to employees who have left the plant and are recalled for some emergency work.

CALL PAY. The guarantee of payment of a specified number of hours' wages to employees when they report for work at their usual time and find no work to do.

CAPTIVE MINES. Coal mines whose output is used almost exclusively by the steel companies which own them.

CASUAL WORKERS. Workers employed for short periods of time who attain no seniority status with either the employer or the union. When employed in a union shop they are given a special permit card by the union. (See Decasualization)

CERTIFICATION OF UNION. An official action or order of the proper government agency (for example, the National Labor Relations Board) specifying that a union is free from employer domination and includes a majority of the employees in its membership, and hence must be recognized by the employer as the collective bargaining agent for all the employees in the collective bargaining unit.

CHAPEL. In the printing trades, a subordinate unit of a local union which is composed of members within a single shop.

CHECKOFF. The practice whereby the employer, by agreement with the union, withholds union dues and assessments from the pay of union members and turns the funds over to the union. Formerly, some employer-union agreements provided for the automatic checkoff for all union members, but the 1947 Labor-Management Relations Act permits checkoff only for those employees who individually authorize the employer to make such withholdings.

CHECKWEIGHMAN. In coal mining, one who weighs or measures the coal produced by each miner who is paid on a tonnage basis.

CLOSED SHOP. A company operating under an agreement which specifies that no persons shall be employed who are not members of the union and that all employees must continue to be members in good standing throughout their period of employment. Closed shops were declared illegal by the 1947 Labor-Management Relations Act. (See also Union Shop)

CLOSED UNION. A union which, through prohibitive initiation fees or restrictive membership rules, seeks to limit its membership or to keep certain persons from becoming members in order to protect job opportunities for present members.

COLLECTIVE BARGAINING. The process of employer-union negotiation for the purpose of reaching an agreement as to the terms and conditions of employment for a specified period. (See also Bargaining Unit)

COMPANY STORE. A retail store owned and operated by a company primarily engaged in other business for the use of its employees and their families. Term is sometimes given a more limited meaning to refer to stores in company towns, or where wages are paid in scrip redeemable at the company store, or where other coercive measures are used to compel employee patronage.

COMPANY TOWNS. A community inhabited solely or chiefly by the employees of a single company which owns a substantial part of all the real estate and homes. Typically, company towns are unincorporated and are usually isolated from other communities. The isolation may be due to natural reasons, for example, mining and lumber towns, or it may be due to the employer's desire to escape unionization or avoid higher taxes and wages.

COMPANY UNION. Structurally and technically an employee organization whose membership is confined to the employees of a single plant or company as contrasted with labor unions which have a broad regional, national, or international coverage. Since such employee associations, or "representation plans" as they were frequently called before the passage of the National Labor Relations Act, were usually established and largely administered by employers to forestall unionization, the term "company union" is commonly regarded as being synonymous with "company-dominated union."

COMPETITIVE WAGE. In economic theory, the wage within a given labor market required to balance the demand for and the supply of labor of a particular type. More popularly, the wage level a company must maintain to compete with other firms in the same labor market.

COMPULSORY ARBITRATION. The process of settlement of employer-labor disputes by a government agency (or other means provided by the government) which has the power to investigate and make an award which must be accepted by all parties concerned; not to be confused with voluntary agreements between employers and unions to have their disputes submitted for final determination by an impartial agency. (See Arbitration, Impartial Chairman, Umpire)

COMPULSORY CHECKOFF. (See Checkoff)

COMPULSORY UNION MEMBERSHIP. Applied to closed or union shops where employees must be or become members of the union as a condition of employment. (See Closed Shop, Union Shop)

CONCILIATION. An attempt to settle disputes between employers and workers by a third party, usually a government agent, who however has no power to compel the disputants to come to an agreement. The term is used interchangeably with "mediation."

CONTINUOUS PROCESS. A term applied to jobs which by their very nature require uninterrupted operation and thus necessitate round-the-clock work scheduling, that is, multiple shifts. Not to be confused, however, with multiple-shift schedules established for the sole purpose of increasing production.

CONTRIBUTORY WELFARE PLAN. A retirement pension or other benefit plan whose cost is shared (not necessarily equally) by the employer and the employees.

COST-OF-LIVING INDEX. A measure of the change in the retail prices of goods, rents, and services paid by families of wage earners and lower salaried workers. The most widely known index, that of the Bureau of Labor Statistics, is issued every month and represents the average change in prices of living essentials in representative cities; correctly termed "Consumers' Price Index."

CRAFT UNION. A labor organization whose jurisdiction is limited to one or several allied skilled trades. (See Industrial Union)

CUTBACK. A sudden reduction in work resulting in layoffs.

CYCLICAL DEPRESSION. Periodic recession in general business activity resulting in widespread and prolonged unemployment; contrasted to seasonal depressions which occur in some industries more or less regularly once or twice a year.

DAYWORK. Usually refers to work where wages are a fixed amount per hour or day in contrast to incentive or piecework. Also used to designate day shifts under multiple-shift arrangements, or casual labor in contrast to employment having some degree of permanence.

DEADHEADING. In the transportation industries, the process of taking empty cars, trucks, and buses to a terminal or other station; also the travel time of transportation workers who are required to report for work at points far removed from their home terminals.

In some other industries the term is used in connection with the practice of not promoting (deadheading) a person where seniority entitles him to a higher position, but who is not qualified to do the work, and allowing junior employees to move around him.

"DEAD TIME." Lost time for which the employee is not responsible (machine breakdowns, delays in receiving materials, etc.) and for which an incentive worker usually is paid his regular wages. (See also Allowed Time)

DEAD WORK. Used in mining to refer to nonproductive work, including the removal of rock, debris, and other waste matter, from the product mined.

DECASUALIZATION. Most commonly applied to longshoring where centralized hiring halls are substituted for the "shape-up," thus tending to regularize the work of individual longshoremen. (See Shape-up)

DISCHARGE. Involuntary dismissal of an employee for cause. A discharged employee, unlike one laid off, loses his seniority rights to reemployment.

DISCRIMINATION. Unfair treatment of a particular group or individual in matters affecting their employment status: employer discrimination against union members in hiring, layoff, or promotion; employer or union discrimination against accepting Negroes.

DISMISSAL WAGE. Payment by the employer of a sum of money to an employee who is permanently and involuntarily laid off through no fault of his own; usually based on length of service and in the form either of a lump sum payment or weekly payments equivalent to a specified per cent of wages for a given number of weeks.

DISTRICT COUNCIL. (See Joint Council)

DOWN GRADING. The reassignment of workers to tasks with lower skill requirements with lower rates of pay. May occur when there is a change in products or in methods of production; also during periods of reduction of work force through the bumping process.

DOWN PERIODS. Brief shutdowns for purposes of cleaning and repairing.

DUAL PAY SYSTEM. A wage system in the transportation industries whereby employees are paid on a dual mileage and hours basis; that is, a day's wages are based on a specified number of hours or miles, whichever is greater, depending upon the speed of the train.

EARNINGS. Total remuneration for services rendered or time worked, including overtime, bonuses and commissions, and other premium pay. (See also Wages, Incentive Wages, "Real" Wages)

EMPLOYEE ASSOCIATIONS. Usually refers to worker organizations whose membership consists of employees of a single company. (See Company Union)

EQUAL PAY FOR EQUAL WORK. A wage plan or legal provision for the payment of the same compensation to all employees within an establishment, or other bargaining unit, who are performing the same kind and amount of work, regardless of race, sex, or other characteristics of the individual workers.

ESCALATOR CLAUSE. A provision in a union agreement allowing or requiring the automatic adjustment of wages in accordance with specified changes in the cost of living or price of product, or some other criterion. (See also Improvement Factor)

EXPERIENCE RATING. The system under which employers' contribution rates for unemployment insurance, or premium rates for workmen's compensation, are adjusted according to each industry's or individual employer's unemployment or accident risk.

FAIR EMPLOYMENT PRACTICE. Legislation which makes it unlawful for an employer to discriminate in the hiring, tenure, or promotion of employees, or for unions to discriminate against applicants for membership, because of race, color, religion, or national origin.

FAIR LABOR STANDARDS ACT. The federal law which establishes a minimum wage, time-and-a-half rates for hours worked in excess of 40 per week, and regulations pertaining to child labor in establishments producing goods or services entering interstate commerce.

FEATHERBEDDING. A term of opprobrium loosely applied to any union work rules which allegedly place limitations on the maximum utilization of manpower or machines, thus creating jobs for a greater number of persons than is actually necessary. The term is most frequently used in connection with certain practices on railroads, such as the mileage and full-crew rules. (See also Full Crew Rules, Work Restriction)

FEDERAL LABOR UNION. A local union chartered by and directly affiliated with the AFL–CIO.

FIXED SHIFTS. Where two or more shifts are employed, the arrangement whereby the hour schedule remains the same for each of the several crews in contrast to the periodic rotating of crews. (See Rotating Shifts)

FLAGS OF CONVENIENCE. Ships owned by American companies but licensed by foreign powers such as Panama, Liberia or Honduras, in order to escape union-wage and other labor standards required by the U.S. government or by American unions.

FLEXIBLE SCHEDULES. Arrangement of work time in which the number of hours per day or days per week varies, but total hours worked within the period do not exceed the number for which straight-time wages are paid.

FREE RIDER. A union term for a worker who does not belong to a union who nevertheless receives the benefits derived from a union negotiated contract or other union activity.

FRINGE BENEFIT. A benefit supplemental to wages received by workers at a cost to employers, such as paid holidays, pensions, health insurance, etc.

FULL CREW RULES. Regulations which require an engineer, fireman, conductor, brakeman, and flagman on every train.

GAIN SHARING. An incentive wage plan which provides progressively smaller bonuses or premiums per unit as output increases, based on the theory that expanded production is the result of both management and worker's effort and that both should share in the gains.

GARNISHMENT. An order issued by a court and executed by a public officer (sheriff, constable, or marshal), directing the employer of a debtor to pay part or all the wages due the debtor to the court officer who in turn transmits it to the creditor. In some states garnishment orders may be issued only against wages due and payable upon a given date; other states allow an order to serve as a continuing levy until the debt is paid. The proportion of any week's wages which may be taken varies among the states.

GENERAL STRIKE. A widespread sympathetic strike in which workers attached to various industries and unions participate, in contrast to a *general industry strike* which is confined to one union or one industry even though plants may be widely scattered over the country. (See Sympathetic Strike)

"GOLDBRICKING." (See "Soldiering")

"GOON." A hired thug to break up a strike or picket line. (See Strikebreaker)

GRAND LODGE. Title used by the Machinists, some of the railroad brotherhoods, and other unions to refer to their national organization, "lodge" being used with reference to their locals.

GRAVEYARD SHIFT. Under continuous operation schedules, the shift which begins around midnight. Sometimes referred to as "lobster shift."

GUARANTEED EMPLOYMENT. A plan established by an employer or through employer-union negotiations, whereby employees are assured a specified number of days' work per week or weeks per year or the equivalent in wages. (See also Annual Wages)

HOLD-BACK PAY. Any wages withheld by an employer; most generally used in connection with the two or three days' wages earned between the end of the pay period and payday.

HOMEWORK. Production of commercial goods in private residences from material furnished by an employer for which the worker is paid by the hour or by the piece. Frequently restricted or regulated by law because of its association with low wages and tenement house conditions.

HOT CARGO. Products manufactured or transported under nonunion conditions or where a union is in dispute with the employer. Most commonly used in trucking, construction and garment industries.

ILLEGAL STRIKE. Technically, a work stoppage forbidden by law because specified legal procedures have not been followed prior to the stoppage, or because of an injunction forbidding the stoppage. In union parlance, the term does not necessarily relate to a strike prohibited by a law but refers to a stoppage by union members which has not been authorized by the proper union officials or voted upon in accordance with the union's rules. (See "Quickie" Strike)

IMPARTIAL CHAIRMAN. An outside person employed jointly by the union and employer (or employers), usually for a definite period of time, to assist in negotiating and administering the collective agreements. (See also Arbitration, Mediation, Umpire)

IMPROVEMENT FACTOR WAGE INCREASE. Periodic (e.g. annual) wage increases provided in union agreements which are based upon the assumption that there will be increased productivity in the plant and that workers should receive a share of the benefits from the improvement.

INCENTIVE WAGES. A method of wage payment by which earnings fluctuate more or less in accordance with actual output, thus providing an immediate financial stimulus to increased effort and output. (See also Piecework, Time and Motion Study, "Standard Time")

INDEPENDENT UNION. A national or local union not affiliated with the AFL–CIO.

INDUSTRIAL UNION. A labor organization whose jurisdiction includes all or most occupations, skilled and unskilled, within an entire industry.

INJUNCTION. A judicial order commanding an individual or a union to refrain from doing certain acts, such as picketing or engaging in a strike or boycott.

INTERNATIONAL UNION. In this country "International" refers to unions having members in Canada as well as in the United States.

JOB CLASSIFICATION. The money value (base rate) attached to a job on the basis of a formal method of evaluation.

JOB EVALUATION. The qualitative rating of jobs to determine their position in a job hierarchy according to skill, experience, responsibility, and other special requirements, for purposes of determining relative wage rates.

JOB FREEZE. A contractual or other stipulation providing that there shall be no layoffs for a specified length of time.

JOINT AGREEMENT. An agreement signed by several unions with one employer or several employers with one union, or several unions and several employers. Joint agreements are frequent among allied craft unions and employers within the same industry.

JOINT COUNCIL (or Board). A delegate body composed of representatives of various locals of the same National union within a given city or other area. Some are known as District Councils.

JOINT HIRING HALL. An employment office administered jointly by a union or union central body and an employers' association.

JOURNEYMAN. A worker in a skilled trade who has served an apprenticeship to qualify himself for such work. (See Apprentice)

JURISDICTIONAL DISPUTE. A dispute (which may or may not develop into a work stoppage) between two or more unions concerning the right to gain or retain the control of jobs in a particular trade, or the assignment of workers to these jobs. (See Rival Union Dispute, Union Jurisdiction)

KICKBACK. The return of a portion of an employee's wages to his employer or foreman upon threat of the employee's losing his job or as a bribe for obtaining a job. (See Anti-kickback Law)

LABEL. A tag or imprint on a product to indicate that it has been made under union conditions.

LABOR GRADE. The category to which a particular job is assigned on the basis of skill, experience, and other requirements, each grade from common labor to those including the highest skilled occupations having progressively higher minimum and maximum wage rates. The practice of labor grading is common in large plants having a multitude of different kinds of jobs, the purpose being to simplify the wage structure and facilitate transfers of personnel. (See Job Evaluation)

LABOR RACKETEERS. Men, often with criminal records, who worm into the labor movement and either take over existing organizations or establish "paper" organizations for the purpose of extortion.

LABOR TURNOVER. A statistical measure of changes in personnel, usually expressed in rates per month; that is, the number of accessions and separations per 100 on the payroll.

LAYOFF. Most frequently used in connection with dismissal from a job because of lack of work although sometimes used to refer to a temporary suspension for disciplinary reasons in contrast to a permanent discharge. Laid-off employees usually retain seniority rights to reemployment for more or less extended periods of time.

LEARNER. A beginner in an occupation which requires a relatively shorter time to learn than a skilled trade where apprenticeship is required. Unlike apprenticeship, there is no formal responsibility on the part of the employer or the union in the matter of instruction although the length of the learner periods may be specified for purposes of wage setting. (See also Apprentice)

LEAVE OF ABSENCE. Allowed time off from a job with the right of reinstatement and without loss of seniority.

LOBSTER SHIFT. (See Graveyard Shift)

LOCAL UNION. Although the term could be applied to any labor organization whose membership is confined to a single locality, the term is generally used to refer to local organizations which have been chartered by, and are affiliated with, a national union.

LOCKOUT. A temporary withholding or shutting down of work by an employer, in protest against employee actions or to coerce them into accepting his terms. (See Strike)

LONGEVITY PAY. Wages based on length of service; may be in the form of graduated wage rates or an extra bonus or per cent added to regular or base earnings. (See also Automatic Wage Adjustment)

MAINTENANCE OF MEMBERSHIP. An arrangement whereby employees who voluntarily join the union must maintain their membership for the duration of the agreement as a condition of continued employment.

MAJORITY REPRESENTATION. A determination by an appropriate agency (for example, the National Labor Relations Board) that a certain union shall be the collective bargaining agency for all the employees within the bargaining unit on the basis of an election that such union is favored by a majority of the employees. (See Bargaining Unit)

MAKE-WORK. Used in two connections with same basic meaning: (1) public works of dubious necessity whose primary purpose is to provide jobs for the unemployed; (2) union rules which restrict reduction of labor force even though the jobs are no longer needed. (See Featherbedding.)

MAKE-UP WAGES. Difference between actual piecework earnings and earnings at guaranteed rates, or statutory minimum rates.

MAKE-UP WORK. Work performed outside regular hours to make up for time lost because of absences; for example, work done on Saturday or an employee's usual day off.

MARGINAL WORKER. A worker who by reason of age, mediocre skill, or other reason, is able to obtain employment only during periods when the labor supply is limited.

MASTER AGREEMENT. A union agreement signed by the dominant employer or several of the largest employers in an industry, or by an employers' association which includes most of the employers in the industry. Since the terms of such agreements usually establish the pattern of the agreements to be negotiated subsequently in the balance of the industry, there is in effect little difference between a Master Agreement and a Standard or Model Agreement. (See also Standard Agreement)

MEASURED DAY RATE. A wage plan wherein each individual's hour (or day) rate is periodically adjusted according to his average efficiency during the preceding period. (See Incentive Wages)

MEDIATION. An effort by an outside person to bring the employer and worker representatives into agreement. Mediation in its very essence implies voluntarism, the mediator's sole function being to assist the disputants to reach a settlement rather than in making a settlement for them as in the case of an arbitrator. (See Arbitration, Conciliation)

MERIT INCREASE. A wage increase granted to an individual worker because of his improved efficiency or quality of work in contrast to a longevity increase based on length of service, or a promotion increase due to a transfer to a more highly paid job, or an increase resulting from a general rise in wage levels.

MERIT RATING. A formalized periodic rating of employees' efficiency and other qualifications to be used as a basis for wage increases and promotions and, in some plants, as one factor taken into consideration to determine order of layoff. Also used in connection with some state unemployment compensation laws with reference to reducing contributions of employers who meet specified standards of employment regularization. (See Experience Rating)

MODEL AGREEMENT. (See Standard Agreement)

MODIFIED UNION SHOP. An agreement between an employer and a union requiring all present members to retain their membership and all new employees to become members, but does not require employees who were not members at the time the agreement was signed to join the union.

MOONLIGHTING. Holding more than one job.

"MORE FAVORABLE TERMS." An agreement by a union that it will not grant more advantageous terms (for example, lower wage rates) to any competitor of the employer signing the agreement.

MOTOR CARRIERS ACT. An act passed in 1935 giving the Interstate Commerce Commission authority to regulate maximum hours of work of employees responsible for the safe operation of passenger and freight motor vehicles operated in interstate or foreign commerce.

MULTICRAFT UNION. A craft union whose jurisdiction covers several distinctly different skilled occupations.

NONCONTRIBUTORY WELFARE PLAN. A health or pension program for the benefit of employees which is financed entirely by the employer.

NONPRODUCTION BONUS. An extra payment to an employee based on a factor other than the output of the worker, such as a Christmas bonus, attendance bonus, or payment in reward for waste elimination.

ON-SITE LABOR. Labor used at the location of a construction project as distinguished from labor associated with activities incidental to the project, such as the production and delivery of materials and equipment.

OPEN-END AGREEMENT. A collective bargaining agreement which has no fixed termination date but which is in effect indefinitely, subject to a specified number of days' notice by either party that it considers the agreement at an end.

OPEN SHOP. Theoretically, a shop where both union and nonunion members are employed. Before union discrimination became illegal, the so-called "open shop" campaigns conducted by employers were in reality an effort to keep unions and union members out of their plants. "Open shop" thereupon became a term of derision, unions declaring that it signified "closed to union members."

OPEN UNION. A union which accepts into membership any qualified person employed in the trade or industry over which the union has jurisdiction; a union whose initiation fees are not prohibitive and whose membership rules are not restrictive as to race, sex, etc.

OUTLAW STRIKE. (See Illegal Strike)

OVERTIME. Time worked beyond the standard established by law, employer-union agreements or company regulations, for which "penalty" rates, that is, higher than regular wage rates, are paid. Sometimes used to refer to the wages paid rather than the actual overtime worked, for example, referring to two hours' actual work at time and one-half rate as being three hours' overtime.

PACE SETTER. An unusually fast worker selected by the employer for use in gauging the amount of work that can be done in a given time as basis for establishing piece rates.

PACKAGE INCREASE. A combination of benefits, including wage increases, insurance, paid holidays, etc. The term generally implies that during the bargaining the parties agreed that a specified number of cents increase is to be applied toward pay increases and the financing of specified benefit programs.

PATTERN INFLUENCE. The effect which a newly negotiated agreement with a major company has upon the contracts signed later by other companies.

PENALTY RATES. Commonly applied to extra rates paid for overtime and for Sunday and holiday work as well as hazardous or onerous work; also sometimes used to designate higher rates for nightwork, although more commonly these are referred to as shift bonus or shift differential rates. (See also Premium Pay)

PERMISSIVE WAGE ADJUSTMENT. Provisions in employer-union contracts allowing either party to reopen the question of wage rates whenever any one or a number of specified changes in conditions have taken place either inside or outside the plant, for example, changes in cost of living or general economic conditions or changes in methods of doing the work. (See also Automatic Wage Adjustment)

PERMIT CARD. A card issued by the union to a nonmember, which permits him to accept temporary employment with an employer who has a union shop contract.

PERMIT FEE. Money charged by a union to a nonunion applicant, which permits him to accept temporary employment on a "union job."

PERQUISITES. Goods or services furnished by an employer which could be considered as an addition to wages; for example, free meals or lodging, right to buy goods from the employer at a discount, etc.

"PICK." (See Run)

PICKETING. The posting by a labor organization of a person or persons at the approach of a work place during a labor dispute for the purpose of (a) informing the public and employees that a dispute exists, (b) persuading workers to join or continue the strike or boycott, (c) preventing persons from entering or going to work.

Mass picketing is a parading of large numbers before the entrance and is used for its dramatic effect or when considerable resistance from the employer or nonparticipating employees is anticipated.

Cross picketing denotes picketing by two or more rival unions, each of whom claims to represent the employees of the establishment.

Informational picketing is solely to inform the public of a labor dispute and does not imply a barrier to crossing the picket lines.

Reserved gate picketing refers to picketing before a gate reserved for employees of a neutral subcontractor whose work is unrelated to the normal operations of the employer with whom the union is in dispute.

Secondary picketing refers to the picketing of an employer not directly involved in the labor dispute but connected through ownership or business dealings with the employer against whom the union is engaged in a dispute.

PIECEWORK. A form of incentive wages which pays a fixed sum for each article produced or worked on. (See also Incentive Wages, Timework)

PORTAL-TO-PORTAL PAY. Payment for time spent on company premises in getting to and from the work place; for example in mining, the computation of hours worked to include travel time between the mine entry and place of work of each miner.

POSTING. (See Bidding)

PREFERENTIAL SHOP. A company operating under an agreement whereby union members are afforded preference over nonmembers in some aspect of employment; for example, requiring that they be the last to be laid off and the first to be rehired. (See Union Shop)

PREMIUM PAY. Variously ascribed to extra payments over normal wage rates to which employees are entitled because of work beyond or outside of regular hours, or for output beyond established minimum standards, or for especially hazardous or onerous work. (See Penalty Rates, Overtime, Incentive Wages, Shift Differential)

PREVAILING WAGE LAW (DAVIS-BACON ACT). An act passed in 1931 (with subsequent amendments) requiring the payment of minimum rates, which are equal to those prevailing throughout the industry, on all federally financed public works contracts.

PROBATIONARY EMPLOYEE. A new employee on a trial basis who is usually not covered by seniority or other protective rules and, under most union shop arrangements, is not required to join the union. (See Learner, Trial Period)

PRODUCTION BONUS. (See Incentive Wages)

PRODUCTIVITY. Amount produced in relation to effort or time expended; a measurement of unit output per worker or per man-hours or days worked.

PROFIT SHARING. A plan by which employees receive a specified proportion of the company's net earnings or of earnings above a specified amount; usually prorated according to employees' service records or other formula.

PROGRESSION WAGES. Graduated wages, within specified limits for each job, based on length of service or merit ratings in contrast to increased wages resulting from promotions to higher jobs.

PUBLIC CONTRACTS ACT (WALSH-HEALEY ACT). An act passed in 1936 which requires that persons employed on United States government contracts for materials, supplies, articles, or equipment be paid no less than the prevailing wages in the industry, that time and one-half be paid for all time worked in excess of 8 hours per day or 40 hours per week, that no convict or child labor be used, and that safe and healthful working conditions be maintained.

"QUICKIE" STRIKE. A spontaneous stoppage of work by a group of employees without the sanction or approval of the union.

"RAT." A union term of opprobrium for a strikebreaker.

RATE CUTTING. A term sometimes applied to any reduction of established piece rates; more accurately applied to the arbitrary reduction of rates by an employer where no changes in the job have taken place in contrast to revision of rates due to changes in methods or machinery used.

RATE RANGE. A range of rates for the same job, with specific rates of individual workers within the range determined by merit, length of service, or a combination of merit and length of service.

RATIONALIZATION. Sometimes used as synonymous to "scientific management," that is, techniques for internal shop management which decrease costs and improve efficiency; also used in connection with plans and controls for an entire industry, such as cartel arrangements.

"RATTING." Accepting employment at lower than union wage rates. Term commonly used by union printers.

"REAL" WAGES. The purchasing power of a dollar of wages; that is, money wages in relation to cost of living or price levels. For example, if wage rates have increased 10 per cent and cost of living has also increased 10 per cent during any period, then "real" wages have remained the same.

REFEREE. (See Umpire)

REPORTING PAY. (See Call Pay)

RESTRICTION OF OUTPUT. (See Work Restriction)

RETROACTIVE PAY. (See Back Pay)

RIVAL UNION DISPUTE. A dispute between two or more unions over the issue of which one shall represent a particular group of workers as their collective bargaining agent. A rival union dispute differs from a jurisdictional dispute in that the latter is concerned with claims to jobs or kinds of work, whereas in a rival union dispute the unions are contending for the right to represent the workers on the jobs. (See Jurisdictional Dispute)

ROTATING SHIFTS. Where two or more shifts of workers are employed, the practice of having the several crews change their hour schedules at periodic intervals so that each in turn works on the day and night shifts. On continuous seven-day operations there might also be rotation of day schedules causing days-off to fall on different calendar days. (See Fixed Shifts, Swing Shift)

"RUN." A term used, especially in the transportation industry, to designate a work assignment; in local transportation a run usually refers to an entire day's or week's working schedule of an employee as distinct from one trip. Sometimes referred to as "pick" because of the customary procedure for employees to pick or choose their runs on the basis of their seniority.

RUNAWAY RATE. A piece rate or other incentive rate which results in earnings that are out of line with earnings in other jobs of similar requirements. May occur because of changes in methods or from faulty rate setting. Sometimes referred to as "loose" rates.

RUNAWAY SHOPS. Businesses which have changed location to escape from union conditions or state labor laws. Especially used in connection with establishments which have moved from New York City to outlying communities in neighboring states, or from Northern states to the South.

SABOTAGE. Act of obstructing or interfering with processes of work by an employee or employees in order to coerce the employer. Sabotage is associated with "direct action" tactics and ranges from peaceful restriction of output to the destruction of machines and materials.

The origin of the term is not fully known and is variously ascribed to the habit of irate French workmen of throwing their wooden shoes (*sabots*) into the machinery and to the dragging, clumsy movements of wooden shoes worn by workers. It was adopted by the French organized labor movement in 1897. "Soldiering" is the American and "ca' canny" is the British equivalent to peaceful sabotage. In recent years the term "sabotage" is more especially used in connection with the destruction of employers' property rather than deliberate slowing down of effort.

SCAB. An employee who continues to work during a strike; also a person who accepts employment in a nonunion shop or under nonunion conditions at a time when the union is trying to organize the industry.

SCIENTIFIC MANAGEMENT. A term used by Frederick Taylor and his successors to refer to certain job techniques carefully worked out (by an engineer) to decrease costs and improve efficiency—for example plant layout, work scheduling, time and motion study, job analysis and incentive wage systems. (See Time and Motion Study, Incentive Wages, Rationalization)

SCRIP. A certificate issued by an employer in lieu of cash wages, usually redeemable only at a company store.

SEASONAL INDUSTRY. A term loosely applied to any industry which normally has one or two periods of full employment each year interspersed by general layoffs or part-time employment. Under the Fair Labor Standards Act the term is limited to those industries which in periodic recurring parts of the year are forced to cease production because "the materials handled, extracted or processed are not available owing to climate or other natural conditions."

SEASONAL TOLERANCES. Waiving of penalty overtime rates for extra hours worked, or waiving of hours limitations, during peak periods of production as provided in some employer-union agreements and in some state laws as well as the Fair Labor Standards Act for certain seasonal (for example, agricultural processing) industries.

SECONDARY BOYCOTT. A concerted effort to impair the business of an employer whose own employees are not directly involved in a dispute with him. Thus workers may refuse to handle or work on any materials, equipment or supplies produced or delivered by nonunion workers or members of a rival union; or a union may declare a boycott against a retail outlet for goods produced in a plant whose employees are on strike.

SECONDARY STRIKE. A strike against an employer who uses or sells materials from a struck plant; differs from a sympathetic strike in that there is a business connection between the employers involved in the initial and the secondary strikes.

SENIORITY. Employment rights and privileges based on length of service; the measure of a claim, in relation to other employees, to a particular job.

SEPARABILITY CLAUSE. A stipulation in an employer-union agreement which protects the validity of the remainder of the contract should any particular provision be declared illegal or void for any reason.

SEVERANCE PAY. (See Dismissal Wage)

SHAPE-UP. In longshoring, the system of having men line up ("shape") at least once a day at the piers or other places where representatives of the steamship or stevedoring companies select those they wish for the day's work or job at hand.

SHIFT. (See Fixed Shifts, Rotating Shifts, Swing Shift)

SHIFT DIFFERENTIAL. Special remuneration for work performed on other than the regular day schedule; may include a per cent or amount over the day rate, or shorter hours with full pay, or both. Differentials may vary between shifts, that is, a higher rate for the midnight than for the afternoon shift.

SHOP CHAIRMAN. A union steward usually chosen by the department stewards from among their own number, although he may be elected by the members within the plant, to serve as chairman over all the stewards in the plant and to deal with top management officials in adjusting matters not settled satisfactorily by the department stewards and foremen. (See Business Agent, Steward)

SIT-DOWN STRIKE. A protest stoppage in which the workers involved remain at their workplace, in contrast to a strike where workers leave the plant and establish picket lines.

SLIDING SCALE. Wage rates which are automatically adjusted to changes in the selling price of the commodity produced in accordance with a fixed formula.

SLOWDOWN. A deliberate lessening of work effort for a definite purpose and time. In motive a slowdown is similar to a strike and differs from the latter only in degree of stoppage involved.

SOLE BARGAINING. The legal or contractual right of a particular union to bargain for all employees, union and nonunion, within the bargaining unit. (See Collective Bargaining, Bargaining Unit)

"SOLDIERING." Loafing on the job. Differs from a "slowdown" in that it involves no motive to bring pressure upon the employer for any particular purpose.

SPEED-UP. A term used by workers to apply to conditions which force them to increase their efforts with no compensating increase in earnings. Speed-up may take the form of a direct increase in work load or it may be the result of rate cutting which forces workers to push up their output in order to maintain their earnings. (See also Rate Cutting, Stretch-out)

SPIES. (See Stoolpigeon)

SPENDABLE EARNINGS. Money earnings less routine deductions for social security, income taxes, union dues, etc. Sometimes referred to as "take-home pay."

SPLIT SHIFT. A work schedule in which there is a daily break—for example, that of restaurant employees who work several hours at noon and again in the evening.

Standard Agreement. A collective agreement prepared by the National union for use by its locals. The purpose of a standard agreement is not only to relieve the locals of the task of drafting their own agreements but also to promote the standardization of working conditions throughout the industry. (See Master Agreement)

"Standard Time." A general term applied to any kind of wage incentive system which uses units of time rather than number of pieces produced for measuring premium earnings; for example, 5 hours' pay for performing a designated 5-hour task in 4 hours.

Steward. A person elected by the employees within a plant or department to represent them in the adjustment of their grievances with the employer. (See Business Agent, Shop Chairman)

Stoolpigeon. A person in the hire of the employer (or a detective agency servicing the employer) who joins the union to spy on union members and their activities and to create confusion and suspicion among the members in order to break up the union.

The term is sometimes used interchangeably with "spy" but the latter may work from the outside while a stoolpigeon wangles his way into union membership and not only obtains information for the employer but also actively seeks to disrupt the union. (See also Strikebreaker)

"Stoop Labor." Farm labor which requires bending or kneeling—for example, cotton picking and cultivation of vegetables.

Straight Time. Regular time or wages exclusive of overtime.

Stretch-out. Requiring an operator to tend more machines or do more work without a commensurate increase in pay. In effect, stretch-out is synonymous with speed-up, the term "stretch-out" being most frequently used in the textile or other industries where machines are largely automatic.

Strike. A temporary stoppage of work by a group of employees in order to express a grievance or to enforce a demand concerning changes in working conditions. Government statistics exclude all strikes lasting less than one day or involving fewer than six workers, and make no distinction between strikes and lockouts. (See also General Strike, Illegal Strike, Sit-down Strike, Sympathetic Strike)

Strikebreakers. Outside persons hired during a labor dispute to fill the jobs of those on strike; more especially those hired for the duration of the strike where there is no intention of retaining them as permanent employees. Also used to refer to spies and "strong-arm" men employed to break up a strike by fomenting confusion and violence. (See also Anti-strikebreaking Act, "Rat," Scab)

Substandard Employee. A worker who, because of physical or mental handicaps, is unable to maintain normal production standards and who, therefore, may be paid less than the regular rate.

SUPERANNUATED RATE. A rate of pay below the prevailing level or union rate for a worker above a certain age. Some union agreements require the employer to employ a specified ratio of older workers, allowing them to be paid less than the going union rates.

"SWEETHEART" CONTRACTS. Agreements entered into by a union official and an employer where there has been no previous discussion or approval by the employees involved. Associated with corrupt union officials who either receive bribes from the employer or use threats on the employer to compel him to sign.

SWING SHIFT. The fourth shift or fourth crew of workers on continuous operation schedules; sometimes refers to the entire four-shift arrangement. The name is derived from the necessary expedient on round-the-clock operations of having one shift (or all four shifts depending upon the nature of the "swing") rotate to different days and hours at specified intervals.

SYMPATHETIC STRIKE. A strike of workers who are not directly concerned with the matter in dispute but have participated in order to demonstrate worker solidarity and thus broaden the group pressure upon the employer against whom there is a strike for a specific cause. (See also General Strike, Secondary Strike)

SYNDICALISM. A French term for trade-unionism. In this country the term is connected with the revolutionary philosophy based on the idea that syndicates or unions should take over, own and operate the industries, as opposed to the trade union philosophy that unions are instruments to improve the condition of workers under private capitalism. The best-known syndicalist movement in this country was the Industrial Workers of the World, active before and during World War I, which was strongly tinged with political anarchism.

TAKE-HOME PAY. (See Spendable Earnings)

"TANDEM" WAGE INCREASE. An increase automatically given a group of employees as the result of an increase negotiated with another group. For example, a pay increase to office workers similar to that negotiated with production workers.

TASK. Under wage incentive systems the amount of production per unit of time which is necessary to earn the base rate of pay, sometimes referred to as "standard time" or production or job standard. (See Base Rate, Incentive Wages)

TECHNOLOGICAL UNEMPLOYMENT. Displacement of workers owing to introduction of or improvements in machinery and new methods of production.

TEMPORARY EMPLOYEE. One who is employed for a short period of time and who therefore does not have seniority rights or other privileges incident to permanent status. Under union-shop agreements may be given a working permit in lieu of union membership.

TERMINAL JOBS. Jobs which have no promotion possibilities; "blind alley" jobs.

"TEST HANDS." Persons selected for time study in establishing job standards and piece rates. (See also Time and Motion Study, Incentive Wages)

TIME AND MOTION STUDY. Observing the motions and measuring the time which an operator takes to perform a job or job element, usually with a stop watch, for purpose of establishing job standards and incentive wage rates.

TIMEWORK. Employment where wages are based on a fixed amount per hour or day in contrast to piecework or other form of incentive pay.

TOUR. A term used in some industries instead of "shift."

TRIAL PERIOD. The time a new employee (or an old employee on a new job) is given to prove his competency and thus qualify for permanent status. (See Apprentice, Learner, Probationary Employee)

TRICK. A work period, such as a shift.

UMPIRE. An outside person employed jointly by the union and the employer, usually for a definite period of time, to whom are referred for final decision disputes over the interpretation or application of provisions of the agreement. Although arbitrator, impartial chairman, referee, and umpire are sometimes used indiscriminately, the latter three are more commonly applied when such persons serve in a permanent capacity as distinguished from an arbitrator who is appointed to settle a particular dispute.

"UNFAIR" EMPLOYER. Specifically, an employer who has committed an unfair labor practice as defined by law. In union parlance it may refer to any nonunion employer.

UNION JURISDICTION. The kinds of work (in some instances an entire industry) which a union claims, or which its federated body has assigned to it as a basis for its membership. (See Jurisdictional Dispute)

UNION-MANAGEMENT COOPERATION. In its broadest sense, refers to any peaceful management-union negotiations including bargaining over terms of employment. More commonly the term is given a limited meaning to refer to those jointly sponsored activities which are directed to the improvement and expansion of the business, such as cost savings, improvement in production procedures and quality of output, sales promotion, etc.

UNION SECURITY. Term commonly applied to provisions in collective agreements which grant the union shop or require maintenance of membership of those who once join the union.

UNION SHOP. An agreement between an employer and union which requires all employees immediately after hiring or after a specified probationary period, to become and remain members of the union.

UNION-SHOP CARD. A card issued by the union for display by the employer to indicate that he is operating under union conditions. Commonly used by barbershops, restaurants and other retail and service industries. Analogous to use of union label in manufacturing.

UNLICENSED PERSONNEL. Seamen who are not required to have a license; that is, ordinary seamen, stewards, cooks, firemen, etc. as distinct from masters, mates, pilots, and engineers.

VERTICAL UNION. A union whose claimed jurisdiction covers all occupation from the production of raw materials to fabricated products. There is no clear line of distinction between a vertical and an industrial union.

VOLUNTARY CHECKOFF. (See Checkoff)

WAGE AND HOUR ACT. (See Fair Labor Standards Act)

WAGE ATTACHMENT. (See Garnishment)

WAGE AWARD. The specified wage rates determined by an arbitrator or government agency.

WAGE DIFFERENTIALS. Established differences in wages paid for the same kind of job because of differences in working or living conditions, for example, day versus night rates or rates adjusted to differences in cost of living between communities.

WAGE RATE. Amount of pay for a specified unit of labor, such as an hour's work. (See also Piecework, Timework)

WAGES. As distinct from "earnings," wages usually refer to regular wage rates or remuneration for work performed under normal conditions, that is, exclusive of overtime and holiday work or work performed under other special circumstances. (See also Earnings, Incentive Wages, "Real" Wages)

WAGE STABILIZATION. Any plan to keep wages in an area or industry at established levels. Used particularly with reference to government plans for preventing inflation during war periods.

WAITING TIME. (See "Dead Time")

WALSH-HEALEY ACT. (See Public Contracts Act)

WATCH. The specified time when a seaman is on duty. Comparable to shift or work period in other types of employment.

WELFARE MANAGEMENT. Activities conducted by the employer for the comfort and improvement of his employees; industrial paternalism. Sometimes used as a term of derision for companies who offer welfare programs as substitutes for collective bargaining.

WHITE-COLLAR WORKER. Normally used to refer to one who works in an office rather than a factory, whose work is primarily mental rather than physical, whose preparation requires more formal education than a factory employee and who is usually paid on a salary rather than an hourly wage. (See Blue-Collar Worker)

WILDCAT STRIKE. (See "Quickie" Strike, Illegal Strike)

WORKING EMPLOYER. One who employs others but more or less regularly performs the same kind of work as is done by his employees. Some unions restrict the amount and kind of work employers may do in order to prevent persons not subject to the terms of the agreement from doing work which the union believes should be done by its members.

WORK LOAD. The quantitative measure of an hour's or a day's performance on a job. The term is usually applied to a standard of output which is supposed to represent reasonably efficient production without risk to health or safety. (See also Speed-up, Task)

WORKMEN'S COMPENSATION. Insurance systems established by law providing weekly cash benefits and medical services to workers who suffer physical injury during the course of their employment.

WORK RESTRICTION. A tacit understanding or planned movement among a group of employees to limit output below the standard of efficiency which could be maintained without risk to health and safety. Restriction of output may be (1) a temporary act to gain an immediate definite concession from the employer in which case it takes on the nature of a slowdown strike or (2) an effort to prolong a job and prevent unemployment. (See Featherbedding, Sabotage, Work Load)

WORK SHARING. A definite plan introduced by an employer, or through collective agreement by an employer and union, by which the reduced amount of work during slack seasons is "spread" among employees by reducing each worker's daily or weekly hours.

YELLOW-DOG CONTRACT. A term of derision to refer to the document which many employers formerly compelled their employees to sign as a condition of employment, wherein the employee promised that he would not join a labor union or otherwise participate in concerted action.

UNION DIRECTORY

All unions are affiliated with the AFL-CIO except those designated "Ind." Unions are listed alphabetically by the key word identifying the craft or industry. Membership figures are as of 1962.

NAME	MEMBERSHIP
Actors and Artistes of America, Associated	55,000
Actors' Equity Association	
American Federation of Television and Radio Artists	
American Guild of Musical Artists, Inc.	
American Guild of Variety Artists	
Hebrew Actors' Union, Inc.	
Italian Actors' Union	
Screen Actors' Guild, Inc.	
Screen Extras' Guild, Inc.	
Air Line Dispatchers Association	630
Air Line Pilots Association, International	13,500
Aluminum Workers International Union	22,000
Asbestos Workers, International Association of Heat and Frost Insulators and	10,000
Associated Unions of America (Ind.)	5,500
Automobile, Aircraft and Agricultural Implement Workers of America, International Union, United	1,136,000
Bakery and Confectionery Workers' International Union, American	85,000
Barbers, Hairdressers, Cosmetologists and Proprietors' International Union of America, Journeymen	75,000
Bill Posters, Billers and Distributors of the U.S. and Canada, International Alliance of	1,600
Boilermakers, Iron Shipbuilders, Blacksmiths, Forgers and Helpers, International Brotherhood of	140,000
Bookbinders, International Brotherhood of	64,000
Brewery, Flour, Cereal, Soft Drink and Distillery Workers of America, International Union of United	60,000
Brick and Clay Workers of America, United	24,000

Bricklayers, Masons and Plasterers' International Union of America	155,000
Broadcast Employees and Technicians, National Association of	5,900
Broom and Whisk Makers' Union of America, International	150
Building Service Employees' International Union	272,000
Carpenters and Joiners of America, United Brotherhood of	800,000
Cement, Lime and Gypsum Workers International Union, United	39,400
Chemical Workers Union, International	79,000
Cigar Makers' International Union of America	5,800
Clothing Workers of America, Amalgamated	377,000
Communications Association, American (Ind.)	8,000
Communications Workers of America	260,000
Coopers' International Union of North America	3,500
Die Sinkers' Conference, International (Ind.)	4,000
Directors Guild of America, Inc. (Ind.)	2,150
Distillery, Rectifying and Wine Workers' International Union of America	34,400
Electrical, Radio and Machine Workers, International Union of	288,000
Electrical, Radio and Machine Workers of America, United (Ind.)	160,000
Electrical Workers, International Brotherhood of	771,000
Elevator Constructors, International Union of	11,400
Engineers, American Federation of Technical	13,000
Engineers, International Union of Operating	291,000
Federal Employees, National Federation of (Ind.)	53,000
Fire Fighters, International Association of	95,000
Firemen and Oilers, International Brotherhood of	53,000
Flight Engineers' International Association	3,250
Furniture Workers of America, United	50,000
Garment Workers of America, United	35,000
Garment Workers' Union, International Ladies'	446,500
Glass Bottle Blowers Association of the U.S. and Canada	54,250
Glass and Ceramic Workers of North America, United	40,000
Glass Cutters League of America, Window	1,450
Glass Workers' Union of North America, American Flint	30,700

Glove Workers' Union of America, International	2,200
Government Employees, American Federation of	70,300
Grain Millers, American Federation of	42,000
Granite Cutters' International Association of America, The	3,700
Guard Workers of America, United Plant (Ind.)	8,500
Guards' Union of America, International (Ind.)	1,682
Hatters, Cap and Millinery Workers International Union, United	40,000
Hod Carriers', Building and Common Laborers' Union of America, International	442,500
Horseshoers of the U.S. and Canada, International Union of Journeymen	290
Hosiery Workers, American Federation of	5,300
Hotel and Restaurant Employees and Bartenders' International Union	443,000
Independent Unions, Congress of (Ind.)	500
Industrial Workers of America, International Union, Allied	68,000
Insurance Agents, International Union of Life (Ind.)	2,000
Insurance Workers International Union	22,000
Iron Workers, International Association of Bridge, Structural and Ornamental	148,000
Jewelry Workers' Union, International	12,700
Lace Operatives of America, Amalgamated (Ind.)	975
Lathers' International Union, The Wood, Wire and Metal	16,800
Laundry and Dry Cleaning International Union	22,000
Laundry, Dry Cleaning and Dye House Workers International Union (Ind.)	65,700
Leather Goods, Plastic and Novelty Workers' Union, International	32,000
Leather Workers International Union of America	9,500
Letter Carriers of the U.S. of America, National Association of	138,000
Letter Carriers' Association, National Rural (Ind.)	38,300
Lithographers of America, Amalgamated (Ind.)	37,100
Locomotive Engineers, Brotherhood of (Ind.)	43,200
Locomotive Firemen and Enginemen, Brotherhood of	81,100
Longshoremen's Association, International	50,000

Union	Membership
Longshoremen's and Warehousemen's Union, International (Ind.)	60,000
Machine Printers' Beneficial Association of the U.S. (Ind.)	1,400
Machinists, International Association of	898,150
Mailers Union, International (Ind.)	3,800
Maintenance of Way Employes, Brotherhood of	164,500
Marble, Slate and Stone Polishers, Rubbers and Sawyers, Tile and Marble Setters' Helpers and Marble Mosaic and Terrazzo Workers' Helpers, International Association of	9,860
Marine Engineers' Beneficial Association, National	11,000
Marine and Shipbuilding Workers of America, Industrial Union of	30,000
Maritime Union of America, National	40,000
Masters, Mates and Pilots, International Organization of	10,000
Meat Cutters and Butcher Workmen of North America, Amalgamated	333,500
Mechanics Educational Society of America	38,000
Mechanics and Foremen of Naval Shore Establishments, National Association of Master	495
Messengers, The National Association of Special Delivery	2,000
Metal Polishers, Buffers, Platers and Helpers International Union	18,000
Mine, Mill and Smelter Workers, International Union of (Ind.)	100,000
Mine Workers of America, United (Ind.)	600,000
Molders' and Allied Workers' Union of North America, International	53,850
Musicians, American Federation of	266,600
Newspaper Guild, American	31,400
Newspaper and Mail Deliverers' Union of New York and Vicinity (Ind.)	4,000
Office Employees' International Union	53,000
Oil, Chemical and Atomic Workers International Union	174,000
Packinghouse Workers, National Brotherhood of (Ind.)	*
Packinghouse, Food and Allied Workers, United	102,600
Painters, Decorators and Paperhangers of America, Brotherhood of	192,600
Papermakers and Paperworkers, United	140,000
Pattern Makers' League of North America	13,900

Petroleum Workers Inc., International Union of (Ind.)	3,500
Photo-Engravers' Union of North America, International	17,000
Plasterers' and Cement Masons' International Association of the United States and Canada, Operative	68,000
Plate Printers', Die Stampers' and Engravers' Union of North America, International	700
Plumbing and Pipe Fitting Industry of the U.S. and Canada, United Association of Journeymen and Apprentices of the	251,300
Porters, Brotherhood of Sleeping Car	6,000
Post Office and General Services Maintenance Employees, National Association of (Ind.)	7,400
Post Office Motor Vehicle Employees, National Federation of	5,000
Post Office and Postal Transportation Service Mail Handlers, Watchmen and Messengers, National Association of	4,000
Postal Clerks, United Federation of	135,000
Postal Employees, National Alliance of (Ind.)	18,000
Postal Supervisors, National Association of (Ind.)	19,250
Postal Union, National (Ind.)	32,000
Postmasters of the U.S., National League of (Ind.)	13,000
Potters, International Brotherhood of Operative	25,000
Printing Pressmen and Assistants' Union of North America, International	114,000
Protection Employees, Independent Union of Plant (Ind.)	2,000
Pulp, Sulphite and Paper Mill Workers, International Brotherhood of	170,500
Radio Association, American	1,500
Railroad Signalmen, Brotherhood of	14,400
Railroad Telegraphers, The Order of	57,500
Railroad Trainmen, Brotherhood of	159,400
Railroad Yardmasters of America	4,500
Railroad Yardmasters of North America, Inc. (Ind.)	*
Railway Carmen of America, Brotherhood of	125,000
Railway Conductors and Brakemen, Order of (Ind.)	25,000
Railway Employees, International Association of (Ind.)	450
Railway Patrolmen's International Union	3,000
Railway and Steamship Clerks, Freight Handlers, Express and Station Employes, Brotherhood of	300,000
Railway and Airline Supervisors Association, The American	6,300
Railway Trainmen and Locomotive Firemen, Association of (Ind.)	250
Retail Clerks International Association	342,000

Retail, Wholesale and Department Store Union	143,300
Roofers, Damp and Waterproof Workers Association, United Slate, Tile and Composition	20,300
Rubber, Cork, Linoleum and Plastic Workers of America, United	170,000
Seafarers' International Union of North America	75,000
Atlantic, Gulf, Lakes and Inland Waters District	
Inland Boatmen's Union of the Pacific	
Marine Cooks and Stewards' Union	
Pacific Coast Marine Firemen, Oilers, Watertenders and Wipers Association	
Sailors' Union of the Pacific	
Sheet Metal Workers' International Association	100,000
Shoe and Allied Craftsmen, Brotherhood of (Ind.)	4,300
Shoe Workers of America, United	58,000
Shoe Workers' Union, Boot and	40,000
Siderographers, International Association of	40
Stage Employers and Moving Picture Machine Operators of the U.S. and Canada, International Alliance of Theatrical	62,000
State, County and Municipal Employees, American Federation of	210,000
Steelworkers of America, United	1,152,000
Stereotypers' and Electrotypers' Union of North America, International	11,000
Stone and Allied Products Workers of America, United	12,400
Stone Cutters' Association of North America, Journeymen	1,200
Stove Mounters' International Union of North America	9,500
Street, Electric Railway and Motor Coach Employes of America, Amalgamated Association of	132,100
Switchmen's Union of North America	17,200
Teachers, American Federation of	56,200
Teamsters, Chauffeurs, Warehousemen and Helpers of America, International Brotherhood of (Ind.)	1,484,500
Telegraphers' Union, The Commercial	27,400
Telephone Unions, Alliance of Independent (Ind.)	90,000
Textile Workers of America, United	40,000
Textile Workers Union of America	192,000
Tobacco Workers International Union	34,400
Tool Craftsmen, International Association of (Ind.)	1,400

Toy Workers of the U.S. and Canada, International Union of Doll and	19,000
Train Dispatchers Association, American	3,500
Transport Service Employees, United	3,000
Transport Workers Union of America	135,000
Truck Drivers, Chauffeurs and Helpers Union of Chicago and Vicinity, Chicago (Ind.)	9,800
Typographical Union, International	105,000
Upholsterers' International Union of North America	56,300
Utility Workers of New England, Inc., Brotherhood of (Ind.)	4,600
Utility Workers Union of America	70,000
Watch Workers Union, American (Ind.)	*
Watchmen's Association, Independent (Ind.)	2,130
Welders, International Union, United (Ind.)	1,200
Woodworkers of America, International	93,500
Writers Guild of America (Ind.)	
Writers Guild of America, East, Inc.	1,100
Writers Guild of America, West, Inc.	1,900

* Not available.

INDEX

This index does not include references to titles in the Glossary of Labor Terms or the Union Directory.

About the Author

As employment manager of a large shoe company in Ohio during the twenties, FLORENCE PETERSON handled employee grievances of all types in a non-union shop. Her field experience was later used to advantage at the University of Wisconsin where she assisted Dr. John R. Commons on his monumental HISTORY OF LABOR, and earned her doctorate. She served as Chief of the Industrial Relations Division of the U.S. Bureau of Labor Statistics from 1934–1947, directing research into methods of improving collective bargaining.

Miss Peterson was director of the Graduate Department of Social Economy at Bryn Mawr College from 1947–1951, and professor of economics at Rollins College in Winter Park, Florida, until her recent retirement.

She is the author of SURVEY OF LABOR ECONOMICS and has contributed articles to *Atlantic Monthly, Social Science Yearbook, Monthly Labor Review, American Statistical Journal, Encyclopaedia Britannica,* etc.